Praise for Steve Rushin's

Sting-Ray Afternoons

"In his funny, elegiac memoir *Sting-Ray Afternoons,* Rushin mines this ineffably familiar terrain with a sense of irony and deep affection, working hard to capture the look and feel of the 1970s as seen through the eyes of a bookish Catholic-school boy growing up in a rambunctious, sports-mad family of seven...Much of what Rushin writes about—the Sears Christmas Wish Book, leaded gasoline, Johnny Carson's many vacations—will strike a chord with anyone who, like me, grew up in that era."   —Jim Zarroli, National Public Radio

"A touching nostalgic memoir...A vivid and comedic approach to Rushin's personal touchstones for the era."
          —CBC Radio's *Day 6*

"You will not read a better book this summer—and maybe well into the fall and winter, too—than *Sting-Ray Afternoons,* a memoir by the magnificent Steve Rushin. Few writers love the language more, and that's an affinity evident on every page."   —Mike Vaccaro, *New York Post*

"A lighthearted, sentimental look back at a Minnesota childhood with a twist of wryness...Rushin's told-with-a-smile stories of childhood are worth the trip."
          —Casey Common, *Minneapolis Star Tribune*

"Rushin's childhood, from the ages of three to thirteen, was perfectly encapsulated in the 1970s, and he celebrates the excesses and excitement of the decade with ardor...His everykid upbringing and the touchstones of childhood he recounts make *Sting-Ray Afternoons* a fun-filled and charming trip."　　　　　　　　　—Bridget Thoreson, *Booklist*

"If you existed in the 1970s and had any awareness of the world around you, *Sting-Ray Afternoons* is going to hit you like the smell of Clairol Herbal Essence Shampoo. Smart as heck, laugh-out-loud funny, and warm, Steve Rushin's memoir does for 1970s childhoods what Jean Shepherd did for 1940s Christmas. This book is nothing short of a Nadia Comăneci perfect 10."
　　　　　　　—Julie Klam, author of *The Stars in Our Eyes*

"Rushin uses his family as the book's focal point, capturing the nonstop zaniness of growing up with four siblings...But it's Rushin's dad, a child of the Depression, who steals the show. Whether quoting his father as he describes his five kids...or retelling stories about him being drunk on what was the then new Boeing 747, it's through his father that Rushin captures the mystery and magic of childhood."　　—*Publishers Weekly*

"Steve Rushin's *Sting-Ray Afternoons* is a fun and often hilarious account of growing up in the Midwest in the 1970s. Throughout the book I was pleasantly reminded of things from my own past—Rushin revisits the TV shows, the toys, the games, of the era while telling his family's own story. *Sting-Ray Afternoons* captures both the freedom of youth and the universal longing for experience in a bigger, more adult world. If you grew up in the 1970s, prepare to have your memory triggered."

—Craig Finn, songwriter and guitarist, the Hold Steady

"Rushin's use of the English language not only paints a complete picture of what it was like to score a touchdown in a game of football in the front yard or get that strikeout in the garage but connects those who grew up in a different time."

—Jason Olson, *Bloomington Sun Current*

"The nostalgic sweetness of Rushin's memories...provides convincing evidence that life in the 1970s wasn't as chaotic as it's often made out to be."

—*Kirkus Reviews*

"Charming and heartfelt, hilarious and touching, Rushin's *Sting-Ray Afternoons* is a pitch-perfect portrait of growing up in Middle America during the *Brady Bunch* era. A gem of a memoir, a tribute to family, and a delectable slice of American history."

—Nina Sankovitch, author of *Tolstoy and the Purple Chair* and *The Lowells of Massachusetts*

"A wild ride through Rushin's '70s boyhood...A fiercely funny memoir about family, sports, music, food, and fads."

—Priscilla Kipp, *BookPage*

Sting-Ray Afternoons

A Memoir

Steve Rushin

BACK BAY BOOKS
LITTLE, BROWN AND COMPANY
New York Boston London

Copyright © 2017 by Steve Rushin

Hachette Book Group supports the right to free expression and the value of copyright. The purpose of copyright is to encourage writers and artists to produce the creative works that enrich our culture.

The scanning, uploading, and distribution of this book without permission is a theft of the author's intellectual property. If you would like permission to use material from the book (other than for review purposes), please contact permissions@hbgusa.com. Thank you for your support of the author's rights.

Back Bay Books / Little, Brown and Company
Hachette Book Group
1290 Avenue of the Americas, New York, NY 10104
littlebrown.com

Originally published in hardcover by Little, Brown and Company, July 2017
First Back Bay trade paperback edition, July 2018

Back Bay Books is an imprint of Little, Brown and Company, a division of Hachette Book Group, Inc. The Back Bay Books name and logo are trademarks of Hachette Book Group, Inc.

The publisher is not responsible for websites (or their content) that are not owned by the publisher.

The Hachette Speakers Bureau provides a wide range of authors for speaking events. To find out more, go to hachettespeakersbureau.com or call (866) 376-6591.

All photographs are from the collection of the author, unless otherwise noted. The Alan Page anecdote on pages 189–192 originally appeared in slightly different form in *Road Swing* by Steve Rushin, © Doubleday, 1998. Portions of "Thanks, Your Honor" and "Cold Comfort" reprinted from *Sports Illustrated*, © 2000, 2005 by Time Inc.

ISBN 978-0-316-39223-5 (hc) / 978-0-316-39225-9 (pb)
LCCN 2016958350

10 9 8 7 6 5 4 3 2 1

LSC-C

Printed in the United States of America

For the faces on the stairs—
    Jim,
      Tom,
        Amy,
          John

Contents

Sting-Ray Afternoons

Introduction

Sting-Ray Afternoons

I'm a product of the 1970s. Like other products of that age—the Boeing 747 and the Schwinn Sting-Ray bicycle—I was conceived in the 1960s but fully flowered in the decade that followed, when I saw my first Sting-Ray through a heat shimmer on West 96th Street in Bloomington, Minnesota. It was electric-green—called "Flamboyant Lime" in the catalogue—with "ape-hanger" handlebars and a banana seat bedazzled with glitter. These were little silver flakes embedded beneath a rubberized clear-coat, so that a Sting-Ray seat shone like the kitchen linoleum in a Mop & Glo commercial.

Everything gleamed or glinted on TV in the '70s, from the "flavor crystals" in Folgers coffee to the yellow dentures dipped in Polident and instantly restored to pristine, piano-key whiteness. This cleansing was often done by a fastidious mascot: Mr. Clean or the Ty-D-Bol man or those kamikaze Scrubbing Bubbles, who scoured the tub then dived to their death down an echoey drain.

My mother was a fastidious mascot in her own right—a Swiss Army knife of housekeeping implements, armed to the teeth with feather duster and Bissell broom and lemon-scented Pledge. With the ease of a riverboat poker dealer, she could flick five coasters beneath as many sweating Kool-Aid glasses from ten yards away.

She often found me, the idlest of her five children, beached on a burgundy love seat, watching a wood-paneled Zenith that was camouflaged in a wood-paneled living room. "Stop gathering dust," she would say while she gathered up dust. I came to understand that it was really the dust that bothered her more than the indolence. In later years, she'd arm-sweep the entire contents of my brother John's cluttered dresser top into the wastebasket, then tip the wastebasket into the garbage can in the garage, where John would find—playing a hunch, after a frantic search—his wallet, his driver's license, and his life savings of twenty dollars.

When Mom snapped off the TV, the image would shrink toward the center, as if also disappearing down a drain. I would pass my hand across the warm surface of the screen. It would crackle with an electromagnetic force field, literally drawing me to it, the fine hairs on my arm bending toward its bottle-green glass.

"Out," Mom would say. A banana-yellow finger, gloved in Playtex, pointed to the screen door.

The index finger of her other hand would be poised on the trigger of an aerosol can of Glade. Mom might not have torn the hole in our ozone layer on her own, but she substantially enlarged it with her Cool Lime fumigations of the bathroom.

"Out," Mom would say again. "Get some fresh air."

The air freshener did not count as fresh air, despite my making the point that it should, and I was eventually flushed from my own house every summer afternoon, like Fred Flintstone put out by his cat.

This was never a happy development. I was a second-generation indoorsman, following in the house-slippered footsteps of my father, who avoided nature when he wasn't selling eight-track tapes for the 3M Company in Saint Paul. And also when he was. To him, nature was a perversion, so much so that he had a private nickname for the guy who walked his dog by the little brook across from our house every morning: the Creek Freak.

"Get a loada the Creek Freak," he'd say, peering through a gap in the curtains. "He's walking the dog." He said this as if dog walking was a euphemism for some comical perversion.

Needless to say, we had no cabin Up North. We didn't camp or boat or hunt. We had no pets: no dogs, no goldfish, no weekends hosting the hamster on loan from Saint Stephen's Nursery School. In fairness, my mother once descended to our basement to get a steak out of the freezer, and when she pulled the chain to light the room, she saw a garter snake coiled at her feet, cooling itself on the concrete floor. She screamed. If the basement had had windows, she'd have leapt onto the curtains and clung to them, teeth chattering, like Scooby and Shaggy when they saw a ghost.

Between screams, Mom managed to cover the snake with a bucket, which she duct-taped to the floor, so that when Dad came home from work eight hours later in a suit and tie he found, in the dark, an enraged reptile—coiled and claustrophobic—waiting to strike. He just managed to slide a copy of the REO Speedwagon album *You Can Tune a Piano, but You Can't Tuna Fish* between the concrete floor and the bucket and in that manner conveyed the snake upstairs, out the front door, and into the marshy parkland across the street.

Snakes were one of the reasons not to be outside in Minnesota on a summer afternoon in the 1970s, but there were many others, including tornadoes, mosquitoes, stray dogs, dragonflies, gnats, bees, killer bees, wasps, ticks, and—to judge by a terrifying line repeating on the radio—"alligator lizards in the air." More fearsome still were bullies and "hippies," who hung out in the elm trees in the park across the street, many of which were marked for execution—the trees, not the hippies—with a spray-painted *X*, the scarlet letter of Dutch elm disease.

Of the many perils of being out of doors, the worst by far was boredom. "There's nothing to do," I'd say.

"Find something," Mom would reply.

"We played Kick the Can," Dad would say. "We kicked a can down the street. There's always something to do."

In the garage, out of the sun, I would sit on Dad's olive-green army footlocker, a relic of his peacetime service between Korea and Vietnam but long since filled with sporting goods worn to nubbins by five kids. Sitting on all those footballs and basketballs and tennis balls for thirty minutes or longer, wondering how to pass the time, I half hoped they might hatch. And in a manner of speaking, they did.

With the empty afternoon hours stretching to the horizon, I'd head soccer balls in the driveway, keeping a meticulous account of my personal record for consecutive touches, which eventually ran into the hundreds. I'd bash tennis balls against the brick wall in the garage with a Wilson T-2000 racquet or hit fungoes to myself in the front yard, towering pop flies that I'd try to catch bare-handed. Settling under what baseball announcers always called a "tall can of corn," I'd compose lines in my head for Carnac the Magnificent, Johnny Carson's soothsayer, who was given the answers and then had to divine the questions on *The Tonight Show.* Every night at 10:30, staccato laughter from a Burbank studio leaked into my bedroom from beneath the door, accompanied by a golden beam of hallway lamplight.

> *Answer: Fungoes.*
> *Question: What's the first thing that goes when Mom turns off the TV?*

Wordplay, as its name suggests, is a form of play. I first discovered it in the school library at Nativity of the Blessed Virgin Mary, in a book called *300 Best Word Puzzles,* which took as its epigraph a line from Hamlet: "Words, words, words." Among the words on the pages that followed were the first palindromes I ever laid eyes on, including "Was it a rat I saw" and "Rise to vote, sir." I spent that first recess after library telling puzzled classmates, "Draw, O coward!"

In truth, I was the one who was puzzled, comprehensively puzzled. The phrase "You can tune a piano, but you can't tuna fish" had not just transported that snake in the basement but me as well. I loved the Knights of the Round Table in a Bugs Bunny cartoon: "Sir Loin of Beef," "Sir Osis of Liver." At the parties my parents hosted, grown-up guests, drinking and smoking in sport coats and tennis dresses, told me punning titles of "books" I might like: "You should read *Fifty Yards to the Outhouse* by Willie Makeit, illustrated by Betty Won't."

No, what I liked was *300 Best Word Puzzles*. It was first published in 1925 as *World's Best Word Puzzles* by—according to the jacket flap—"England's most distinguished puzzlist," Henry Ernest Dudeney, who was born in 1857. The Nativity of the Blessed Virgin Mary library was not known for its contemporary collection. Its shelves apparently had been stocked once, when the school opened in 1951, so that a quarter century later a boy bewitched by the aerial acrobatics (and mushroom-cloud Afro) of the Philadelphia 76ers star Julius Erving would be chastened to find, in the basketball section, books with titles like *Comeback Cagers* and *Sink It, Rusty*. On the cover, our frail white hero, in buckled satin shorts and ginger crew cut, always heaved a two-handed set shot at a wooden backboard.

The stamp on the little index card tucked in the envelope glued to the endpaper of each of these books I read invariably showed it had last been checked out on November 3, 1954. Coincidentally, it was the last time anyone had checked out the librarian too. Or so we said in eighth grade, as adolescence and the 1980s both beckoned, a decade and a childhood running down together.

In the shadow cast by our driveway basketball hoop, lying on my stomach at the curb, using a Popsicle stick to burst the tar bubbles that blistered the road surface on a summer day—this was where I saw my first Sting-Ray.

It was meant to resemble a motorcycle, so that while biking to buy baseball cards at Pik-Quik, two or more eight-year-olds on Sting-Rays could—when viewed through a heat haze—just about look like Hell's Angels. Heck's Angels, perhaps, or maybe Hell's Hall Monitors.

The Sting-Ray was the brainchild of a Schwinn executive named Al Fritz. In the early 1960s, a bicycle salesman in Southern California told Fritz that kids in suburban Los Angeles were tricking out old twenty-inch bike frames with banana seats and chopper handlebars. If you were too young for hot rods, but too old for Hot Wheels, this new style—called the "hi-rise"—could serve as the halfway house between your toddlerhood and your teens. Six hi-rise bikes parked side by side turned any suburban cul-de-sac into the parking lot of a biker bar, as Fritz was quick to recognize. At the laminate bar of a kitchen countertop, you could down a shot of Hawaiian Punch, then crush the Dixie Riddle Cup in your fist before jumping on a Sting-Ray and laying a patch of rubber in the driveway.

That was the whole point of childhood, or of boyhood, or at least of boyhood in the 1970s in the South Brook subdivision of Bloomington, Minnesota: to look and act as old and as hard-boiled as possible against all evidence to the contrary. In the spring of 1973, when I was six, researchers at the University of Chicago reported that "young school children at play are similar in a number of ways to young baboons or monkeys," a fact any boy could have told them. "Boys play aggressively in large groups," the report said, "and social rank [is] equated with 'toughness.'"

Toward that end, candy cigarettes with trademark-evading names like Marboro and Cool were enormously popular at Pik-Quik, the Bloomington convenience store that promised six nickel items for a quarter. Outside its glass door, a thousand grade school Grouchos gesticulated with bubble gum cigars. Big League Chew—shredded bubble gum in a chewing-tobacco pouch—would not arrive on Pik-Quik's shelves until 1980, but that hot-pink weed was sown in the 1970s, cultivated by the decade's kid culture.

And so a fourth-grader with a red-tipped Lucky Spike dangling from his lip and a die-cast metal cap gun tucked into the waistband of his Toughskins, riding through South Brook on a Sting-Ray the color of grape soda, was an adolescent American badass circa 1974—especially if he had a temporary tattoo from a Cracker Jack box adhered to one or both of his pipe-cleaner biceps.

Al Fritz was also an American badass. The Chicago-born son of Austrian immigrants, Fritz left school after eighth grade to study stenography before serving on the staff of General Douglas MacArthur in the Philippines, where he was wounded by a Japanese mortar. After the war, Fritz returned to his old Chicago neighborhood and to its dominant employer, the Schwinn plant, where he took a job on the factory floor and soon parlayed his stenography skills to become secretary to Frank W. Schwinn. Schwinn's father, German-born Ignaz Schwinn, not only founded the bicycle company that bore the family name but also owned the Excelsior Motorcycle Company from 1911 until 1931, at which time the Great Depression forced him to end production—and his career as an esteemed designer—of American motorcycles.

Ignaz Schwinn had been dead for eighteen years by the time Al Fritz—having worked his way up to vice president for engineering, research, and development—sold Frank Schwinn on a ready-made, factory-fresh, motorcycle-inspired bicycle whose in-house name (model J-38) was unlikely to resonate with America's eight-year-olds. Leafing through a dictionary, Fritz saw a line drawing of a stingray, its pectoral fins raised on either side, and its profile put him in mind of those ape-hanger handlebars.

At the time, Schwinn sold more than three hundred different bike models, and the bestselling among them moved maybe ten thousand units a year. In 1963, the Sting-Ray's first year of production, with a pool of 23.4 million American children between the ages of six and eleven, Schwinn sold 46,630 Sting-Rays at $49.95 a pop. By 1970, hi-rise-style bikes—sometimes called "muscle bikes," sometimes called "wheelie bikes"—made up most of the American bicycle market. In that first year of the new decade, 3.4 million hi-rise bikes were sold in the United States. The Sting-Ray and its many cheap knockoffs rose in tandem with the career of Evel Knievel. On a million plywood driveway ramps, kids braver or tougher or cooler than I was tried (and often violently failed) to jump rows of galvanized-steel trash cans.

What made this bike so bewitching? To begin with, there were those candy-shop colors—Flamboyant Lime, Kool Lemon, and the insuperable Radiant Coppertone. For a time, Sting-Rays came in the vivid purple of cough medicine, which also happened to be the color of Bloomington's most famous residents, the Minnesota Vikings. These colors, set off by chrome fenders, with a reflective bicycle license issued by the City of Bloomington adhered to the seat tube, gave the lucky Sting-Ray riders a pride of ownership, something to take care of. A bike was our first licensed anything, before a driver's license, before a hunting license, before a real estate or forklift or marriage license.

A bicycle was independence, a magic carpet, freedom of movement, but also a belled or tasseled expression of our developing personalities, even if my bike was a burgundy CCM Mustang Marauder festooned with Valvoline and STP stickers, stuck to the seat by my older brothers, who'd gotten them free at the gas station.

The ape-hanger handlebars on a Sting-Ray made it easy to pop a wheelie. In its chrome fenders was reflected the fish-eye image of the bike's blissful owner. A cable lock coiled around the seat post like a steel serpent kept the Sting-Ray secure when parked in the bike rack of the Penn Lake branch of the Hennepin County Library, where it was the envy of all who passed it. The racing-slick back tire was designed for fishtailing or leaving the longest possible driveway skid marks.

But of course you couldn't say "skid marks" without irony, without thinking of underpants, without someone chanting "Fonzie's cool! He's not square! Skid marks in his underwear!"

Underwear, not incidentally, was white, the porcelain white of toilets and tubs, of T-shirts washed in Tide or teeth brushed with Topol ("The smoker's tooth polish"). The colors that would come to be associated with the 1970s—harvest-gold; avocado-green; the brown-and-orange scheme favored by Burger King and the San Diego Padres—had nothing on white: white tennis shoes, white tube socks, our tighty-whities scored with skid marks, awaiting the cleansing touch of Fab or Bold or Cheer.

My mother aspired to the dazzling white bedsheets of detergent commercials, but there were also the white loafers and belt of the esteemed architect Mike Brady, the white jumpsuit of Evel Knievel, the white spikes of the Swingin' Oakland A's, the white-smocked Mr. Whipple (squeezing the Charmin), the white cleats that spawned the nickname of Billy "White Shoes" Johnson—kick-return specialist of the Houston Oilers and early adopter of the end-zone celebration dance. The '70s era was the gleaming white of storm-trooper armor, of Travolta's suit in *Saturday Night Fever.*

White was also the color of heaven in the movies, and I spent the '70s at Nativity of the Blessed Virgin Mary, K through 8, wanting this spotlessness, to feel Scrubbing-Bubble clean coming out of confession or Christmas Mass. I wondered if the conscience could be cleansed of its ring around the collar, if there were—as in the Calgon commercial—an "ancient Chinese secret" for scrubbing the soul.

Heaven, I knew even then, would be an uphill battle. The tenth commandment was against coveting thy neighbor's goods, and there were so many goods to covet growing up in that decade, not least of all the Flamboyant Lime Sting-Ray, gliding past me now on West 96th Street, its owner—a freckled twelve-year-old from Washburn Avenue—fixing me with his gaze and saying, "What are *you* looking at?"

"Your bike," I said with the innocence of an eight-year-old.

But he was already past me, and he shouted over his shoulder, "No shit, Sherlock!"

Even as my face flushed and my armpits ignited, I could appreciate the alliteration. (It was the alliteration as much as the candy itself that bewitched me at Pik-Quik: Chunky, Chuckles, Chiclets, Charleston Chew.)

As the bike was pedaled into the distance, the white letters of "Sting-Ray" painted on the chain guard rearranged themselves into an anagram: "It's-Angry."

The Sting-Ray was undeniably beautiful, but before I ever laid eyes on one, there were Big Wheels and Green Machines to lust after, and Topps baseball cards, just as later would come boom boxes, pinball machines, custom vans, and—at the very end of the decade—girls. Women, rather: Charlie's Angels and the Farrah poster my brother Tom put up in the room we shared for twelve years and the newspaper ads featuring Bo Derek in *10*.

All my father would say on returning, lightly flushed, from seeing *10* at the Southtown Theatre with my mother in 1979 was "You can see it when you're forty."

Charles Foster Kane was fixated on his sled, but childhood has a thousand Rosebuds. The 1970s escorted me from age three to age thirteen, from the onset of memory to the onslaught of puberty. My childhood ran precisely in parallel with that decade. As such, the '70s don't seem to recede at all with the passage of time but follow me, the way the moon always followed our car at night when I'd pretend to fall asleep in my seat and be carried into the house and upstairs to bed.

There, my mother would tuck me into a quilted, baby-blue bedspread emblazoned with tin soldiers and toy cannons, $7.99 in the Sears Christmas Wish Book of 1972. The Sears Christmas Wish Book, thick as a telephone directory, was more than a catalogue of consumer goods. It was a glossy catalogue of children's dreams, a hard-copy rendering of an eight-year-old's id.

Beneath that Sears blanket, my fingers did their nightly inventory of bugbites—like rereading the day in Braille—and I drifted into many a Sting-Ray dream.

In those dreams, I parked my Sting-Ray in a friend's driveway, angled just so, the sun glinting off the silver fenders, the kickstand sinking into the softening blacktop. (It always did this. Every driveway was kickstand quicksand.) The metallic green chain guard painted with that white hyphenate magically angled to the right—*Sting-Ray,* as if in forward motion—was to me what the Cadillac badge would become to my dad: a token of arrival that was always just an inch out of reach.

Dad didn't have a Caddy, and I didn't have a Sting-Ray. I had something *like* a Sting-Ray, which is to say something not at all like one, something by the Canadian Cycle and Motor Company, more famous for its hockey skates, though it might just as well have been by Huffy or Raleigh or even Sears, purveyor of the Spyder 500. Sears also sold a tennis shoe—"Made by Converse, just for Sears"—with *four* stripes. Sears, protesting too much, called it "The Winner."

"Four stripes," Mom would say, stroking my hair. "That's one better than Adidas." But she and I both knew this wasn't the army, and that extra stripe didn't signify a higher rank but rather its opposite.

Sears also sold a cut-rate version of Converse All Stars called Jeepers. They didn't fool anyone, even if they did have something called "action-traction soles."

We were suckers for these copywriter coinages. Certs with Retsyn ("It's two mints in one!"). SSP Racers with "the howl of power from sonic sound!"

Still, so powerful was Sears's hold on American mothers

that the company, at the dawn of the '70s, was the largest retailer in the world, a title it claimed for half a century. In 1924, the company founded a 50,000-watt radio station in Chicago, WLS, whose call letters stood for "World's Largest Store." In 1970, Sears began to build a headquarters suitable to its place in the firmament: the Sears Tower in Chicago was to be the tallest building on earth, an edifice honoring all the Spyder 500s and Winner shoes it was then selling to frugal moms, which was just about all of them, as far as I knew.

The lives of American children were full of these name-brand knockoffs. We got the Old Dutch Twin Pack of "Rip-L" potato chips in a cardboard box instead of stackable Pringles, which were vacuum-packed into something like a tennis ball can and made the same satisfying *whoosh* when you opened it.

Mom, not entirely oblivious to the social status at stake with every shoe purchase, didn't buy The Winner but something slightly less objectionable: Jox by Thom McAn. These looked enough like the Onitsuka Tigers I coveted but were just dissimilar enough to avoid legal action. Target—"Tar-zhay," as Dad called it—carried another brand, with two stripes, when all any of us ever wanted were the three-striped Adidas or the Onitsuka Tigers or the blindingly white Nike Cortezes.

Tennis shoes had nothing to do with tennis. There were only two kinds of shoes for Catholic grade-schoolers: tennis shoes (sometimes called "gym shoes") and good shoes (sometimes called "church shoes"). Tennis shoes were what our cousins in Cincinnati called "sneakers," one of many exotic words they had for everyday objects: Our "pop" they called "soda." Our "suckers" they called "lollipops." Our "burnouts," "freaks," or "dirtballs"—the phrases applied to any kids who smoked— they called "wubs."

We played Duck, Duck, Gray Duck; they played Duck, Duck, Goose. What we called "ketchup" they called— hilariously and inexplicably—"catsup."

Tennis shoes were the primary way to distinguish ourselves at Catholic school, where there was a uniform but no real uniformity. To the outsider—to a public-school kid at Hillcrest Elementary—we all looked the same in our navy-blue pants and light blue shirts. But on the inside, on our exercise yard of a playground (bordered by a twenty-foot noise-barrier wall that protected us from the cars speeding by on I-35W, and also protected the cars from us) our uniforms encoded all manner of social signifiers.

Long-sleeve or short-sleeve shirt? Button-down or not? Oxford cloth or polyester? Some shirts had a small loop of fabric sewn between the shoulder blades that was (and remains) of mysterious utility. It was barely noticeable, really, until it one day became known as a Fag Tag or a Fruit Loop, after which nobody wanted one. Which was fine, since they were usually torn off at recess during games of Smear the Queer.

According to Nativity legend, Sister Mariella had once hung Jay Campbell on a hook in the broom closet of the fifth-grade classroom and left him there in the dark for over an hour, dangling from his Fruit Loop.

Nobody doubted the veracity of this story. Sister Mariella was the only nun at Nativity still teaching in the full-penguin habit. Her face, squeezed by her wimple, gave her the look—and the disposition—of a woman perpetually caught between elevator doors.

For reasons known only to her, Sister Mariella kept a ceramic mug on her desk in which she hoarded a small collection of walnuts and acorns as well as paper clips and rubber bands. She called this receptacle her "nut cup," and she appeared not to notice the stifled laughter and ten-year-old embarrassment whenever she announced, as she frequently had cause to, "Mr. Matthews, please place your Juicy Fruit in my nut cup *this instant*."

If Ned Zupke failed to stow his galoshes in the cloakroom, where they belonged, she would say, "Has someone forgotten his rubbers?"

She called rubber bands "rubber binders."

When Sister Mariella wrote on the blackboard with her back turned to the class, the more brazen among us would attempt to shoot spitballs into her nut cup. This was done by removing the little blue plug from one end of a BIC Cristal pen and removing the little blue cap from the other end. Pushing the ink stem out turned the BIC's empty barrel into a cannon. A corner of notebook paper, steeped in saliva and rolled into an angry pellet, was loaded into the BIC and—with a sharp intake of breath—blown like a poison dart toward the nut cup. If that dart missed its target, it would land—with a moist *splat*—on Sister Mariella's desk. It was not uncommon for her to return from the blackboard to find a dozen or more of these spitballs, adhered to—and hardening on—her weathered work surface.

Anyone caught red-handed might hang in the broom closet from his Fruit Loop, as far as we knew, or be exiled to the cloakroom to stare for half an hour at Ned Zupke's soiled rubbers. But nobody ever got caught. Of the thirty suspects in class, all thirty were packing BIC Cristals. Indeed, for the entirety of the 1970s, every child in the school—every child in every school—had a BIC Cristal with a pointed blue cap poised on his or her lips. This is hardly an exaggeration. By the end of the decade, BIC was selling tens of thousands of these pens *every day,* and the name of the pen's inventor—Marcel Bich—was literally on the tips of all our tongues.

Bich was born in Turin in 1914 but emigrated to Paris at an early age. By the time he was making pen and pencil cases in a leaky shed in suburban Clichy, he had become a French national. This was after World War II, at the same time Al Fritz began working on the floor of the Schwinn factory in Chicago. The two men, an ocean apart, were already conceiving a '70s American childhood long before any of us American children were actually conceived.

Bich didn't invent the ballpoint pen—Laszlo Biro, a Hungarian newspaper editor, fathered the modern ballpoint in 1938—but Bich went a long way toward perfecting it when he introduced the Cristal in 1959. Through its clear polystyrene barrel, you could watch the ink drop like the mercury in a thermometer. This transparency would remain a distinct advantage over the Cristal's own loudmouthed brother, the BIC Banana, whose opaque yellow barrel achieved a devoted following in the '70s, when bananas were enjoying a brief vogue in pop culture: *The Banana Splits* TV show of the late '60s gave way to banana seats on bicycles and, by the middle '70s, the banana section on the TV game show *Tattletales.*

In 1972, BIC would enter the disposable lighter market and create a second icon of the era, one that illuminated the encores of every concert in the decade and beyond. But even the toughest among us in fifth grade were not yet lighting up real Lucky Strikes or flicking our BICs at Led Zeppelin concerts, despite Led Zep's regular visits to Bloomington to play the Met Center arena. And so the BIC Cristal remained the greater influence in our daily lives.

This perfect object was practically free, a price that appealed to all our parents. In 1970, the tuition at three-quarters of Catholic schools in America was less than a hundred dollars. Likewise, the price of a BIC Cristal in 1979 was the same as it had been in 1959: twenty-nine cents. Purchased in a multipack, the pens could be had for as little as seven cents apiece.

All these pennies made Marcel Bich a very rich man by the time the fifth-graders at Nativity had weaponized his pens in our assault on Sister Mariella's nut cup. Bich drove a Bentley, became a baron, fathered ten children, contested the America's Cup yacht race, and generally lived as large as he deserved to on the proceeds of his world-conquering pen-slash-spitball bazooka.

To this day I cannot see a BIC Cristal without wanting to field-strip it and load it with a spitball made from spiral-bound Mead notebook paper steeped in my saliva. And I'm hardly alone in that compulsion, given the ubiquity of BIC's invention. The one billionth BIC Cristal was sold in 2006, and it has joined the collection of the Metropolitan Museum of Art, alongside Van Gogh's *Starry Night* and Dalí's melting clocks, as a timeless (if not quite priceless) work of art.

Likewise, Schwinn Sting-Rays of the '60s and '70s now sell, fully restored, for five thousand dollars or more. In 2016, when I showed one to my brother Tom, with whom I shared a bedroom for much of the 1970s, he squinted at the Flamboyant Lime model and said, "Five thousand dollars? For *that* piece of shit?"

In truth, it looked humbler than either of us remembered, deprived of its '70s sunshine and harshly lit on eBay. But then Tom gazed a little closer, lost himself in a long reverie, and finally said, more softly this time, "That sissy bar needs to be higher."

True, they're only objects, and you can't take them with you. But are they really? And why can't you? A retired Procter & Gamble engineer named Fredric Baur, when he died in Cincinnati in 2008, was cremated, per his wishes, and had his ashes interred in his greatest creation, another coveted totem of my childhood. His children had purchased this vessel at Walgreens expressly for that purpose, on their way to his memorial service in Springfield Township, Ohio, where Fred Baur is now riding out eternity in the Pringles can he invented. After a brief debate over which flavor to choose, his children went with Original, because Fred Baur was sui generis, much as his contemporaries Al Fritz and Marcel Bich had been.

It's a paradox. One man's entire life can be interred in an emblematic object of his age. But it takes a hundred more of these objects to capture the lightning flash of a single childhood.

1.

Eight-Track Mind

Dad holds a finger to the sky. "Look," he says. The moon is a waxing crescent, a children's book moon. It looks to my father like Bob Hope in profile.

On a summer night in 1969, in the moon glow of the motor court of the Shady Lawn Motel, five and a half of us spill out of a Chevy Impala station wagon; Dad cradles me in a forearm, the way he used to hold a football. Jim and Tom, my big brothers, race ahead of us to the check-in desk. Mom, five months pregnant, presses a palm to her lumbar. She doesn't know it yet, but she will get the daughter she has instructed us to pray for every night—my little sister, Amy.

Jim, Tom, and Amy. Our parents named us as if we were telegrams, as if they were being charged by the letter.

And so the Shady Lawn is cheap, the kind of motel Mom and Dad are partial to, with an air conditioner rattling in the window. In its man-made breeze, the single-ply toilet paper dances like a little lace curtain.

A thrumming soda machine stands guard outside the lobby, lit from within and stocked with exotic pops, the kind of soft drinks we can only have—and can only *find*—on vacation. Tahitian Treat. Cactus Cooler. Bubble Up.

Dad squeezes the coins in his pocket to stop them from jangling. He doesn't want Jim or Tom asking for change for a Shasta cola or an Orange Crush. Vending machines, my father knows, are untrustworthy, prone to rob a man of his hardearned nickels while leaving the desired treat agonizingly out of reach.

He has already been betrayed by countless inanimate objects, and many animate ones. The superlemon that is our wood-paneled Ford LTD Country Squire station wagon is still a few years and a few dozen repairs in our future. So are a succession of unsatisfactory armchairs. The spring-loaded suspension of one such chair—his "Archie Bunker chair," as we will come to call all of them—seems to give out the moment he drives it off the lot at Levitz. From that day forward, whenever he hears the Levitz commercial jingle—"You'll love it at Levvv-itz"—Dad sings softly to himself, "It's lousy at Levvv-itz."

And yet the mechanical failure of any man-made good—be it toaster or transmission—confirms his hard-won knowledge of the universe and seems to put him at peace. It proves him right, that relying on other people, to say nothing of their mechanical offspring, is foolhardy. The larger the failure, the greater the gratification, so that when the furnace finally blows, he can sigh and say what he always does: "The joys of homeownership." Or when he is feeling especially philosophical: *"C'est la Guy."* None of us knows it is *"C'est la vie,"* least of all Dad, who prior to flying to Paris for work will buy a book called *French Made Simple.* He'll never even open it, leaving it on our basement bookshelf for two decades while he wings it *en français,* developing his own versions of that and other languages. French Made Even Simpler. When he tells us to eat in Italian— *mangia*—it comes out as a kind of Chinese: "Mon-jai! Mon-jai!"

In January of 1970, a forty-year-old man named Robert Goines inserts a few coins into the soda machine at his own filling station in Indianapolis. Then he presses a button and watches, with growing fury, as nothing at all happens. In previous years, by Goines's own estimate, that machine had taken twenty-five dollars in nickels and dimes from him and his customers, and now—God dammit—he has had enough.

"So I walked over to the desk drawer, got out my .22 revolver, and shot it dead," Goines tells a judge after his arrest for discharging a weapon within the city limits. Upon firing the fatal bullet, his .22 still smoking in his hand, Goines says to the vending machine, "That's the last time you're going to cheat anybody."

The judge, unmoved, sentences Goines to ten days in jail and fines him $160 plus court costs, a fine my father fervently wishes to be paid in nickels. Almost immediately, no fewer than eight lawyers come to the defendant's aid, helping him to file an appeal, presumably on the grounds that shooting a pop machine at the dawn of the 1970s is justifiable homicide.

In the years to come, children will find other ways to get revenge. Slugs—the smooth circles of metal punched out of electrical boxes—sometimes work in the absence of coins. Friends become adept at sliding a hand up the chute and manipulating the machine's inner workings. They are soft-drink ob-gyns, expert at digitally extracting a Mello Yello or a Mr. Pibb.

In the 1970s, I will learn to remove the pull tab from a can of Coke and casually insert it into the beverage, hoping to swallow the one but not the other. It is as tough as any eight-year-old can hope to look without benefit of a candy cigarette or a souped-up Sting-Ray.

But on this night in the late summer of 1969, I am not quite three and struggling to stay awake, freshly fed at a greasy spoon in the resort town of Wisconsin Dells. "The Dells," as everyone in the Upper Midwest knows, are the largest single tourist attraction in Wisconsin, outdrawing even the Mars Cheese Castle or the House on the Rock.

The Dells in 1969 has fifty-six swimming pools, "twenty-two man-made attractions," and one hundred thirty motels, enough to attract 1.9 million guests a year. And every one of these motels—the Pine Aire, the Black Hawk, Landeck's Auto Court, their neon NO VACANCY signs buzzing—is conveniently adjacent to one of the town's fifty-five restaurants. In a town with fifty-five restaurants and fifty-six swimming pools, a day does not pass without a thousand mothers instructing three times as many children to wait forty-five minutes after eating before going for a swim.

Each of these fifty-five restaurants is the kind of joint favored by Dad, a car-based salesman with a weakness for alliteration: Country Kitchen. Korner Counter. Coffee Cup. To the eternal question "Where were you when Kennedy was shot?" Dad can always answer "The Pie Pan, off the Edens Expressway."

Even beyond the pancake houses and the pop machines, the Dells are, for any child under ten, a wonderland of unearthly delights. You can't throw a rubber tomahawk in any direction without hitting an Indian Trading Post selling fringed buckskins, hand-tooled wallets, peace pipes, tom-toms, cowboy hats, bows and arrows, and beaded moccasins.

At the center of it all is Fort Dells, a reproduction pioneer outpost and Western-themed amusement park that steals from Disneyland in broad daylight. It is divided into sections named Frontierland, Adventureland, and Indianland. Kids can be locked up for a jaunty photograph in one of the fort's many stockades. A famous statue of a saloon girl—"Lady Lou"—is seated on a park bench in Frontierland, her dress hiked to mid-thigh. Teenage boys rest their heads on her emerald-clad bosom while dads—posing for Polaroids—snap the garter belt on her fiberglass thigh.

An array of glossy brochures racked in the lobby of the Shady Lawn Motel advertise the Tommy Bartlett Water Show on Lake Delton. It is the best of its kind, the Pyramids of pyramid-based waterskiing spectacles. Amphibious duckboats decommissioned from World War II ply the streets and waterways of the Dells, where middle-aged men—also decommissioned from World War II—reenact Old West shootouts. In Wisconsin Dells, from mid-May to September, Black Bart is killed every hour on the half hour.

All of this is to say that three boys aged eight, four, and two can fall asleep in a cheap motel on a midsummer night in Wisconsin Dells and never run out of dreams for the next morning: of go-kart tracks, wax museums, haunted mansions, ghost towns, lost canyons, enchanted forests, storybook gardens, and prehistoric lands.

But these rituals of a Dells vacation are all in a distant future, in the decade that is looming but not quite here. We made a brief flyby of these various attractions before checking into the motel, enough to whet our various appetites, but on this trip in the summer of '69, we are not on holiday. There will be no Cactus Coolers or Tahitian Treats. On this night, rather, Wisconsin Dells is chosen strictly for its location: equidistant between suburban Chicago (where we had lived until this very morning) and our unfurnished new home in suburban Minneapolis (where we will take up residence tomorrow afternoon).

Our growing family is leaving Illinois and starting a new life in Minnesota. Dad has been transferred—summoned, *promoted*—to the international headquarters of the Minnesota Mining and Manufacturing Company, known to its employees the world over as Mickey Mouse Mining, and known to the rest as 3M. Dad shortens the employees-only phrase further—every night at the dinner table, in his sigh-heavy conversations with my mother—to Mickey Mining.

A Mayflower moving van with all our possessions trails us by a day. When my father says, "Look," as he holds me in his arm outside the motel on this Sunday night, I gaze up at that waxing crescent moon. Like us, it's looking west, toward Minnesota. It's a cartoon moon, the kind suspended above a high school stage. All the way here in the car, the moon has followed us, and now we are following it. The whole world is following it.

My 1970s childhood begins in earnest on this night, on July 20, 1969, at the Shady Lawn Motel in Wisconsin Dells, Wisconsin, with my dad hooking an index finger at the moon and whispering, "Someone's up there. Right now."

In a few years' time I won't be able to look at the moon without thinking of an anagram from Henry Ernest Dudeney's *300 Best Word Puzzles.*

astronomer = moon starer

I share a bed at the Shady Lawn with Jim and Tom. I was meant to be Dan, three-lettered like my brothers, but Dad vetoed the name in the hospital room. His new boss was named Dan, and Dad told Mom he'd be damned if he was going to be the ass-kisser who walks into the office on Monday morning having named his new son for the new boss.

In spite of (or perhaps *because* of) Don Rushin's unwillingness to brownnose, that new boss now requires Dad's presence at 3M headquarters in Saint Paul, on the Mickey Mining mother ship.

I sleep bracketed by my brothers, Three Stooges–style, in a room adjoining Mom and Dad's. On the other side of a thin door, Dad turns on the TV and manipulates the rabbit ears. At 9:56 p.m. central daylight time, I softly snore as Neil Armstrong sets foot on the moon.

The men on the moon, and the colonies to follow, will surely need Scotch brand recording tape for all their magnetic-tape needs. Don Rushin, a magnetic-tape salesman, who is also a magnetic tape salesman—behold, the power of the hyphen!—might one day add the moon to his sales territory.

With our move to Minnesota, he is already adding all of earth to his purview, moving up in the world, from car-based salesman to international jet-setter at the most propitious time in aviation history.

As if preparing for Dad's new-won responsibilities, Boeing is, at this very moment in 1969, putting the finishing touches on an engineering wonder, a winged *Titanic* called the 747. It will be the first "jumbo jet," twice the size of Boeing's 707, which itself was twice the size (and twice as fast) as the prop plane it usurped, the Stratocruiser. The 707 was the first jet to achieve commercial success as a passenger plane. On its debut in 1958, Pan Am ushered in the age of jet transport and created the jet set. But Pan Am founder Juan Trippe had also worked to ensure that airline travel was not entirely closed off to the common man, that international destinations could be aspired to. And so he created a second class of seating—tourist—in an effort to democratize global travel. As early as 1949, Trippe appeared on the cover of *Time* magazine above the line "Now the world is every man's oyster."

"Mass travel by air—made possible in the jet age—may prove to be more significant to world destiny than the atom bomb," Trippe said. "For there can be no atom bomb potentially more powerful than the air tourist, charged with curiosity, enthusiasm, and goodwill, who can roam the four corners of the world, meeting in friendship and understanding the people of other nations and races."

Trippe was convinced the masses would be drawn to travel in the 1970s. In 1965, Pan Am forecasted a 200 percent increase in international travel by 1980. Planes would have to get bigger to accommodate the demand of an eager public to see a shrinking globe.

Enter the 747, the love child of Juan Trippe and Boeing chief Bill Allen. It's bigger than anything previously dreamt of. Six stories tall, with a fuselage twenty feet across, it necessitates all manner of new parts and designs and even words, beginning with "wide-body." It holds three hundred fifty passengers, and two aisles are required to evacuate them in ninety seconds, as the FAA mandates. The ceilings are eight feet high, with no center overhead baggage bins, so that stepping onto a 747 will feel like walking into an airy cathedral.

The plane weighs 355 tons fully loaded. To look at a 747 on the ground is to fail to imagine such a thing airborne. But Pratt & Whitney have built a revolutionary engine called the JT9D, four of which are sufficient to carry the beast away, like a baby borne aloft by the four corners of a stork's blanket. Each of those four engines is seven feet nine inches in diameter, large enough for a stewardess to stand up in. And stewardesses frequently do precisely that in promotional photographs, which tease a public longing for this sexy new conveyance.

The 747 is meant to be only a stopgap until Trippe can shrink the world even further. It is designed to move passengers only until the mid-1970s, when the new supersonic transport planes—SSTs, already a joint project of the French and British—are expected to become the workhorses of commercial air travel, ushering passengers from New York to London in three hours. Toward that end, Trippe insisted the 747 be bi-level, with the cockpit on the upper level, and the front nosecone lifts straight up so the plane can be easily converted to a cargo carrier by the time everyone is flying on the Concorde or its equivalent in America's looming bicentennial year.

I don't know it in the predawn darkness outside the Shady Lawn Motel in 1969, but Trippe is already carrying my father Up, Up, and Away from me.

When Trippe placed his massive initial order for the 747, one of his longest-serving employees was living in Darien, Connecticut. Charles Lindbergh would take the New Haven Railroad into Grand Central, then walk to the iconic Pan Am Building for consultations on the project. Lindbergh approved of the 747, which was somewhat better appointed than the *Spirit of St. Louis* had been. "He frequently flies to Paris," wrote Lindbergh biographer Walter S. Ross in 1968, "and the jets he takes follow the same great-circle route which he was the first to fly successfully."

A little more than four decades after Lindbergh's first Atlantic crossing, that great-circle route is about to become a swinging cocktail party in the skies. Of all the 747's technological innovations, the upstairs lounge is the greatest: at the top of a spiral staircase, conveniently adjacent to the cockpit, is an open bar, groovily appointed—some have Wurlitzer organs—where a wide-tied businessman might drink all night from the United States to Europe. Continental Airlines enlists Playboy Bunnies to ply the aisles on its Chicago to Los Angeles route. Other weeks, magicians roam the cabins doing card tricks. To a child of the 1970s, the name itself—747—holds a strange magic.

At Boeing, model numbers in the 500s are reserved for turbine engines, 600s are for rockets, and 700s are devoted to jet aircraft. The round number 700 had been deemed insufficiently alluring for Boeing's first release, so the marketing department—liking the bookend cadence of two 7s—called it the 707. It was followed, over the years, by the 717, the 727, and the 737, those 7-and-7s hinting at the cocktail-fueled flights to come on the 747.

Even before the jet's maiden voyage, airports fear massive human logjams when the 747 attempts to unload three hundred fifty passengers at a time. The long lines anticipated at toilets after overnight flights have airlines contemplating waking the passengers in shifts to empty their bladders. But the truth is, passengers are already wetting themselves in anticipation of flying the 747, Dad included.

Juan Trippe's gamble begins to look like a stroke of genius. "If anyone ever flies to the moon," said James Landis, head of the Civil Aeronautics Board, as the plane was still in development in the middle 1960s, "the very next day Trippe will ask C.A.B. to authorize regular service."

Well, as of this summer night, someone *has* flown to the moon, just hours earlier, and Dad will soon be in flight as well: Pan Am plans its 747 voyages to begin when the new decade does, in January of 1970.

That date promises an age of wonder in which just about anything can happen. A leading cancer researcher, Dr. James T. Grace Jr., has confidently asserted that cancer will be a memory by 1979. "I predict that we can enter the decade of the '80s without the specter of cancer hanging over our people," Grace says, a statement that everyone can suddenly affirm with the brand-new sentence starter: "If they can put a man on the moon, surely they can [fill in the blank with your wildest dream]."

With the moon still out and fresh with footprints, we rouse from our beds at the Shady Lawn Motel and are on the road before dawn on this Monday morning, heading for Minnesota. The Impala wagon is butterscotch with a butterscotch interior. Its menacing seat belts are safely tucked in the crevice between the bench seats and the backrests so that no one will be struck by a swinging buckle if Dad has to swerve at eighty miles an hour, which is the speed of traffic on the highway, where the posted limit is seventy-five.

"What's the best thing to come out of Wisconsin?" Dad asks before answering his own question: "Interstate 94."

I am bobbing on Mom's lap in the front seat, so in the event of an accident in these days before the air bag, I will be the thing deployed to save the lives of my mother and unborn sister.

Motorists happily heave their donut bags out their windows on the interstate. Jelly-roll filling spatters the faces of motorcyclists unencumbered by helmets.

We drive, and our windshield wipers sluice off the remains of a paper cup of Tab jettisoned from a tractor-trailer. The median of every American highway is a riot of crushed cans, mateless socks, and windblown burger wrappers. In a single afternoon in the spring of 1970, the Marsh family of Bangor, Wisconsin, will collect 389 *pounds* of litter along just 4.5 miles of Highway 162 in America's Dairyland, a haul that includes, by their account, "beer and soft drink containers, old hubcaps, iron bars, plastic bags, and whatnot."

It's the "whatnot" that is endlessly diverting on long car trips—the baby buggies and toilet seats and aluminum lawn chairs blown free from roof racks, all the stuff we spy on the side of the road in what will become a game of Garbage Bingo. In 1969, half of all Americans admit to intentionally littering. By one estimate, 20 million pieces of litter are loosed on the streets and sidewalks of America this year, and they consist of almost every conceivable object. In Maryland alone in 1969, an estimated 160,000 abandoned cars litter the countryside.

The most commonly discarded object is the cigarette butt. At a time when smoking is legal in all places, and compulsory in many of them, cigarette butts are ubiquitous. Dad doesn't smoke, but stewardesses hand him promotional four-packs of cigarettes whenever he boards an airplane. He gives them to a grateful seatmate, who blows the smoke into his face for the duration of the flight. Nobody finds this arrangement the least bit disagreeable. On the contrary, smoking cigarettes is necessary for the production of cigarette butts, our grossest national product, found snuffed out in beach sand, afloat in street gutters, or flicked out car windows and throwing up sparks as they hit the pavement. Our carful of nonsmokers even has armrest ashtrays that somehow smell of cigarettes and polished metal, if I put my nose right into them and draw deeply, which I will later do often.

The ashtrays also smell of ABC gum. "Want some ABC gum?" America's third-graders are fond of asking each other, my brother Jim included. When one of them replies in the affirmative, their eight-year-old interlocutor will remove a wodge of gum from his mouth and say, "Here—it's Already

Been Chewed." One will also learn to decline the offer of a Hertz Donut, which consists of a punch to the biceps and a rhetorical question: "Hurts, don't it?" Nor should we ever say yes when one's big brother approaches with a deck of cards and says, "Wanna play 52 Pickup?"

And one should never, ever accept the following invitation: "Open your mouth and close your eyes and you will get a big surprise."

The butts, the cans, the ABC gum—this is the American roadside in 1969. "We are a nation of pigs," the *Roanoke Times* editorializes this summer. "And anyone who says it's not so hasn't left his house in years."

In Indiana, two trucks collide on I-65, scattering to the breeze thousands of copies of a forthcoming *Playboy* center-fold; Miss July 1969, Nancy McNeil, wears little more than a bouffant hairdo and a look of mild astonishment, as if she were just noticing the photographer snapping away as she lounges around the house in the altogether. To any Indiana farm boys downwind of the accident, the naked lady falling from the sky must seem miraculous. A *Playboy* centerfold is certainly one of the few pieces of litter a citizen will even con-sider collecting voluntarily in 1969.

"Next time you throw an empty beer can out your car win-dow," a writer for the *Chicago Tribune* will admonish readers, "remember it will cost Illinois taxpayers 63 cents to pay for collection crews to pick it up and dispose of it." In other words, shotgunning a beer while at the wheel of a massive American automobile is fine, in and of itself, so long as you don't then hand-crank the window down and toss out the empty, which is more costly bereft of beer than when full.

Beer, after all, is very nearly free. A six-pack of Ballantine can be had for seventy-nine cents, or thirteen cents a can, half a buck less than it costs taxpayers to retrieve the empty can on its own.

The solution is not to reduce the production of beer and soda cans (by imposing onerous bottle-deposit laws on Big Soda and Big Beer) or to discourage the consumption and concomitant production of cigarettes. Rather, Philip Morris and Coca-Cola, among other companies, fund a nonprofit organization called Keep America Beautiful to urge individual consumers to stop littering. Keep America Beautiful will place the onus of litter squarely on the American consumer, who in turn doesn't know—and likely won't care—because the organization will produce a surpassingly effective piece of commercial art and artifice.

Keep America Beautiful commissions a public-service announcement featuring what appears to be an American Indian chief, Iron Eyes Cody, paddling a canoe past belching smokestacks, making landfall on a littered riverbank, then standing beside a highway just as a motorist throws a sackful of fast-food leftovers onto his moccasins. In what *Ad Age* will later call one of the top one hundred ads of the twentieth century, Cody turns to the camera and sheds a single tear from an iron eye in despair for his native land.

The spot is no less beautiful for it being mostly bullshit. Cody is Italian American, just for starters, the son of Sicilian immigrants. He was born Espera Oscar De Corti and raised in Louisiana before moving to Los Angeles to pursue an acting career. He will appear in a hundred Westerns and get a star on the Hollywood Walk of Fame for roles that will not always require the same gravitas displayed in the litter spot. As an Indian on the warpath in a 1950s Borden commercial, he ceased tomahawking a white man to death only after being offered an Elsie brand Popsicle. "When that Injun tasted the fresh fruit flavor," went the voice-over, "his war paint melted into a great big happy grin."

In his buckskin and braids, Cody would look right at home at Fort Dells—a reproduction American Indian in a reproduction American Indian campsite—right down to the mock mocs on his feet.

And yet if the commercial Cody makes is fiction, it is the best kind of literary fiction: a lie that tells the truth. Cody is by all accounts genuine in his love of Native American culture. He married a Native American woman, adopted and raised two Native American children, and will pass as Native American for the rest of his life. As such, he doesn't want to look weak by crying on camera in the Keep America Beautiful spot. So the director does two takes: one with the tear and one without. In the take that will become famous, Cody's single tear is a drop of glycerine.

But that not-quite teardrop shed by that not-quite Indian tells a truth about America. For a time in the 1970s, Keep America Beautiful will report getting two thousand letters a month from volunteers wanting to clean up their own communities. Casual littering quickly attracts public scorn. I will shame my own father when he absentmindedly lets a Kleenex fall from his pocket in the park near our house, and that is almost entirely down to Iron Eyes Cody.

As a child of the 1970s, and thus the fresh-faced hope for world change, I will soon be urged by a succession of cartoon characters to take personal responsibility for the state of the planet. Told by Woodsy Owl to "Give a hoot! Don't pollute," we'll give a hoot, my friends and I, refusing to pump toxic waste from our factories into our rivers while at recess. It will be frightening to hear Smokey Bear say "Only you can prevent forest fires" when I don't live near a forest or have access to the matches in the cabinet above the stove. But I will dutifully obey. Told to "Think metric," we'll think metric (at least in a half-assed way, for a brief time, during school hours) until we come home and live proudly among ounces and feet.

None of that yet concerns us while traveling westbound on I-94 in Wisconsin on the morning of July 21, 1969. Behind me, as we fly toward the Minnesota state line, Jim and Tom are fighting over who gets to lie across the hump that conceals the drive train, with its pleasing, spine-numbing vibrations. They are in costumes, pretending to be adults, Jim dressed entirely in flannel, in a replica Cubs jersey, while Tom wears the pin-striped overalls of a train engineer. Whenever Jim spots a Volkswagen Beetle he shouts "Slug Bug" and punches Tom in the biceps.

Jim is about to become a '70s alpha boy: dibs caller of car seats, hogger of second helpings, chooser of channels, permanent Monopoly banker, all-time quarterback of backyard football, giver of charley horses on long car rides, and slugger of Slug Bugs with no punch-backs.

The very substance speeding us on our way—leaded gasoline—is already being phased out by law. In just a couple of years "loony gas," as it has been known since the 1930s for its deleterious effect on the brain, will be replaced by something called "unleaded." ("Regular or unleaded?" the grease monkey always asks on summer car trips across the country, while wiping the back of his neck with a filthy rag. And Dad will affect the accent of wherever we are and say, "Fill 'er up with unleaded.")

But for now—in the dog days of summer, in the dog days of a dying decade—we are still inhaling leaded gas, and those fumes aren't the only heady aromas about to evaporate forever. It is the last moment to let litter fly from the car window with society's sanction, while a two-year-old gently snoozes in his mother's lap, unfettered by a seat belt, in the shotgun seat of a Chevy Impala. Soon we will be making our own giant leap into the unknown, the dawn of a new decade, on a mission—*Impala 11*—to a new world.

But first we take a valedictory pass through the old world. Hitchhiking is illegal on the interstate highway system, but the hitchhikers are stationed at every other on-ramp, thumbing a ride or bumming a ride or—as a song by the British group Vanity Fare will put it at the end of 1969—"Hitchin' a Ride." The song will become a top-five hit in the United States, where thousands of young people this summer hitchhike to and from Woodstock: "I came upon a child of God. He was walkin' along the road…"

Dad doesn't know it, but those hitchhikers are already an endangered species by the time he is blowing past them at eighty miles an hour in a butterscotch blur, and even the cigarette butts those hitchhikers are scattering to the wind will soon be reduced in number.

Dad smoked two packs a day until he was thirty. In high school, he lived in an eighteen-by-thirty-six-foot trailer in Fort Wayne, Indiana, with a single mother who chain-smoked, so he was already steeped in the stuff, like a hickory-cured ham, by the time he went off to play football at Purdue, where he figured he might as well see what firsthand smoke was like and took up Marlboros.

Mom smoked all the while she was pregnant with her first child, and when that child was born, Dad liked to photograph him in his high chair, a cigarette dangling from one-year-old Jim's lower lip.

Dad, Mom, and baby Jim had all quit smoking by the time Tom was born in 1965—Dad abstemiously declined to hand out cigars, as he had done with Jim—and the scant evidence of their ever having smoked is a black-and-white picture from a party in 1954: Dad has three cigarettes fanning out from his mouth and nine empty beer bottles on the table in front of him. He is decanting the contents of a tenth beer bottle into his right ear. In his left arm is my mother-to-be, aged nineteen, looking at the camera with a half smile as unreadable as the *Mona Lisa*'s.

The clock is already running out on Big Tobacco. On January 1, 1971, cigarette ads will be banned on TV and radio, and print ads and cigarette packages will carry a warning: THE SURGEON GENERAL HAS DETERMINED THAT CIGARETTE SMOKING IS DANGEROUS TO YOUR HEALTH.

This determination was made in no small part by two doctors, E. Cuyler Hammond and Oscar Auerbach, who conducted an extraordinary study. Dr. Auerbach taught eighty-six beagles to smoke up to two packs of cigarettes a day. The smoking was done through a tube inserted in their throats—the beagles had been given tracheotomies—and not, to my disappointment, while leaning up against a building in the rain. But still, the beagles took to smoking with gusto. After two weeks, some of the beagles wagged their tails in anticipation of their next heater. Twelve of those beagles developed lung cancer.

Dad would have probably let us get a dog if it was a chain-smoking beagle, an animal close to his own denatured nature.

Cigarettes and hitchhikers wouldn't be the trip's only imperiled sights. Our drive itself is among the last of its kind, a summer car ride without benefit of seat belts or air-conditioning or FM radio, and nothing to pass the time but the sack of Tootsie Roll Pops Mom stows in the glove box to keep our mouths occupied on long trips. Those suckers keep our hopes up too. If one of our Tootsie Roll Pop wrappers features a boy dressed as an Indian, aiming his bow and arrow at a shooting star, we will win free Tootsie Roll Pops for life. Everybody knows that, even if nobody we know will ever collect on it.

This particular urban legend will gain such cultural purchase in the 1970s that hopeful children who mail their lucky wrappers to Tootsie Roll Industries on Cicero Avenue in Chicago (and for a time more than a hundred children a week will do this) eventually receive by way of reply not a Mayflower moving van full of Tootsie Roll Pops, backing up their driveway, but a letter headlined "Legend of the Indian Wrapper," facsimile-stamped TOP SECRET in red ink. The letter tells the story of an American Indian chief who shot an arrow at a star and in doing so created "lollipops with a chewy candy center." The letter is signed "Chief Shooting Star"—he sounds made up, like Iron Eyes Cody, not an authentic American Indian—and its bureaucratic tone becomes an early lesson for many children in the manifold disappointments life has in store for them.

A child who studies television closely enough in the 1970s will quickly learn the secret code that signals things are not really what they appear to be. Among the adult phrases that whisper something is a rip-off are "Batteries not included," "Some assembly required," "These items sold separately," and the agonizing "Six to eight weeks for delivery."

Television exerts an outsized influence on our lives, a cathode-ray hypnosis. The moon landing is not even the first time TV and space have conspired to mark a watershed in my young life. I was born twenty minutes before sunset on the last summer day of 1966, "The Long, Hot Summer," as a headline in that day's *Chicago Tribune* put it, the summer The Lovin' Spoonful sang "Hot town, summer in the city." The end of that summer meant the start of a great many other things: me, of course, and fall, a season fraught with the giddy anticipation and inevitable disappointment of a powerful annual event, the start of a new television lineup.

I was born at the start of the most exciting fall season of all, the first season in television history in which every prime-time program (bar news specials and old movies) on all three networks was broadcast in color. "In living color" was the vital phrase of the day, because for all the supernatural powers conjured by the sorceress in *Bewitched* or the genie in *I Dream of Jeannie,* they were still rendered in a monochrome that defied magic. That changed when I was born, at the moment the world—as in *The Wizard of Oz*—abruptly switched from black-and-white to Technicolor.

At 7:30 p.m. central time on the evening of September 22, 1966, while I was passing my first forty-five minutes of life at Elmhurst Memorial Hospital, a new show on NBC, *Star Trek,* in an episode titled "Where No Man Has Gone Before," marked the network television debuts of Captain Kirk, Sulu, and Scotty. "Welcome aboard the United Space Ship *Enterprise.* Where it goes, no program has ever gone before..." read the display ad in the *Tribune,* which my father had folded into quarters in the waiting room, at which he had hastily arrived from O'Hare, having just flown in from urgent Mickey Mining business in Cleveland.

It is not impossible that Mr. Spock's was the first face my mother saw after giving birth to me, or the second face after mine, given the time of *Star Trek*'s airing and—more crucially—the series of bowl haircuts she would direct me to get, in the basement, as my father manned the electric clippers for years to come.

My older brothers, Jim and Tom, will be exempt from these bowl cuts—Jim because he will cultivate a russet 'fro that will wax and wane throughout the 1970s, expanding and contracting as if it were a paper bag into which God was hyperventilating. Tom's Brillo-pad hair likewise won't lend itself to any form of basement taming. By the time Tom is seven, Bernie the Barber, scissors snipping in one hand, will survey his head from every angle and finally grab a handful of hair in exasperation: "Your hair," he will announce, "belongs on a dog's butt." The statement is no less cruel—and possibly a great deal *more* cruel—for being true.

Still, there is something about his hair and his ears and his freckles that suit Tom. His constituent parts, like the various accessories of a Mr. Potato Head, are not much to look at separately. But assembled on the blank tuber of his face, they complement one another. Everyone says Tom looks like the *MAD* magazine cover boy Alfred E. Neuman. Hearing this often enough, Tom will take on Neuman's behavioral traits as well. He will become a stirrer of pots, lighter of farts, collector of friends, and charmer of girls, forever riding his bike away from me.

So I, the third-born of three boys, will get the bowl cut, and Mom, to compensate for bedhead, will blow it dry and crimp it with a curling iron on school picture day, Macing me with a cloud of Final Net hairspray through sixth grade, the only flourish to the Spock bangs I'll wear through junior high, evidently in homage to my birth at the birth of *Star Trek*.

To say that Mom might have wanted her third child to be her first girl is a matter of historical record. "What happened to the girl?" asked a well-meaning neighbor in a congratulatory card, which my parents thoughtfully preserved for me in a Tupperware memory box. Dad was pleased with a third consecutive son—indeed, *My Three Sons* was airing on CBS opposite *Star Trek* that night. I've been told he said, "I maintain my perfect record," clapping his hands together in the waiting room. My father idly thumbed the *Tribune* while waiting for news of my arrival. The day's horoscope contained a small addendum:

If Your Child Is Born Today: He or she will be a very practical person and want security from earliest youth. Otherwise the nature will be an unhappy one.

*   *   *

I am happy on this day, in this car, as we speed toward the Minnesota state line with windows halfway rolled down. Dad changes the station whenever our AM radio is fouled by music, including the ubiquitous hit in the middle of its six-week run at number one, "In the Year 2525," a dystopian vision of man's nightmare future.

For a guy making his living in the consumer electronics industry, Dad does not much care for consumer electronics or the pop culture they convey. He often boasts of having "completely missed" Elvis and the Beatles, and the only popular music he will ever bother committing to memory is—for reasons known only to him—the chorus to Willie Nelson's "On the Road Again" and the title phrase in "Bad, Bad Leroy Brown."

Rather, the car radio is for dispensing news. That news is sonic boredom, a tedium delivered by auditory nerve to numb the brain and deaden the body. Dad wants a complacent backseat on long car rides so that he never has to make good on his frequent threats to come back there, to pull over, to stop this car right now. He makes do instead with the occasional backhanded swat, whose accuracy is a source of wonder since he never takes his eyes off the road.

One phrase seems to come up so often on the car radio— "House Ways and Means Committee"—that I will eventually come to think of it as a musical act of the era: House, Ways, and Means, like Emerson, Lake, and Palmer or Earth, Wind, and Fire or Crosby, Stills, and Nash.

The man responsible for our car radio is also responsible, not incidentally, for my father's livelihood. Bill Lear and his partner, Elmer Wavering, created the first commercially practical car radio in the 1920s, for the Galvin Manufacturing Company in Chicago. By then, car radios had been preemptively banned in many cities for the potential havoc they might cause distracted drivers, who might be tempted to Lindy Hop along to the radio. Lear installed his radio in the Studebaker owned by his boss, Paul Galvin, who suggested they call the new device a Motorola.

Wavering would one day become president of Galvin's company, which they renamed Motorola, which itself was a nod to the Victrola, which allowed people at home to play their own music. By the mid-1950s, there was still no satisfactory way to listen to anything in the car other than whatever the radio happened to play. And so, in three of its 1956 models, Chrysler offered the Highway Hi-Fi, an in-car record player that could play specially manufactured 7-inch discs at 16⅔ rpm, for about an hour of music on either side. The system worked surprisingly well: as the DeSoto traversed potholes and S curves, the records were not prone to skipping.

In its 1961 models, Chrysler offered a less expensive record player, which it called the Auto Victrola. As with the Highway Hi-Fi, the stylus seldom jumped the groove, but there was still something inherently ridiculous about playing records in a moving vehicle, never mind storing and flipping those LPs at the wheel. There had to be a better way to free oneself from the tyranny of the radio disc jockey.

At about this time, after decades of making airplane radios and navigation devices—mostly for the military—Bill Lear set about designing and manufacturing a private jet that could fly as fast as a 707 or DC-8. The new plane was targeted to wealthy businessmen like himself. Shortly after the Learjet got off the ground in 1963, Lear flew one from his home base in Wichita to the airport in Santa Monica. There, one of his daughters collected him in a Lincoln Continental she had borrowed from a friend whose father was the zany entrepreneur Earl "Madman" Muntz.

Madman Muntz was a wildly successful automobile salesman who had pioneered the loud television hard sell to move cars off his lot. His dealership billboards all over the Southland read I BUY 'EM RETAIL AND SELL 'EM WHOLESALE— MORE FUN THAT WAY. Another claimed I WANNA GIVE 'EM AWAY—BUT MRS. MUNTZ WON'T LET ME. SHE'S CRAZY! (In fact, there would be seven different Mrs. Muntzes over the years.) Madman Muntz also manufactured and sold televisions, and was the first to measure the screens diagonally, to make them appear bigger than his competitors' in advertisements. Muntz so prospered selling TVs this way that he named one of his daughters Tee Vee.

When Bill Lear arrived at Santa Monica Airport that day in 1963, he saw that Muntz had rigged his latest brainchild to the dashboard of his son's Lincoln—a four-track tape player Madman called the Muntz Autostereo. Fascinated, Lear brought several of the four-track cartridges and playback machines back to Wichita. He dissected the cartridges and decided he could create a better system from scratch. His would have eight tracks instead of four, two hours of music spooling on an infinite loop, so the driver never had to flip the tape over.

Lear was interested in installing this eight-track system on his Learjet, of course, but he also saw it as a consumer product of much broader interest. There was no evidence for this—at the time there was no appetite at all for the eight-track tape, in part because no one yet knew of its existence—but that scarcely mattered to Bill Lear.

He leased from Motorola a fifty-four-thousand-square-foot warehouse in Detroit and set about manufacturing eight-track cartridges, anticipating a market that didn't yet exist. "Tape playback in automobiles is going to be the next big thing," he said. "I'm going to be in the position of a man with a boat full of life jackets following a ship he knows is going to sink. He won't have any trouble selling them."

Like Muntz, Lear was an eccentric man, a serial philanderer who married four times and enjoyed calling business associates from the phone in his executive bathroom so that—in the words of one colleague—"they could hear him tinkle" as he talked.

Colleagues could actually picture him selling life jackets to the passengers of a sinking ship, except Lear could also be charming and convivial, and most endearingly—at least to me—he had a love of wordplay, to judge by the name he gave one of his daughters.

He was picked up in the borrowed Lincoln that fateful day at Santa Monica Airport by his daughter Shanda.

Shanda Lear.

Ford first offered the Lear Jet Stereo Eight player and compatible eight-track tapes in some of its 1966 models. I am a 1966 model myself, lightly used, now crossing the border from Wisconsin into Minnesota on July 21, 1969, not yet old enough to be grateful to Bill Lear for inventing the eight-track tape that my father sells for Mickey Mouse Mining.

I am likewise ignorant of Lear's friend and former partner, Elmer Wavering, who invented the automotive alternator, which made possible power windows, power steering, and air-conditioning, none of which we yet have in the butterscotch Impala now yielding to the gravitational pull of the Saint Paul suburbs.

The Impala didn't come with any add-ons, save a free yard-stick bearing the logo of the dealership, Lattof Chevrolet in Arlington Heights, Illinois. For years to come, Mom will use that yardstick to whack us across the ass whenever one of us—The Boys—gets out of line while Dad is out of town, borne to some far corner of the world by another 747, on a mission to sell the planet on Scotch brand eight-track record-ing tapes.

Lear and Wavering and Muntz were all native Illinoisans who moved elsewhere to give the greatest possible expression to their genius. Al Fritz, inventor of the Sting-Ray, stayed in Illinois—he would die in suburban Chicago at age eighty-eight—and my mother likewise never wanted to leave Chicago for Minnesota, just as she hadn't wanted to leave her native Cincinnati for Chicago. But Dad had to abandon subur-ban Chicago for his own genius to fully flourish, and so Mom reluctantly gave the move to Minnesota her blessing.

The Impala slows in the metropolitan traffic east of Min-neapolis. On the cusp of that city, on the cusp of a new decade, everything seems suddenly possible. They have put a man on the moon; there is nothing they—which is to say, *we*—cannot do.

Or so I'll be told, many times, by Mom and Dad, who today walk into their new house—*our* new house—in a brand-new subdivision called South Brook, in the burgeoning suburb of Bloomington, Minnesota.

Surely this is Tranquility Base. The Impala has landed.

One of These Things
Is Not Like the Others

Shortly after our arrival in Bloomington, Minnesota, I suffer a grand mal seizure—I have no memory of it—and the doctor tells Mom a seizure could recur at any time, especially in strobe lighting, so that I will have a fear of discos later in this decade above and beyond my fear of disco music itself.

The streets of South Brook are gratuitously broad, every one of them a paved Mississippi. A week after my seizure, Mom spots me through the curtains of the family room, motionless on the banks of Southbrook Drive, head at the curb, feet in the yard, flat on my belly.

The screen door bangs. The only other sound is the rainwater running past the curb to the storm drain down the street.

"Jesus, Mary, and Joseph!" Mom cries. "Steven, are you okay?!"

My right fist holds a long stick. The gap between my front teeth shows when I smile.

"I'm fishing," I say, eyes still locked on the cut grass and dandelion fuzz floating by.

Mom lifts me to my feet and hugs me to her chest. She smells like Oil of Olay and Tide. I can feel her heart beating inside her blouse.

"Your mother is a worrywart," Dad occasionally says to me. She worries about the stocks he handpicks from the newspaper, worries that Tom is having too much fun and I am having too little, worries that her boys aren't eating enough and that we are eating her "out of house and home."

There is no such thing as a carefree childhood, only a childhood that shifts the burden of care onto someone else. She is that someone else.

Bloomington has two Chinese restaurants: Fong's on the east side and Wong's on the west. Its high schools are named for coin-worthy presidents—Lincoln, Jefferson, and Kennedy—and its nine-mile creek is called Nine Mile Creek. Our subdivision, South Brook, is south of that creek, which the developers call a brook. The brook-slash-creek passes near two city parks: Brookside and Creekside. Directly across the brook from South Brook, on the crest of a hill, is Hillcrest Elementary School.

That Bloomington has named all its landmarks with literal-minded haste is a sign of how rapidly it has grown. The city has risen from the prairie at once, fully formed, as if from the pages of a pop-up book. In the early 1950s, Bloomington had 9,902 residents scattered over 38 square miles and not a single traffic light. By 1961, there were more than 50,000 citizens, a Major League Baseball team, *and* an NFL football team, with an NHL hockey team on the way. Much bigger cities—places people have actually heard of, like Houston, Phoenix, and Miami—don't have a single team in any of these leagues. They aren't major-league in the way we now think of ourselves.

By 1970 a family moving to Bloomington from suburban Chicago can plausibly persuade itself that this is a step up to the big leagues. The population has swollen to 81,970, and beginning this year Howard Cosell bestows on every one of us a national legitimacy (and a fourth syllable) over the ABC television network: "To Buh-*loom*-ing-ton, MINN-uh-soda," he says while narrating the halftime highlights on *Monday Night Football.* "To the *Icebox!* Met-ruh-pol-i-tan Stadium…"

Cosell's prime-time benediction for Bloomington, bequeathed in a canary-yellow blazer, isn't our only network-TV validation. Beginning this year, every Saturday night on CBS, in the opening credits of her titular sitcom, Mary Tyler Moore drives pensively up the freeway to her new life in Minneapolis. In doing so, Mary had to pass through Bloomington, her brown eyes taking in our motel on the cloverleaf interchange (called the Cloverleaf Motel), our Ford dealership on the freeway (called Freeway Ford), our bowling alley by the airport (called Airport Bowl), even our racquet and swim club on West 98th Street (called the 98th Street Racquet Swim Club), before throwing her hat in the air on Nicollet Mall in downtown Minneapolis.

In subsequent seasons, in the show's updated title sequence, this virginal Mary will stir confused longing in me as she sloshes a soapy rag across the blue hood of what looks like a life-sized Hot Wheels car while wearing the purple number

10 jersey of Vikings quarterback Fran Tarkenton, ticking all the boxes of Catholic-school/Bloomington/adolescent erotica. And so Mary Tyler Moore joins Maria from *Sesame Street* and the illustrated Little Debbie (blue-eyed, red-haired, sunbonneted beauty on the Little Debbie snack cake boxes) in the pantheon of my early, unrequitable crushes.

Bloomington's biggest cultural ambassadors by far are the Vikings, regal in purple, who go to the Super Bowl during our very first winter in town. Naturally, they lose—the first of four Super Bowl losses in the 1970s—an act of one-downmanship that is quintessentially Minnesotan. Unlike Chicago, Minneapolis will build its skyscrapers to be just shorter than the tallest building extant, and the state will sacrifice a string of vice presidents and presidential runners-up to the nation, among them Hubert Humphrey, Walter Mondale, and perennial presidential candidate Harold Stassen.

The stadium in east Bloomington that serves our metropolis, Metropolitan Stadium, is next door to Metropolitan Sports Center, where the Minnesota North Stars play National Hockey League games bereft of any helmets, if you don't count their own flowing manes of hockey hair. The North Stars share their arena with the world's most decadent rock bands, sometimes on the same spring Sunday.

With an ex-footballer father who can provide all the blank recording tape the company store can stock, Bloomington—with its Vikings games and Zeppelin concerts—is (or might well be) the center of the universe.

Led Zeppelin plays Bloomington on April 12, 1970. "The Zeppelin, a British four-man group that specializes in hard, cerebral rock, made a din that made a North Stars crowd in full cry sound like a mewling baby," Dad reads to Mom from the next day's *Minneapolis Star.* "The rock concert was set back an hour and a half to accommodate the play-off activities of the local icemen…As the lights dimmed and the musty, sweet aroma of burning 'grass' lifted from all parts of the crowd, much of the throng swept out of the aisles closer to the loudspeakers that were set up on the ice sheet."

Peering over the paper for reaction, Dad arches his eyebrows in silent ridicule. Yes, Dad calls on record labels, recording studios, and television networks to sell them Mickey Mining's audio and video recording tapes, but he hasn't the slightest interest in almost any of the popular musicians or actors who are recorded for posterity on those tapes. As far as he's concerned, Scotch brand recording tape reaches its peak of perfection when it rolls off the factory floor, before being vandalized by the likes of Led Zeppelin. The canvas is the masterpiece; the paint is graffiti. (He later says that even the set of the beloved *Tonight Show,* which he will visit when calling on NBC in Burbank, looks much shabbier in person than on TV.)

The newspaper he is reading, the *Star,* is the afternoon paper—the one we get, the one Mary Tyler Moore clutches to her breast in the opening credits of her show. The *Minneapolis Tribune* is for readers who prefer to face their news head-on first thing in the morning. News is not a fluid construct, but a product delivered to our doorstep once a day and consumed in a single sitting—in my father's case, after dinner, when he can digest both his meatloaf and the world's events simultaneously, toothpick in mouth, from the comfort of his Archie Bunker chair as the network news plays on TV. He likes to get the headlines over quickly, a bad-news Band-Aid ripped at once from his skin.

The anchorman looks gravely into the camera and says, "Federal agents tonight are searching for..."

From behind the *Star*, Dad finishes the sentence in the anchorman's voice: "...the guy who gave me this haircut."

Anchorman: "A Texas jury has sentenced to death..."

Dad: "...the man who sold me this tie."

He is undercutting for my benefit the gravity of whatever grim news is to follow.

The TV is on a four-wheeled cart—in the event of a house fire, we can wheel it straight through the front doors with a bang, like a hospital stretcher at an ER—and I lie prone before it, chin on palms, in the deep-pile carpet that serves as elephant grass for our army men. The plastic soldiers, their bayonets bent like scythes, hack through the thick brush of the green shag as John Chancellor announces the day's developments in "Viet Nam," or possibly in "Vietnam": in TV graphics and newspapers, I will come to notice, the war is seldom spelled the same way twice, as if the very name of the country has been contentiously split in two and is being reunited by force. I certainly don't understand the war, but in those alternate spellings, I manage to infer some sense of what it's all about. Such is the power of words, of letters, even the absence of letters—"Viet Nam," divided at the seventeenth parallel of a single keystroke of white space.

My earliest "memories" are memories of home movies. Christmas morning in the split-level house on Dover Drive in Lisle, Illinois. Crawling over a rubber tugboat to get to a book: *1,001 Riddles.* The images are intercut with footage from Dad's business trips abroad. Double-decker buses at Trafalgar Square in London. A Danish street protest of the war in Vietnam: USA UD AF INDO-KINA. And before Dad can throw himself onto the projector as if it were a live grenade, the camera pans a Copenhagen sex-shop exterior: MAGAZINES—LESBIAN—HOMO—ANIMALS—BIZARRE.

We gather to watch these home movies in the basement in Bloomington: Dad aiming the Super 8 projector at a bed-sheet on the wall, threading the film, dousing the lights, the twitching hair in the lens dominating the frame, the laughter at seeing ourselves as babies, the projector bulb abruptly burning up a frame, our family going up in flames, the basement lights suddenly flooding the room again and returning us—with a great sigh of disappointment—prematurely to the present.

Science says permanent memory kicks in at age three, and for me it arrives exactly on time, on my third birthday, in our lemon-yellow, avocado-green, harvest-gold kitchen in Bloomington. I blow out the candles on my cake, and while they're still smoldering, Jim and Tom each grab one and pretend to smoke it like a cigarette, so I do the same, the three of us chain-smoking as Dad films. But then anything will stand in for a cigarette: pencils, Tootsie Pop sticks, Cheetos, BIC pens. We hold any of them between our index and middle fingers and pretend to puff away.

After cake, presents. My trembling hands unwrap the first one, from Jane Selander, our nearest neighbor and my first playmate. Mom stands by, already elated for me. But even before the box inside has been entirely denuded of its wrapping paper, I burst into tears. And then I scream, *"Just* what I didn't want!"

Jane's mother is the first friend Mom has made in Minnesota. Mom looks at Mrs. Selander, stammers apologies, then chases me down the hall, the yardstick from Lattof Chevrolet raised behind me like a riding crop. I spend the remainder of the afternoon in my bedroom, crying into my Sears rib cord bedspread and listening to my own party through the door.

The offending present is a pair of Romper Stompers, two inverted yellow cups, each attached to a green loop of plastic cord, that children "ages 2½ to 6" can walk on. I have seen a girl enjoying these on *Romper Room,* and while they look like great fun, I am left with the impression that Romper Stompers are exclusively a girls' toy, a suspicion confirmed by the pig-tailed blond on the box.

What I feel for Romper Stompers is the opposite of desire, the flip side of the usual aching for some object. This pining, this prayer *not* to get something, is of equal intensity to the wanting of a toy, the kind of fevered anticipation that sometimes comes with an actual fever. In Illinois, Jim had so desperately desired a windup, ice-skating circus clown called Clancy the Great that he nearly became ill with anticipation in the weeks leading up to Christmas. The commercial jingle that stoked his fever—"Clancy the Great! Look at him skate! Fun for a girl or boy!"—still resonates in our house, and will for decades to come.

When Jim finally tore open the package containing Clancy the Great on Christmas morning, his horny hands quivering, he couldn't cope with the ensuing avalanche of emotion. His wildest dream finally fulfilled, he descended—as some lottery winners do—into a manic cycle of elation and despair, joy and rage. By nightfall, Clancy the Great (Look at him skate!) was upside down in a trash can at the curb, skate blades glinting under the streetlamp, dispatched there by my father, who had recognized the evil in the ice-skating clown.

It was hardly Jim's fault. As birthdays or Christmas draw near, childhood desire becomes all-consuming. Even Easter is preceded by an agonizing interval of anticipation. Jim raced down the stairs one Easter morning, found a dyed, hard-boiled egg hidden behind the sofa, and bit into it like a hand fruit.

"Mmmmmm!" he said, smiling, as bits of eggshell fell from his face like plaster from a ceiling. Then he took another bite.

The *Romper Room* logo that features prominently on my box of Romper Stompers is a little pink house with an orange roof and a yellow chimney over which flies the *Romper Room* mascot, a cartoon bumblebee who teaches proper manners. Though Mom and I don't know it—and nor, presumably, do the creators of *Romper Room*—that bumblebee's name is also a "grass" reference. H.R. Pufnstuf, Puff the Magic Dragon, and the voracious Scooby Dooby Doo are part of the same grand tradition that has given us Do-Bee, the *Romper Room* mascot who produces a gentle buzz.

Romper Room was conceived in 1955, by a Baltimore teacher named Nancy Claster, as a televised kindergarten classroom. "Miss Nancy" broke the fourth wall by speaking directly to kids in "Televisionland," sometimes through her Magic Mirror, in which she could uncannily spot children at home: "I see Tommy and Susie and Janie and Billy..." (If you are a Jamal or a Dingxiang, you are evidently invisible.)

The Magic Mirror comes as a terrifying revelation, confirming my suspicion that while I am watching the TV, the TV is also watching me. Nancy Claster and her producer husband, Bert, franchised *Romper Room* to local markets while still hosting the Baltimore show, and by 1960 more than ninety cities had signed on. The show would eventually air in one hundred fifty cities in the United States, Canada, England, Japan, Italy, and Australia.

Our *Romper Room* teacher on channel 9 in Minneapolis is a brunette (and occasionally blond) teacher named Miss Betty. Whenever Miss Betty picks up the Magic Mirror and says the magic phrase—"Romper, bomper, stomper, boo; tell me, tell me, tell me do..."—she becomes one more agent of espionage in my life. My world is full of these Orwellian figures. Santa and God are scarcely distinguishable, two white-bearded, supernatural supreme beings watching over me as I sleep. Santa: "He sees you when you're sleeping. He knows when you're awake." God: "Now I lay me down to sleep, I pray the Lord my soul to keep." Throw in Mom and Dad, the bogeyman, my guardian angel, and Miss Betty, and there is an entire secret police conspiring to keep an eye on me—to catch me, literally, with my hand in the cookie jar.

Romper Stompers were inspired by Nancy Claster's father, who wouldn't let his daughter walk on stilts and thought tin cans tethered to strings served the same purpose just fine. In 1969, Nancy and Bert Claster sold *Romper Room* to the Hasbro toy company, resulting in the Romper Stompers that I can hear, through my bedroom door, now being enjoyed by my party guests.

They sound like a blast. They have quasi-mystical, almost divine powers. "Some time ago I received a letter from a woman in Pennsylvania who had a child who was in leg braces and also wore a waist brace because of a muscular deficiency," Miss Nancy tells an interviewer in 1970. "The child was only out of the braces about twenty-five minutes a day. One day the youngster asked her mother for some Romper Stompers. The mother asked an orthopedic man who said, 'By all means get them for her.' Three weeks later, the child was able to stay out of braces for more than three hours a day. She saw other children using the Romper Stompers and had the desire and courage to try."

And so I quickly grow to love my Romper Stompers, just as Mom and Dad grow privately fond of—or at least amused by—my initial objection to them. Frequently (and for the rest of their lives) they'll repeat my line whenever bad news or an unwelcome social invitation arrives. Dad, plunger in hand, whenever a toilet backs up: "*Just* what I didn't want." Mom, hand cupped over the mouthpiece, whispering the words after a caller has invited her to another Tupperware party: "*Just* what I didn't want." Dad again, after a diagnosis of melanoma: "*Just* what I didn't want."

It turns out the Romper Stompers *are* just what I want. On them, I clomp around the kitchen's linoleum floor like a colossus. "Teaches coordination and helps develop balance," it says on the box, but I don't care about that. Romper Stompers make me feel taller, and older, and more fearsome, in the way that smoking my birthday candles does. When I alight from the Stompers, I am short again, in the same way that I feel elfin and flat-footed after removing ice skates.

So inside, it's Romper Stompers, and outside, we never take the skates off. There's an outdoor rink within walking distance of every house in Bloomington, in the kind of outdoors that even Dad can endorse. The ice rink is nature tamed—water frozen and floodlit, painted with stripes and circles, fenced by dasher boards, and always overlooked by a "warming house," a small, heated shelter full of happily shivering children. When we walk across the wooden floor on our skates, it sounds like rolling thunder.

Jim is already elegant on the ice—Jimbo the Great! Look at him skate!—but I shuffle like a newborn fawn. The only thing holding me up is the hockey stick I use as a cane. Hockey sticks all have great names, like Sher-Wood and Northland, Koho and Jofa, and, our favorite, Minnesota's own Christian Brothers. To curve the blade, Mom turns on a stovetop burner and Jim holds the blade just above it until it's bendable. The glowing coils of the burner and the stainless steel of a nearby pot make the process feel metallurgical, like we're ironmongers or ore smelters or some other obsolete tradesmen. When we get our skates sharpened—at BIG (Bloomington Ice Garden) or Westwood Skate and Bike or the Met Pro Shop; Bloomington has skate-sharpening services like other cities have dry cleaners—the machine grinding against the blade throws up sparks.

The twin blades of my "double-runners"—like training wheels for hockey skates—splay out to either side, so that the inside of each ankle nearly touches the ice. "Ankle skater," the older kids call me, or "leatherbeater." When my toes go numb, it's a relief to retreat to the warming house. The heat hits me instantly, like Mom opening the oven door. The frozen stalactites of snot extending from my nostrils begin to thaw, and I lick my upper lip, enormously content to be indoors, in this lovely place with its lovely name: warming house.

Mom is happy to have us out of her house. She is due to give birth to her fourth child any day now, and so every night, kneeling beside our twin beds in the room we share, Tom and I do as we're told. We pray for a girl.

We recite the Our Father as best we can. ("And deliver us some evil, Amen.") We say the Hail Mary. ("Blessed is the Fruit of thy Loom, Jesus.")

Tom recites a prayer-in-verse that goes "Good night, my sweet Jesus, the one I love best. My work is now finished, and now I must rest. Today you have blessed me, now bless me this night. And keep me from danger till morning and light. Amen."

But I recognize the prayer's cadence—its rhythms and its rhymes—in songs I've overheard in the park. And though I know it's wrong, and God can see me in the dark, I can't help but silently sing a response to every line that Tom utters.

"Good night, my sweet Jesus..." Tom says, and I silently sing in reply, "On top of Old Smokey..."

"The one I love best..." ("All covered with sand...")

"My work is now finished..." ("I shot my poor teacher...")

"And now I must rest..." ("With a red rubber band...")

"Today you have blessed me..." ("I shot her with joy...")

"Now bless me this night..." ("I shot her with pride...")

"And keep me from danger..." ("I couldn't have missed her...")

"Till morning and light." ("She's forty feet wide.")

Four months after our arrival in Bloomington, and in spite of my silent and serial blasphemies, Amy is born. The doctor finds Dad pacing in the waiting room at Fairview Southdale Hospital and tells him, "Congratulations. You finally got one with indoor plumbing."

Our arrival in Minnesota coincides with the debut of *Sesame Street*, which I sit in front of twice a day, once in the morning and when it repeats in the afternoon, physically incapable of turning away.

Sesame Street has everything that Southbrook Drive does not, including graffiti, high-rise housing projects, suffocating urban heat, fire hydrants, front stoops, and black people.

From its opening theme—"Sunny day, sweepin' the clouds away"—I want to live there. Kermit the Frog sits on a ledge next to the letter *W*. Cookie Monster bites off one of its constituent parts, and the *W* becomes an *N*. Cookie takes another bite, and the *N* becomes a *V*. After another, the *V* becomes a slanted *I*. Letters are Swiss Army knives, and I now see how an *N* is just a *Z* that has fallen on its face, possibly after a grand mal seizure. *O* is just a *Q* that has swallowed its tongue.

I am learning the alphabet and before long how to read, and so Mom lets me stay in to watch *Sesame Street* again in the afternoon while my brothers are happy to play outside. "One of these things just doesn't belong here," I sing along with Susan. "One of these things just isn't the same."

By the time the sad trumpet of its closing theme softly intrudes on the final sketch—playing *Sesame Street* off like an Oscar winner who is speaking too long—I've grown sad and anxious. When Mom hears the sponsors being read—"*Sesame Street* has been brought to you today by the letter *M* and by the number six"—she comes in from the kitchen. By the time they get to "*Sesame Street* is a production of the Children's Television Workshop," she snaps off the set and orders me out of the house, so that the last thing I see on TV every day is the PBS logo. And then I'm set out in the front yard like a garden gnome.

In the fall of 1970, Mom sends me to Saint Stephen's Nursery School. Saint Stephen was the first martyr and the saint for whom I am named, though I'm Steven-with-a-*v*, because when the nurse at Elmhurst Memorial asked my parents how they wanted to spell my name, Dad answered before Mom could: "With a *v*. It's easier." He had already vetoed Mom's first-choice name of Daniel, and now, even with my *v*, I am named after the saint who was stoned to death rather than the one who was tortured and beheaded. Reading my *Children's Book of Saints,* I think of this as a small blessing.

My teacher is a white-haired lady named Mrs. Bakke. At home, I call her Mrs. Bakke-Hockey, and Mrs. Walkie-Talkie. I like pulling words apart and putting them back together, as if they're building blocks or Lincoln Logs or Tinkertoys. Alliteration pleases me as much as it pleases the toy makers, one of which—Tonka trucks—was founded a few towns over in the alliterative suburb of Mound, Minnesota, and named for its alliterative neighbor, Minnetonka, Minnesota.

Romper Room, Sesame Street, Captain Kangaroo. I am not the only child who loves alliteration. "Wanda waved her wand and her washtub filled with warm water," goes a sketch on

Sesame Street. To which Carol Burnett says, "Wow, Wanda the Witch is weird."

Words are toys. You can couple and uncouple them like model train cars. *The Electric Company* will soon hold me spellbound. "Who can turn a can into a cane? Who can turn a pan into a pane? Anyone can plainly see—it's silent *e.*"

Wordplay is all around me, on Popsicle sticks, in knock-knock jokes, in *1,001 Riddles.* Even when I don't understand them, I'm drawn to these jokes and want to take them apart, the way other kids will take apart a radio to see how it works. "If an athlete gets athlete's foot," asks my Dixie Riddle Cup, "what does an astronaut get?" I'm not entirely sure what an athlete is, much less athlete's foot, and the answer to the riddle—"missile toe"—is more mystifying still.

But I don't care, because I'm reading everything—from street signs ("stop" backward is "pots") to newspaper head-lines (I like how "Twins" conceals "win"). I devour whatever is put in front of me. If a hungry mind leaves a clean plate, I read the way my dad eats his dinner: until I can see my re-flection on the page. Tom and Jim are out riding their bikes or making friends while I sit inside reading the labels on clean-ing products. One of these things is not like the others. One of these things just doesn't belong.

"Riboflavin," "niacin"—the words on the cereal box side panels are as far-out as the cereal names themselves. Quake and Quisp, Trix and Kix, plus all the titled titans—King Vi-tamin, Count Chocula, Cap'n Crunch—in the *Burke's Peerage* that is our breakfast table.

Froot Loops. Cheez Whiz. Rold Gold. TV is a smorgasbord of deliberate misspellings, a froot-and-cheez platter that's more appealing by far than the natural foods they approximate. As much as these words have a different way of looking, Minnesotans have a different way of talking. They pronounce "roof" more like "rough." They go for "woks" instead of "walks." If someone says "Can I have a buck?" they're asking for a ride on your bike, not a dollar. And the way the kids in Bloomington pronounce "milk" makes me wonder if it isn't a slightly altered food-like substance along the lines of froot and cheez. Everyone but my family calls it "melk."

In 1970, the Federal Trade Commission opens an investigation into what it calls the breakfast-cereal oligopoly. Ninety percent of America's cereals are produced by Kellogg's, Post, or Minnesota's very own General Mills. I was born among the Keebler elves in Elmhurst, in the shadow of the great city that gave us Hostess Twinkies and Oscar Mayer hot dogs, and Kraft mac and cheese and those magical bricks of Velveeta. And now I'm being raised in the backyard of the Lucky Charms leprechaun, the Pillsbury Doughboy, the Jolly Green Giant, and Betty Crocker.

Every one of these mascots and their products are aimed at me. And they can't possibly miss, given my sitting-duck status three feet from the television screen. When I am four, an Arizona pediatrician concludes that a child spends more hours watching TV before he goes to kindergarten than a college student spends in the classroom over four years. Preschoolers in 1971 spend 64 percent of their waking hours watching TV, says Dr. Gerald Looney, whose Bugs Bunny–evoking surname is unintentionally synonymous with the kind of children's television that I find so hypnotic.

There is a short-lived cartoon on ABC called *Fantastic*

Voyage, based on a movie starring Raquel Welch, in which a miniaturized crew of explorers journeys through a human body in an infinitesimal submarine named *Voyager.* This is what fascinates me most about commercials—their fantastic voyages through the human body. As Pepto-Bismol "coats and soothes," I see the inside of a man in profile, his innards slowly being painted pink. I love the Anacin and Bufferin tablets racing straight to the throbbing, jagged, red-hot source of a housewife's elbow pain. Every adult on TV is in desperate need of pain relief, all the time, theatrically rubbing his or her shoulders or neck or back. And it's not just people: a Cascade commercial pulls back the door on the churning dishwasher, revealing its interior at work—the detergent gently cleaning the clear glass dinner plates, every wineglass gleaming with a sparkling sunburst.

More than anything, it's the musical language of advertising that is so captivating to me. The brand names that are wonders of alternative spelling—Endust, Renuzit, Liv-a-Snaps—are just part of the allure. I haven't the slightest notion what any of them means, but certain phrases are repeated over and over until I've committed them to memory: Steel-belted radials. Rack-and-pinion steering. Substantial penalty for early withdrawal. Use only as directed. Your mileage may vary. In specially marked boxes.

In commercials, as on *The Electric Company,* words are Play-Doh and the rhymes designed to embed in my brain— Shake 'n Bake, flick your BIC, Frito Bandito—succeed in their mission. "Dotsa lotsa mozza-rella," I tell Mom whenever she is making anything. The tongue twisters are even more effective. Libby's Fruit Float is a fruit-infused canned syrup to which you add cold milk, then stir, to get a creamy, pudding-like wonder substance that Mom obstinately refuses to buy us for dessert. Still, at the end of the commercial, the kid always says to his father, "Bet you can't say 'Fruit Float' three times." As a result, I walk around doing just that, uttering the name of the product out loud, a walking advertisement. But I have also committed to my very short memory the company's diabolical corporate jingle: "When it says Libby's, Libby's, Libby's on the label, label, label, you will like it, like it, like it on the table, table, table."

And: "Have another Nutter Butter peanut-butter sandwich cookie."

And: "Renuzit do's it."

By 1971, a commercial airs every 2.8 minutes on Saturday morning, when TV—and the household that surrounds the TV—is given over almost entirely to kids. In the glorious hours before noon, 23 percent of all airtime is devoted to commercials, according to a survey by Action for Children's Television, which wants to ban commercials outright during children's programming. For educators, there is a silver lining in all those ads: they take time away from the exceedingly violent shows. As Evelyn Sarson, the president of ACT, puts it, "So many of the shows [have] chases and people hitting each other over the head." The violence is what my brothers and I love about them—the cartoon lump rising like a vertical baguette whenever a man is beaten over the head with a sledgehammer. By ACT's estimate, 30 percent of dramatic children's shows are "saturated" with violence, and 71 percent have at least one instance of it per segment. These shows, which my brothers and I watch for hours on end on Saturday mornings, are, in the words of the ACT study, "predominantly concerned with either crime, the supernatural, or interpersonal rivalry between characters." Exactly! And so are we, my brothers and I, *especially* violence born of interpersonal rivalry.

Some mornings after Saturday cartoons, Tom and I descend to the basement, still in our pajamas, and lace up the sixteen-ounce boxing gloves that Dad acquired in the army. We throw wild haymakers at each other, swinging as hard as we can, always aiming for the head, never the body. Dad films one of the bouts with his Super 8 camera. A single frame reveals my face collapsing sideways like an accordion as Tom's round-house right connects in a furious blur.

For Dad, prizefighting is a welcome alternative to TV, which he assumes is more likely than the boxing gloves to deliver brain damage. In February of 1970, New York City mayor John Lindsay says that advertising nudges children toward drug addiction, even before they've reached school age. Lindsay tells a gathering of city school principals that the average child will see eight thousand hours of TV before he or she enrolls in school. That child, the mayor says, will be told "to relax minor tensions with a pill; to take off weight with a pill; to win status and sophistication with a cigarette; to wake up, be happy, relieve tension with pills." Truth be told, everything on TV looks good and glamorous, be it Martini & Rossi on the rocks or the come-on "How about a nice Hawaiian Punch?" This question, like the offer of a Hertz Donut, is often met with a real punch on the playground. Even the dog food—the glistening Gaines-burgers, the moist Chuck Wagon in gravy—looks good enough to eat. "Schools," Lindsay says, when he's really blaming television, "are becoming the training ground for the next generation of addicts."

My parents now know from these daily dire news reports that TV is conspiring against me, and against all the other kids in South Brook. Mine is not the only mom snapping off the TV in mid-program and shooing her children from the house.

And while the only pills I'm jonesing for right now are Flintstone vitamins and the only cigarettes I crave are of the candy variety, I am given to anxious crying jags (when I don't get my way) and fits of pants wetting (even when I do). For a time I insist during long car rides that we stop for gas only at Gulf stations. Their blue-and-orange logo soothes me in a way that even the green brontosaurus logo of the Sinclair stations cannot.

It could hardly be otherwise. I was born in Elmhurst, Illinois, in 1966, the year Keebler moved its headquarters there, presumably to a hollow tree staffed by elves. It was a happy coincidence that this large purveyor of advertising aimed at children arrived at the same time I did, and in the same place, just when color television could fully convey to us the psychedelic, pharmaceutical beauty of Trix, Fruity Pebbles, Kool-Aid, and Kaboom.

By 1969, when we moved to Bloomington, television was already singing me to sleep with its moon-landing lullaby. TV is a security blanket, not altogether different from the Sears Orlon blanket on my bed—warm, fuzzy, narcotizing, vividly colored, and crackling with static electricity.

3.

When You Comin' Home, Dad?

We settle into an easy domestic routine in Bloomington. Most evenings around six, we hear Dad's car sighing in the driveway. Mom goes into the bathroom, opens the top drawer of the vanity, retrieves her lipstick, applies a fresh coat, looks in the mirror, and lightly presses her fingers to her hairdo. She kisses Dad when he walks through the door.

Dad sets down his briefcase in the same place every night, beneath the wall-mounted telephone in the kitchen. The phone is banana-yellow and the property of Northwestern Bell. It is literally a ringing endorsement of American engineering and ingenuity. Its receiver feels solid and purposeful in my hand, like a five-pound dumbbell. It's tethered to the base unit by fifty feet of coiled cord, so that I can follow it like a miner's lifeline around corners and down the hall to find who is tying up the line.

If I accidentally bump into it while running through the kitchen, the phone rings out with a single ding, like the bell in a boxing match that signals the start of a fight.

Mom carries the phone cord in her free hand as she talks, like a singer on TV strolling the stage while manipulating the microphone cord. She occasionally gets so wrapped up in these phone conversations with her "cronies," as Dad calls them, that she finds herself tied up in the concertina wire of the phone cord, and a series of pirouettes is required to extricate herself. Once a week Dad takes the phone off the hook and lets the receiver dangle from the cord. That heavy receiver looks like an explorer caught in a vine trap, spinning this way and that, until the cord finally spins itself out and untangles.

Mom makes me commit our phone number to memory. "Eight-eight-eight, two-eight-seven-two," she says. "Can you remember that? In case of emergency?"

I say it so fast it sounds like something else entirely: "Ay-day-date, too-weight-seven-two."

"Again."

"Ay-day-date, too-weight-seven-two."

"Perfect."

What kind of emergency she has in mind, I cannot say. Another seizure? I've heard her—through the kitchen door, after dinner, over the gentle thrum of the dishwasher, the soothing gurgle of the rinse cycle—say to Dad, "He could swallow his tongue." I don't want to swallow my tongue. And without a tongue, how can I call Mom—from a neighbor's kitchen or while coming to consciousness in a hospital room—and tell her I've swallowed my tongue? I hold my tongue between my thumb and forefinger and try without success to say something.

At least I can dial the phone now and hand it off to a tongue doctor to deliver the terrible news. And so I drift off at night, repeating "Ay-day-date, too-weight-seven-two" until I can literally recite it in my sleep.

After Dad kisses Mom and relieves himself of his briefcase, he climbs the stairs to his bedroom to change out of his suit and tie, shedding the cares and work clothes of the day. Then we sit down to dinner, knee-to-knee and elbow-to-elbow, beneath a hanging light fixture. It's a single bulb concealed in a white frosted globe wreathed by fruit slices, alternating wedges of lemon and lime and orange. The fruit appears to be in orbit around the sphere, like the birds that circle the heads of cartoon concussion victims.

We all make the sign of the cross and Dad calls on one of us to say a rote, robotic grace: "Bless us O Lord for these thy gifts…" One night, years from now, I'll say after grace: "Shouldn't it be 'Bless us O Lord *and* these thy gifts'? Because 'Bless us O Lord *for* these thy gifts' doesn't make sense."

"You're right," Dad will say. "I never thought of it." And then he'll call me what he always does: "Our wordsmith."

Regardless of what Mom has made tonight from her steel box filled with recipes on index cards—salmon patties, three-way chili, or chipped beef on toast, which Dad fondly recalls from his army days as SOS, or Shit on a Shingle—we're expected to clean our plates. Dad leaves no trace of food on his. There is a glistening bone where a pork chop used to be. He eats potato skins and orange rinds. Apples are reduced to a stem and seeds.

The only thing on his plate at the end of dinner is his reflection. He eats like one of the animals we see on Mutual of Omaha's *Wild Kingdom.* Mom calls him the Dispos-All. "I was a Depression baby," he says in his defense, before reminding us that no one gets dessert without first joining him in the Clean Plate Club.

He cuts the fat off the "family steak" that Mom buys at Red Owl and gives it to Tom, who likes to chew and suck the fat.

In 1971, General Mills introduces Hamburger Helper, a little miracle that Mom immediately embraces when Dad is traveling. If she is going to embrace anyone when Dad is traveling, we all agree that the Hamburger Helper mascot—a four-fingered glove with eyeballs—is better than the alternatives. But when Dad is home, the meal is always made from scratch, whether or not Mom partakes.

Mom is frequently "on a diet." She eats a Dole pineapple ring that glistens on the plate like a halo. On top of it quivers a scoop of cottage cheese.

Dad enjoins us to sit up straight and put our left hands in our laps. When we forget our manners, he says, "Mabel, Mabel, sweet and able, get your elbows off the table."

Dessert is our birthright. It appears unbidden every evening. We eat it three hundred sixty-five nights a year. It is seldom ice cream. Most often, Mom has made a peanut-butter pie or a carrot cake or some other baked confection, inviting us to lick the twin beaters of the electric mixer when she's finished. Sometimes she makes a chocolate pudding with a rubbery skin on top. We skeptically tap our spoons on its trampoline surface before rolling the skin back like the lid of a sardine tin.

Before clearing the table, we're required to say "May I be excused?" Other nights, we may only be excused after also saying—three times fast, and with proper elocution—"Afghanistan banana stand." In return, we'll challenge Dad to say "Fruit Float, Fruit Float, Fruit Float."

When he's in a good mood, Dad might summon me to his chair at the head of the table and ask me to hold my right thumb and forefinger an inch apart. "If you can catch it, you can keep it," he says, removing a crisp five-dollar bill from his billfold and dropping it lengthwise through my fingers. He is also adept at removing and swiftly reattaching his own thumb and finding loose change in my ears.

Occasionally, he'll ask to see my grip. He has the hands of a stevedore, the grip of a serial strangler. When shaking hands he likes to give me what he calls the Knuckle Floater, rolling the knuckles of my right hand around as if they're a handful of marbles, only releasing his viselike grip when I've cried "Uncle" or "Mercy" or taken a knee.

He brings the same ferocity to Rock Paper Scissors. When his paper wraps my rock or his rock covers my paper, he licks his right index finger before snapping it across my wrist, just below the palm. We play a game in which I place my palms on top of his, and he has to slap the backs of my hands before I can remove them. The ensuing slap always sounds like a whipcrack.

If the dinner has depleted our family-size bottle of Heinz ketchup, Dad will open the new bottle, place the old one on top of it to form a ketchup hourglass, then watch the old one drain into the new one, saving a tablespoon of ketchup from the garbage can.

Every once in a great while, Dad arrives home, kisses Mom, sets down his briefcase, and announces with great solemnity that we are—and we can scarcely believe he is saying this—Going Out to Eat. The ensuing celebration rivals V-E Day. Tonight, we will not eat under the fruit-slice chandelier and fight for the last shred of Banquet fried chicken but instead will choose from a dizzying array of restaurants in which—as long as we don't fill up on bread and have only water before the food arrives—we can drink pop and enjoy an hour or more of central air-conditioning.

We eat out so infrequently, and with such great ceremony, that it hardly matters where we go. Tom asks to go to Mister Steak, whose logo—the best thing about the place—is a cartoon steer in a chef's hat. Dad will point out, after a rib eye whose chief attraction is its $1.98 price tag, that "Mister Steak" might better have been called "Miss Steak." I get this pun and love it. Like wordplay, a sense of humor is a fraternity handshake, a shared secret, a radio signal sent out on a frequency that not everyone receives.

Jim wants to go to The Embers, chiefly for its commercial jingle, repeated endlessly on the radio: "Breakfast, lunch, or dinner! Every meal's a winner! Remember the Emmm-bers."

Any one of us would be happy eating at Perkins, which flies an American flag the size of the rain tarp that covers the infield at Metropolitan Stadium. Perkins also has a wishing well next to the hostess stand. You can reach into its depths like a magician into a hat and pull out a plastic prize. Perkins serves breakfast for dinner, though when my brothers and I talk about where we want to eat, food is seldom mentioned. The sense of occasion occasioned by Going Out to Eat is enough. Some nights we go to Red Barn, whose signature dish is the Barnbuster, a quarter-pound hamburger that is not quite a Quarter Pounder from McDonald's, so that it's the culinary equivalent of Sears's four-striped shoes.

Country Kitchen serves fresh strawberry pie and a signature sandwich called the Country Boy. Its mascot is a hayseed in a straw hat holding a hamburger, in the hope that maybe we'll mistake it for Bob's Big Boy. Mom has an irrational aversion to "hillbillies," so we seldom eat at Country Kitchen, though she remains perfectly comfortable eating in a reproduction red barn at Red Barn.

More often than not, we pile into the Impala and drive to Shakey's Pizza on Portland Avenue in Richfield, with its player piano ghosting out ragtime songs and a waitstaff wearing straw boaters that diners can take home. They can take home the boaters, not the waitstaff, though that may be true too, for these are the 1970s and this is suburbia and Shakey's serves alcohol in copious quantities.

At home, the complimentary "straw" boater—the hat is actually made of Styrofoam—has a twenty-four-hour life span before it's sat on or has a hole punched in its crown or Tom takes a bite out of its brim for a cheap laugh. But so what? It's enough to be here, among waiters in red-and-white-striped jackets, hustling to and fro amid the Olde English décor. There are jokey signs that I don't quite understand but seem to make Dad smirk. WE HAVE A DEAL WITH THE BANK, reads one. THE BANK DOESN'T MAKE PIZZA AND WE DON'T CASH CHECKS.

Shakey's offers twenty-one varieties of pizza, and we can watch each of them being made in the kitchen display window. There are imitation leaded windows in the bar—Ye Public House—from which Dad can get a cold beer delivered to the table. There are "sarsaparillas for the li'l darlings." The whole place is a shotgun marriage of Dixieland and Henry VIII. Every outlet in the Shakey's empire makes a mockery of mock Tudor, and I never want to leave its cool, dark sanctuary for the parking lot just beyond those brown bottle-glass windows.

We often eat out after Dad has returned from a long business trip, to spare Mom another night of cooking dinner for ingrates. We are never shy about expressing our contempt for her homemade spaghetti sauce, made from real tomatoes grown in her garden. "Why can't we have Ragú instead?" Dad's trips last as long as two weeks, and Jim—dominating Little League baseball and football—feels his absence most acutely. The radio holds a terrible poignancy for Jim. I will press PLAY on a cassette recorder in the basement one afternoon to hear him earnestly crooning "Leaving on a Jet Plane." If only there were a Bufferin that could race straight to the source of his red-hot pain.

This fear of jet-enabled abandonment is in the air, or at least on the air, in "Cats in the Cradle" ("When you comin' home, Dad?") and "Daniel" ("Daniel is travelin' tonight on a plane..."). Dad is feeling the reverse sensation, the existential ennui of air travel, as expressed in "Big Ol' Jet Airliner" ("As I get on the 707") and "It Never Rains in Southern California" ("Got on board a westbound 747"). Dad doesn't know these songs or any others, save the few drinking songs he learned while playing college football, which he teaches us while tapping the wheel of the Impala wagon on our Saturday drives to Hardware Hank.

Oh Purdue, Oh Purdue, how you make me quiver
With your old Sweet Shop and your Wabash River
How I love you with my heart and I love you with my liver
Oh Purdue (tap, tap), *by the River* (tap, tap)
Oh Purdue, what a hole, by the River (tap, tap).

He is happy behind the wheel of our butterscotch land yacht, and the names he calls other drivers become a kind of music: "nitwit," "dingbat," "ding-dong," "idiot," "imbecile," "moron," "bozo," and "buffoon." Dad is the Roget of motoring insult. Of these epithets, "bozo" is by far his favorite, a vestigial memory of *The Bozo Show,* airing daily on channel 9 in Chicago when his three sons were toddlers there.

"That's right, bozo, don't use your blinker. Let me *guess* which way you're going."

Errands with Dad are rewarding in other ways too. I get to choose a sucker from a little jar at the liquor store. Then there's a coin-operated horsey outside the Ben Franklin five-and-dime that's always out of order. The car wash is terrifying, a felt-tentacled monster, foaming at the mouth, that eats us up at one end and excretes us at the other. At the dry cleaners, I watch the shirts make their endless ovals around the carousel all day. They travel with a mechanical ease in exactly the way the slot cars in the basement are supposed to work, but never do, always having to be nudged with a finger and then flying off the track at the corners. Every single time Dad pulls the car into the garage after these errands, he says, "Home again, home again, jiggety-jog." It's the second half of a nursery-rhyme couplet that begins "To market, to market, to buy a fat hog."

Before Dad leaves on a "business trip," he crouches down and tells me, "Hold down the fort for your mother." Should something happen to Mom or Jim or Tom, I am fourth in line to the throne, which is to say the Archie Bunker chair, and I feel that responsibility like a physical weight on my frail shoulders. I repeat our phone number to myself, in case of emergency.

On January 15, 1970, First Lady Pat Nixon christens Pan Am's *Clipper Young America* at Dulles airport in Washington. The majestic flying beast is on its way to New York, where six days later it embarks on its maiden commercial voyage from JFK to London Heathrow. Some passengers have booked their tickets two years in advance. "This airplane is the finest piece of aeronautical engineering ever constructed," says the captain, Robert Weeks. Among the passengers on the return flight from London to New York is Raquel Welch, of *Fantastic Voyage,* which is precisely what she has had aboard the 747. "Once you have flown on this plane," says Emmet Judge, a passenger on that first flight, "it will spoil you for everything else."

By summer of that year the 747 carries its millionth passenger. Everyone wants on, as the glamour and vastness of these planes are breathlessly reported. A passenger supposed to be flying across the United States on a TWA 747 has his flight delayed for fifteen minutes when he loses his daughter—on board! Coach passengers can choose smoking or no-smoking sections, movie or no-movie sections, R- or G-rated sections. Travelers on American Airlines can book a dinner table for four with swivel chairs and bone china. Paramount premieres

The Adventurers on a 747 flying from JFK to LAX as stars Candice Bergen and Ernest Borgnine hold court in the upstairs lounge.

At the dawn of jumbo-jet travel, Dad makes his maiden voyage aboard the 747. It's in that upstairs lounge that Dad and his boss drink a French liqueur called Green Chartreuse all night, all the way from Minneapolis–Saint Paul International Airport to Paris Orly, where a French employee of Mickey Mining fetches them at the gate. There is no such thing as airport security, even though hijackings have become commonplace. In the United States alone, more than a hundred fifty planes are "skyjacked" between 1961 and 1973. Fewer than seven months after its maiden voyage, that first 747, the *Clipper Young America,* is hijacked to Cuba.

Every night before bed I pray that Dad's plane isn't hijacked. One of the 1970s' biggest hit movies, *Airport*—the first of the decade's many disaster films—was shot at Minneapolis–Saint Paul International and involves a terrorist trying to blow up a 707 in flight. Is this what Mom means by an emergency? Will Dad recite our phone number—ay-day-date, too-weight-seven-two—in turbulence?

The Frenchman charged with escorting Dad and his boss to their first sales call of the day tries to speed them through customs, but the American executives from Mickey Mining just want to sit down. "We kept telling the guy, 'No, we have to get aspirin,'" Dad will recall forty years after the fact. "But the guy couldn't understand what we were saying and must have been wondering how these two Americans could arrive in Paris first thing in the morning absolutely shit-faced."

Of course, the Frenchman speaks little English, and my father speaks not a word of French, beyond "Tar-zhay" and "grand mal." Eventually he is driven, head aching, to his first sales call, perhaps muttering under his 110-proof morning breath, *"C'est la Guy. C'est la Guy."*

On another trip, the 747 bears him to Berlin. After calling on Mickey Mining's many Teutonic customers, Dad asks a 3M Germany colleague, "What's a good schnapps to take back to the U.S.?"

"There are so many," the colleague replies. "Shall we try a few?" Though Dad is scheduled to fly back to Bloomington the next morning, via London, he tries "a few zillion," as he later confesses. A knock on his hotel door wakes him at three the next afternoon. It is his 3M Germany colleague. "We missed you at breakfast" is all he says.

At home, while Dad is away, Jim beats up Tom, Tom beats up me, and sometimes Jim skips the middleman and beats me up directly. He has a litany of tortures at his disposal. They have names like Indian Burn, Dutch Rub, Purple Nurple, Swirly, Sudsy, and Snuggy—also known as a wedgie—but his favorite is the 99 Bump. He pins my biceps to the floor with his knees. It's like pinning spaghetti noodles to a plate with a fork. With the raised knuckle of his middle finger, he gives me ninety-nine shots to the sternum, pausing for a beat between each blow. Sometimes he enlivens the exercise by hocking up a loogie while kneeling over me and letting the bolus of phlegm dangle pendulously before he sucks it back into his mouth. Occasionally, he sucks too late, and he can't retract the loogie.

If I tell Mom on him, he'll give me some other torment—a

Pit Viper, a Hertz Donut—or narc on me for my own trans-
gressions: spitting back at him, perhaps, or missing the toilet
when I pee. This sometimes happens when Tom and I play
Crisscross Crash, in which we stand at opposite sides of the
toilet and try to make our ropy urine streams intersect in the
hope that one will overpower the other, because even peeing
has to be a violent collision between brothers.

A portrait of Christ above the credenza in the hall sees all
of this, but He keeps His counsel.

Depending on how we've behaved, we ache for Dad's return or dread it. We check our metaphorical bingo cards: Has
Mom claimed to be "on the brink of a nervous breakdown"
from our "constant bickering"? Has she invoked the phrase
"Wait until your father gets home"? If so, the wait can be
agonizing, like waiting for some anti-Christmas. Have we
"smarted off" to her or "talked back" or given her "lip"? Is
there a broken lamp, stained upholstery, a shattered curio re-
sistant to restoration with Krazy Glue?

Long-distance calls are so expensive that Dad phones home
only once during his week (or weeks) away, and when he does,
we follow the coiled yellow cord to Mom's seat in a floral easy
chair in the "living room," the room we are not allowed to use
or even to set foot in unless our parents are hosting company.
(That this is the most prominent room in the house and takes
up a good deal of its square footage is beside the point.) From
a safe remove, we eavesdrop on Mom briefing Dad with news
from the home front. Will she tell him about the 99 Bump or
the loogie hocking or the Crisscross Crash or any of the other
bodily expulsions that have set off our fistfights?

But no. To listen to her chat, it's as if she has been witness to an entirely different house. Mom regales Dad with stories of school achievements, of neighbor illnesses, of Amy's latest milestone. Like Christ above the credenza, she keeps her own counsel, and Dad comes home bearing gifts: a marionette puppet from the Bavarian Alps, a T-shirt emblazoned with the logo of some European soccer team, Corgi brand toy cars from London. And then, our family made whole again, we eat a fatted calf at Shakey's.

Given all the travel, Dad begins to salt his conversation with phrases picked up from abroad, of which *"C'est la Guy"* is just the most badly butchered. He now sends us to bed with *"Bonne nuit"* or sometimes *"Buona notte."* Other drivers are denounced as *"pazzo."* Tom is suddenly "Tomasso" and I have become "Stefanino."

"Buona notte, Stefanino," he says from the Archie Bunker chair every night before bed.

But if we have been very bad, exceptionally bad, or if our many sins have accreted over the week to form a coral reef of misconduct that Mom cannot reasonably ignore, then we must be disciplined with a masculine hand and we dread Dad's return.

It is possible to wear Mom down. If our horseplay turns to roughhousing and our roughhousing turns to fist fighting, and the yardstick from Lattof Chevrolet cannot becalm the house, and a "smart-aleck" comment brings her to tears, we instinctively stand down. But then every night bedtime comes as a shock and an outrage, and we meet it with our usual Kübler-Ross stages of denial, anger, bargaining, and depression before the reluctant last gasp of acceptance, which comes only in the form of sleep.

On exceptionally rare occasions, when Dad comes home after a week or two of such behavior, one or more of us will get a spanking.

Terrified, trembling, already screaming, I'm brought to my bedroom holding my bottom with both hands, and as he peels my palms from my buttocks, my index fingers grasp instead at my belt loops, so that by the time he gets my pants down an epic battle is engaged. And then I am bent over his knee and whacked three times with an open hand, each one sounding like a gunshot.

Those spared a spanking, or those who are next, can hear it through the walls and down the stairs. They will cover their ears and reflexively clench their cheeks. There comes a realization afterward that it didn't hurt as much as I expected, but the humiliation of the de-pantsing, and of being physically overpowered, is excruciating. When I am a little older, I come to think of being embarrassed as being em-*bare-assed*, like the opposite of embraced.

For the rest of the evening I devise theatrical plots to run away, featuring operatic exit lines, after which I'll live as the hoboes do in the *Tom and Jerry* cartoons of the 1940s, which play on Saturday morning. I'll hop aboard a boxcar, filch pies from windowsills, wrap all my possessions in a red bandanna and tie it to the end of a stick. Dad will wonder how he could have been so cruel, and Mom will weep with regret for ratting me out.

The next morning, after a heavy sleep induced by shoulder-heaving sobs, life returns to normal in South Brook, this sceptered isle, this other Eden, this little world, this blessed plot, this earth, this realm, this subdivision of not quite one hundred houses on seven streets and three circles. ("Cul-de-sac" is another French word we don't yet know.)

In most other respects it is a world I am coming to know intimately: which backyards can be used as cut-throughs, which yards have climbable fences, which ones have dogs and "dog doo" and angry homeowners. The two old ladies in the white Colonial—sisters? some say they're twins—are known to neighborhood children as the Sea Hags. They share a name with Popeye's nemesis, a weather-beaten witch who sails the seven seas in her boat *The Black Barnacle*. If our Nerf football rolls into the Sea Hags' yard, we leave it there, to decompose or disappear into their house, where they have, I am certain, the ultimate ball pit, a room filled with Nerf and Itza balls that rolled across their property line.

Tom and his buddy Steve Raich compose a song that goes in part "The Sea Hags across the street, meanest things on two feet. They like to call the heat, on me..."

The 1968 survey map of South Brook is on file at city hall. It bears the stamped logo of the surveying company, Harry S. Johnson Associates, and oh—if he only knew—how Jim and his friends would enjoy that name. *Harry Johnson!* It fits perfectly among the names on the baseball cards—Dick Pole, Pete LaCock—that ballplayers have in the 1970s, cards I will keep meticulously filed away in Velveeta cheese boxes. They are the perfect repositories, as if custom-built for baseball cards, whose glorious subjects stare back at me, each one sporting a mustache and a Windbreaker worn *under* the V-necked pullover of their double-knit jersey and a crazy name screaming grade school innuendo.

The names of athletes in the 1970s—men born and christened in a more innocent age after World War II—are all the better for being real. There is the White Sox outfielder Rusty Kuntz and the Bengals running back Boobie Clark, grown men whose names will make us giggle after the middle of this decade, when calculators will become ubiquitous. The moment the first pocket calculator appears at Nativity of the Blessed Virgin Mary, children will punch in 5318008 and turn it upside down to reveal BOOBIES. For a time, I will be so fascinated by this trick that I begin to fear—in case of emergency—I'll give my phone number as 531-8008 instead of 888-2872.

Jim and Tom are already privy to this kind of information, these secrets that aren't divulged on *Romper Room* or *Sesame Street* or even *The Electric Company*. A Sudsy (or a Swirly) is when a student's head is jammed into a flushing toilet. My brothers swear it is a routine occurrence in the boys' bathroom at Nativity and that a Swirly almost certainly awaits me next week when I start kindergarten in the middle of the year, as the newest and youngest kid in the school.

I have spent a couple of months at Saint Stephen's preschool, but whenever Mrs. Bakke-Hockey reads to the class and turns the book around to show us the illustrations, I silently mouth the words on the facing page. I read the construction-paper letters right off the wall, see them in my dreams like a spilled bowl of Alpha-Bits, and it's probably best for everyone—Mom and Mrs. Walkie-Talkie agree—if I finish the school year in kindergarten at Nativity, where I'm expected to do a nine-year stretch, enduring Sudsies and Snuggics, overseen by the two remaining nuns: Sister Roseanne and Sister Mariella, whom some call Sister Carl Eller, after the Vikings' fearsome defensive end.

It's like a mid-season call-up to the big leagues. And the red rash that spontaneously breaks out on my body? It's called pityriasis rosea, according to Dr. Larsen, our pediatrician, whom we all like for his gentle manner and startling resemblance to our favorite channel 5 meteorologist, Barry ZeVan the Weather Man. "Probably just anxiety induced," Dr. Larsen says. And then, though it barely needs saying, "In anticipation of school."

4

Glory, Glory, Hallelujah, Teacher Hit Me with a Ruler

Consistent with the themes of early education, my school-lunch sandwich is a pile of shapes: a square of Wonder Bread, a circle of Oscar Mayer bologna, and a sharp-cornered square of Kraft American cheese, shiny like vinyl. Its violent orange is vivid against the stark white of the Wonder. We ask Mom to cut these sandwiches diagonally, to make two triangles, but she cuts them horizontally, because she believes strongly that sandwiches should consist of two rectangles. She has strong convictions on what is right and what is wrong. Thank-you notes should be sent within three days of receiving a gift, we should always say hello when adult "company" comes over, and we should never—under any circumstances—use the word "fart" in front of her. "It's 'passing gas.'"

So the sandwiches are two rectangles, mortared together with Hellmann's Real Mayonnaise and placed in a metal lunch box embossed with the Peanuts gang, which I snap shut with exactly the same flourish—and with the same sense of mission—Dad displays when snapping shut his briefcase.

Mom saves the Wonder Bread bags. I wear them over my socks. They make it easy to slip what we call snowmobile boots on and off, and to keep my socks dry while I'm planted in a snowbank at the end of our street, waiting for the school bus. That bus is also a violent shade of orange, vivid against the stark white of the snow. It slows to a stop, the air brakes decompressing with a long sigh, and its doors fold outward, like the arms of a malevolent stranger.

Mom digs a wad of Kleenex from her purse, licks it, and wipes my face. I scratch at my pityriasis rosea and let the bus swallow me whole, and think of Jonah being eaten by the whale in my children's Bible.

As she recedes from view, Mom waves the Kleenex as if it were a hanky and the bus is the *Queen Mary,* pulling out of port on a nine-year voyage around the world.

And so life begins—and begins to pick up speed. Mom wakes me every morning by pulling up the shades and singing in falsetto the theme song from *The Boone and Erickson Show,* the morning-drive juggernaut on WCCO radio: "Good morning, good morrr-ning. It's great to be on hand. Good morning, good morning, to yooooou!" Her predawn cheeriness is something I admire and resent in equal measure.

Supine on my blue bedspread, I stick my legs in the air and bicycle into my underpants. Pulling on a single tube sock, I remain on the bed, lost in thought. Mom sings, "Diddle, diddle dumpling, my son John, one sock off and one sock on."

Dad has already left the house under cover of darkness after his solitary bowl of Post Raisin Bran. ("There're *two scoops* of raisins in Kellogg's Raisin Bran," I tell him, but he doesn't care.) He's taught me to check my gig line every morning when getting dressed. I make sure my shirt buttons, my belt buckle, and the fly seam of my navy-blue pants are ramrod straight, as Dad learned to do in the army, giving us both the illusion that the world—and, by extension, the day ahead—can be ordered, straightened out, or bent to our will.

He wears a suit to work every day, navy-blue or charcoal. They're racked up in the closet in their dry-cleaning bags emblazoned with ONE-HOUR MARTINIZING. Mom launders and irons his white shirts. When Mickey Mining dispatches Dad to Guam, to sell Scotch brand recording tape to the U.S. Army base exchange stores of the Pacific Rim, Dad meets the local 3M rep for breakfast at his hotel. It is 100 degrees at 7:30 in the morning. "What are you wearing?" asks the guy, dressed in a guayabera shirt, regarding Dad, in his navy-blue suit and tie knotted to the neck.

"I'm dressed for business," Dad replies. "What are *you* wearing?"

Dad shaves every morning, seven days a week, even on vacation, before slapping some jewel-colored, mentholated unguent onto his cheeks. When he sees an unshaven face on TV—usually a "wino" or a "bum" in some Quinn-Martin production—he says, "That guy stood too far from his razor this morning."

Despite these best efforts at organizing it—Mom's tidy house, Dad's impeccable gig line—the universe is already in chaos by the time I walk down the aisle of the school bus, hoping in vain to find an empty seat, silently praying that someone will move his book bag and gesture for me to sit.

Most days I'm still standing as the bus lurches to a start, and the force throws me into a seat next to a pigtailed girl who picks her nose and slowly rolls the booger between thumb and forefinger, like a little Chinese stress ball.

And fair play to her: there is much to be stressed about. A kind of reverse segregation system prevails on the bus, in which the overlords sit in the very back and the disenfranchised are forced to remain up front, near the terrifying driver, whose radio plays Led Zeppelin's "Black Dog" on a loop.

From the back of the bus, cruel nicknames are bestowed on all who embark. Pale, frail Michael Amato is "Michael Amato, the Albino Tomato." Gary Fritz easily and inevitably becomes "Hairy Pits." Shame on his parents for not anticipating the taunt. A girl whose address is betrayed, on her mailbox, as 10101 France Avenue is greeted—every single day—with a binary taunt in a haunting, singsong chorus: "One-oh-one-oh-one-oh-one-oh-one-oh-one..."

I gaze out the window and think of *The Electric Company:* Who can turn a bus into abuse? Anyone can plainly see—it's silent *e.*

When my brothers and I walk down the aisle, we hear, "The Rushins are coming, the Rushins are coming," after a 1966 movie that none of us has ever seen called *The Russians Are Coming.* Jim and Tom offer me some measure of protection, though not from the language of the eighth-grade boys at the back. They talk about which girls are "stacked" and which ones don't require "over-the-shoulder boulder holders," a phrase I find enormously pleasing to the ear, if not yet to any other organs.

The seats are pine-green. They smell of vinyl and what

Mom calls "passed gas." It is not possible to pass gas on the bus without an Inquisition. The responsible party must be publicly identified and held accountable.

"Who farted?"

"Not me."

"Whoever denied it supplied it."

"He who smelt it dealt it."

Whenever one of us passes gas in church Mom leans over and whispers, "Are you sitting in your own pew?" It is her favorite joke. But any flatulence on the bus will not be met with good humor, and I resolve to hold it in for the next dozen years.

I rest my forehead against the frozen surface of the bus window. The older kids pinch the locks to lower the windows halfway. The inrush of cold air makes their breath look like cigarette smoke. Following their lead, I learn to press the fleshy side of my fist to the frosted glass and pull it away. The resulting impression resembles a footprint, and with my fingertips I add five dots for the toes.

There is so much to learn on the bus that isn't part of the Nativity curriculum. Our principal is Sister Roseanne. (In a few short years, after the premiere of *Saturday Night Live*, she will become forever—to her everlasting confusion—Sister Roseanne Roseannadanna.) Our janitor is said to be even more terrifying. He's Mr. Sipe, though everyone calls him The Sniper. They say he enjoys running kids down at recess in his orange El Camino, which is like a beast out of Greek mythology: the front half is a respectable sedan with a landau roof while the back half is a pickup truck. It's as if Chevrolet has manufactured a 350-horsepower mullet—business in the front, party in the back. Every student agrees it's the coolest car we have ever seen. The very name "El Camino" sounds Californian and confers the same California glamour on our Midwestern suburb that the Schwinn Sting-Ray does.

The Royal Knight edition of the El Camino has two fire-tongued dragons on the hood, either fighting or French kissing, or possibly both. Already anxious about swallowing my own tongue, I find the El Camino dragons now make me fear that I could swallow someone else's too, or they could swallow mine.

Still, these are my favorite cars by far, the ones with creatures painted on the hoods, not least of all the Pontiac Firebird Trans Am, with its black-and-gold "Thunder Chicken" either breathing fire on the hood or sticking out its tongue. I know if I stick out my tongue on the hood of a car on a cold day in Minnesota it will remain there until spring, long after the rest of me has been prized away by the Bloomington Fire Department.

Counting cars is the principal pastime on the bus, but not the only one. The middle of the bus, representing the middle grades of the school, is alive with songs and chants. My ears reflexively bend toward the rhymes like flowers to the sun.

"Jingle bells, Batman smells, Robin laid an egg! The Batmobile lost a wheel, and the Joker got away—hey…"

And: "The Addams Family started, when Uncle Fester farted. They all became retarded…"

Retarded. Ree-tard. There is a kid who wears a motorcycle helmet at school—in class as well as at recess—and because of this I heard him called a ree-tard. It's another ugly word that gets whispered. The boy is in every other respect exactly like every other kid at Nativity, except for the helmet, which marks him out as alien. No activity in our lives requires a helmet, save for playing football or hockey, or being Evel Knievel, and these happen to be the three coolest things it is possible to be. My yellow canvas book bag is emblazoned with the Vikings' purple helmet. On the bus, it's an amulet warding off ridicule, a token of universal acceptance.

The bus rings out with: "Beans, beans, the musical fruit. The more you eat, the more you toot..."

And: "Liar, liar, pants on fire, hanging from the telephone wire!"

And: "Glory, glory hallelujah! Teacher hit me with a ruler! So I hid behind the door, with a loaded .44, and there ain't no teacher anymore!"

Silence is the safest way to get along, which is all I desire. In life, as in games of tag, I never want to be It. I only want to be Not It.

"Bubble gum, bubble gum, in a dish. How many pieces do you wish?"

It is written in the stars, or at least in the *Chicago Tribune,* that I will want security from earliest youth. Just by listening, I discover the traps to be avoided, the questions better left unanswered, the dozen Hertz Donuts to be declined daily.

"What's under there?"

"Under where?"

"You said 'underwear.'"

Or: "Guess what?"

"What?"

"That's what."

There are rhyming rules to be learned: "Finders keepers, losers weepers."

And: "No cuts, no butts, no coconuts."

And rhyming insults: "I see London, I see France..."

And taunts: "Steve and Wanda sittin' in a tree, K-I-S-S-I-N-G..."

And comebacks: "Sticks and stones may break my bones..."

The bus ride to Nativity is only fifteen minutes, but in that time the alternative lyrics to every television theme song ever are revealed. "Come and listen to a story 'bout a man named Jed, dumb mothesucker wore a rubber on his head..." I don't recognize the compound word that follows "dumb" or even if I heard it correctly. Nor do I know why Jed would wear one of Ned Zupke's galoshes on his head. But I instinctively recognize the epithet as a swear word and thus never to be repeated.

The bus introduces me to another bad word, and I realize from the reaction that this one is the worst of all. "Daniel Boone was a man, was a biiig man! But the bear was bigger so he ran like a nigger up a tree." It is met with a hush, a shaming silence. Even the radio seems to pause in mid-Zeppelin. In that excruciating interval of quiet, my armpits ignite, and not for the last time. I'll hear the word again, replacing "tiger" in "Eeny, Meeny, Miny, Moe," and it will have the same effect. Dad has impressed on each of his children that we're no better than anybody else and are often a great deal worse. He coached the baseball team while stationed at Fort Sill in Oklahoma. When the team bus stopped en route to games at Fort Hood in Texas, black players were often denied service in restaurants. "So of course we all refused to eat there," Dad says. "These were United States servicemen." Like many of Dad's other attributes—his neatness, his self-discipline, his love of black coffee—his embrace of equality was confirmed in the integrated army. He often laments the end of the draft. At the sight of any of our unmade beds he always says with a shake of his head, "A couple of years in the army would do you good."

On the school playground, whenever two boys fight—and it is always two boys, never two girls—a crowd forms a circle and chants, "Fight! Fight! Fight!" On occasion, when a teacher comes to break it up, she finds the boys lying on their bellies, arm-wrestling, and the teacher will shake her head and walk away, to howls of derisive laughter.

More often the fights are real, and the animal aggression on display is scary and thrilling, not least because every fight can conceivably end with The Sniper driving up at high speed, the El Camino throwing up dust and gravel, scattering the chanting children at ringside.

You see his left leg first. It swings out of the cab of the El Camino, ring of keys on his hip jangling like a jailer's. The Sniper is silent, save for the clinking of the keys, which he stills with a hand that looks like it's reaching for a holster. Plank palmed, thick fingered, eyes unblinking behind aviator glasses, The Sniper has many violent tools at his disposal: dust mop, steel bucket, rotary floor buffer. But the greatest of these is the El Camino, whose grille, it's been said, has taken out a dozen or more students, victims of The Sniper's vehicular homicide. The mere sight of that grille, glinting in the distance, is enough to break up most fights.

But The Sniper can't be everywhere. One afternoon on the playground across the street from our house I hear a public-school kid say the word "jigaboo." I don't know what it means. When I idly say it out loud at the dinner table that night, Dad abruptly stops buttering his baked potato, a silence falls over the kitchen, and my ears begin to burn in dread. Pausing in mid-chew, he points his butter knife at me like a bayonet.

"I better *never* hear that word again," he says. "Is that understood?"

"Yes," I say without understanding.

This cultural sensitivity is not applied equally to all. When Viet Nam is reunited as Vietnam and refugees from that country almost immediately begin to arrive in Bloomington, Amy becomes best friends with one of them, a classmate named Oanh, pronounced like "Juan," who attends Nativity with her two younger siblings. Dad collectively calls them, with abiding affection, "Oanh, Two, and Twee."

At age six, it only suggests to me that words exist to be stretched and kneaded like Silly Putty, the way a butterfly can flutter by. Allowed to stay up late one night, I hear someone on *The Tonight Show* describe Elizabeth Taylor as having "more chins than a Chinese phone book." Dad hears me laugh, sees my delight, but says nothing. Months later, after a Northwest Orient 747 safely returns him to Bloomington from Hong Kong, he walks into the house, kisses Mom, opens his briefcase, and silently hands me a sheaf of onionskin pages torn from the telephone directory in his hotel room. Here are all the Chins in a Chinese phone book, and I clutch the paper to my chest as if it's a treasure map.

First grade. 1972. The alphabet is displayed on the wall of our classroom, uppercase and lowercase letters written between two solid lines with a dashed line running along the middle, like a road seen from above, so that the ABCs appear to be perpetually stuck in traffic. I'm an idling letter myself, seated here in alphabetical order between Roxanne Riebel and Joe Saleck, stifling yawns, staring out the window to the range of snow mountains on the edge of the parking lot, where the plow has piled it high.

As we inch agonizingly toward recess—twice a day, mid-morning and after lunch—the second hand of the clock above the blackboard slows down, taking perverse pleasure in its sluggish laps.

The bell, when it finally rings, is the same bell that sends the horses from their chutes at the Kentucky Derby, and with much the same effect. We fly out of the classroom, down the hall, through the double doors, and into the parking lot to play King of the Mountain. The older boys throw the younger and smaller boys off the top of the snow hills. A routine repeats itself for twenty minutes: I ascend to the summit, get dwarf-tossed off by a fifth-grader, and begin to make another icy ascent of this parking-lot Everest. The air is thick with flying children. We are frightened, thrilled, adrenalized, alive—sliding down on the fronts of our fur-fringed parkas like penguins.

Other days at recess we play Smear the Queer, in which the holder of a football is chased by an amped-up mob of shrieking schoolchildren until he—for it is only ever boys—throws the ball away in fear or disappears beneath a writhing pile of winter coats and flying fists, the blows softened by mittens, the screams of the dispossessed ball carrier muted by his own scarf. Lying at the bottom of such a pile, gagged by my Vikings scarf, it occurs to me: this is why they call it a muffler.

In the afternoon, after dismissal, I watch an eighth-grader "skitch" behind a departing bus, grabbing hold of the back bumper with his bare hands and skiing behind it for a hundred yards in his tennis shoes. The big kids go hatless and mitten-less in the dead of winter. They wear socks and gym shoes in the snow. As I board my bus in bread-bagged feet, mortified by their misbehavior, I have my own secret sin on my con-science.

I don't care for my circle-and-square sandwiches but tell Mom that I do. I don't bring them home uneaten for fear of hurting her feelings. Nor do I throw them in the wastebasket in our classroom—we eat at our desks, like harried middle managers at Mickey Mining—for we are told, at home and at school, that starving children in Africa would love to have our bologna sandwiches.

So I put my uneaten sandwiches in the pencil box in my desk and watch them turn green after many, many weeks sealed inside their plastic Baggies. The Wonder Bread, Amer-ican cheese, and bologna are so pregnant with preservatives that it takes ages for them to turn. But after two months, the sandwiches piling up in the pencil box like corpses under the patio begin to stink. Mrs. Streit doesn't yet notice. In a class-room full of six-year-olds, it's just one more strange smell among many. Still, the sandwiches haunt me. The guilt over-whelms me. Even seated at my desk, I am a fugitive on the lam. I want to confess but can't, knowing it's only a matter of days before I'll be led out of the classroom in handcuffs, my classmates pointing and howling at me on the way out, the pencil box zipped into a plastic evidence bag carried by a man in a hazmat suit.

* * *

That pencil box, not incidentally, is the size of a cigar box and every bit as redolent. Before I began stashing my sandwiches in it, the box smelled of pencil shavings, crayons, Elmer's paste, eraser crumbs, and possibilities. The lid of this canary-yellow cardboard coffin is illustrated with fresh-scrubbed boys and girls frolicking beside a puppy in a meadow. Above the tableau are the words MY SCHOOL BOX. There are spaces on the lid for my name, my school, my grade, and my teacher's name. Mom filled it all in, the blank spaces now embroidered with her impeccable Palmer Method cursive.

MY SCHOOL BOX holds the fruit of my first back-to-school shopping spree, which I undertook before first grade, making the pilgrimage that Jim and Tom made before me to Snyder Brothers Drug Store in the Cloverleaf strip mall. There, in a magical aisle, are spiral-bound Mead notebooks in a motley of colors, number-two pencils racked up like bats in the Twins dugout, and bevel-edged erasers the color of bubble gum with "Pink Pearl" stamped on them in an elegant script. They look like a human tongue, or the pink rectangle of bubble gum inside Topps baseball cards.

As for crayons, we are not allowed the sixty-four-pack of Crayolas with the sharpener built into the box but rather the primary colors of the eight-pack. The sixty-four-pack induces crayon envy among the eight-packers in the classroom. The eight-pack deprives us of Peach, the crayon formerly known as Flesh, so crucial to drawing our Caucasian flesh-toned self-portraits. The sixty-four-pack has Peach and even Indian Red, evidently manufactured exclusively for drawing

Indians. Since that first visit to the Dells, a good portion of my thoughts have been devoted to Indians—the rubber-tomahawked Indians of my imagination.

I am beckoned to sit "Indian-style" during story time, and when Kenny Mellenbruch repossesses one of the marbles he has given me—a polished "steelie" that's hard to come by—I call him an Indian giver. The school year itself begins with the false promise of Indian summer. And yet all the Indians I know—the Atlanta Braves mascot, Chief Noc-a-Homa; the Cleveland Indians mascot, Chief Wahoo; Iron Eyes Cody himself—are noble and righteous figures. The Indian headdress on the Tootsie Pop wrapper is a symbol of joy, Willy Wonka's golden ticket.

The Washington Redskins consist entirely of Indians, as far as I can tell. The Redskins are the 1972 NFC champions and have a linebacker whose name is Chris Hanburger but whom I always think of as Chris Hamburger.

Back-to-school shopping concludes with a fitting for uniforms at Korner Plaza. For boys, Nativity requires navy-blue pants and a light blue shirt, a seemingly rigid code that in fact leaves almost endless leeway. For instance, the uniform code allows children, through a celestial loophole, to wear navy-blue Levi's corduroys, provided they can somehow persuade their mothers to buy them. These are the gold standard. At the opposite end, a few boys wear tweed trousers with flecks of white and gray, like a pointillist sign that says KICK ME. The Rushins wear something in between, flat-fronted gas-station Dickies paired with short-sleeved dress shirts.

But it's the shoes that matter most. We beg for Adidas, to whose three stripes we have assigned an imagined hierarchy.

At the entry level are the Roms, followed by the Viennas, topped by the Italias. The names ring out with European so- phistication, and any child leaving Nativity in Levi's cords and Adidas Italias on a Schwinn Sting-Ray is the luckiest child on earth. Levi Strauss has been dead seventy years, Ig- naz Schwinn died a quarter century ago, and Adi Dassler is an old man in his eighth decade. And yet, in Bloomington, these three dominate fashion and adolescent longing unlike any other men of the modern age.

"Shall I box them up," says the shoe salesman, holding my nylon Thom McAns, "or will you wear them out of the store?"

Mom is talking to the clerk but looking at me when she says, "Box them." My shoulders slump.

"We don't wear shoes out of the store," she whispers. "We're not hillbillies."

All around us, hillbillies are walking out of the store in new gym shoes, their old gym shoes in a box beneath their arm.

Our new clothes have to hang in the closet or sit folded in a dresser drawer for several days before we're allowed to wear them. As with America's handgun laws to come, my purple paisley dress shirt with the pterodactyl-wing collar requires a five-day waiting period before I can get my hands on it. I ask Mom why I can't wear it right now, a day after we walked out of Target with it, and she says (as I knew she would), "That's what hillbillies do."

I can't possibly know where she gets her irrational fear of hillbillies. God knows, I have plenty of irrational fears of my own, including a fear of being hypnotized by a pocket watch swinging back and forth on its chain while a soothing voice says "You are getting *verrry* sleepy." It happens in half the shows I watch on TV. As for Mom, she grew up in Cincinnati, evidently fearful that hordes of hillbillies would wade—straw-hatted, barefooted, bib-overalled—across the Ohio River and into her backyard. This might explain Mom's endless cleaning, the neatening of drawers, the discarding of anything that isn't nailed down. If she finds a hole in the toe of my sock, she darns it with a needle and thread. In every cartoon and comic strip, a bare big toe poking out of a hole in the sock is a hillbilly indicator. I might as well walk around with a stalk of hay in my mouth.

When Mom and Dad married and Dad bought their first car—used, from a friend—he had to finance the purchase with a loan. "A loan?" Mom said. "Isn't that what hillbillies do?"

It was Dad's first set of wheels, unless you count the trailer he lived in with his mother in high school. He had to leave the trailer to use a communal bathroom, so when he says "We didn't have a pot to pee in," he is telling the God's honest truth. He would sit on the toilet in that outbuilding, picking the flies off the wall and feeding them to the spiders to pass the time. Growing up fatherless in a Fort Wayne, Indiana, trailer park next to a sewage treatment plant may have instilled a mild hillbilly phobia in Dad, because he told Mom's mom—my Grandma Boyle in Cincinnati—that the used car he bought to convey his twenty-two-year-old bride to Fort Sill, Oklahoma, was not the end of his automotive ambitions. "Someday," he told Grandma Boyle, "I'll drive a Cadillac."

This story is the only time I will ever hear of my father boasting about anything. He trades in self-deprecation—and the deprecation of others, especially motorists and television newsreaders—but he loathes self-promotion and so does Mom. "Don't toot your own horn," she has told me many, many times. And so I just assume it's something better left to the hillbillies that walk among us.

Whatever its source, Mom's aversion to hillbillies does *not* stem from a fear of falling into poverty or a discomfort with poor people. On the contrary. After she graduated from the University of Cincinnati with a degree in primary education, Mom was one of two white teachers to integrate the all-black faculty at an all-black school in one of Cincinnati's poorest neighborhoods. Her rectitude and naïveté were instantly on display in her fourth-grade classroom in the mid-1950s. Students lined up for recess in front of the chalkboard, and when the line marched out of the room, there was often a single word scrawled on that board. She would erase it, and the word would reappear the next day.

After a week, my future mom finally asked the class, "Why does someone keep writing 'Pussy' on the board?"

The children gasped and giggled.

Mom pressed on. "Is Pussy somebody's cat?"

There was more giggling, and a girl raised her hand. "Miss Boyle," she said. "That's something a lady has." This only confirmed Miss Boyle's notion that Pussy was indeed a cat, and she let the matter rest, but not before telling my future dad, who palmed his face in disbelief.

I don't yet know any of these stories, of course, only that I can—simply by putting on a brand-new Izod shirt thirty-six hours after purchasing it or walking out of Famous Footwear in a pair of brand-new Thom McAns—end my parents' hard-won climb up the greased pole of the American middle class and send them (and me and my growing number of siblings) crashing back to hillbilly class.

In truth, the only hillbillies I know from TV are living a life of unimaginable luxury after moving to Beverly (Hills, that is). California holds a fascination for all of us. Viewed through our Zenith, everything there—*The Brady Bunch* house, *The Partridge Family* clothes, the blue-and-yellow license plates on the twelve-lane freeways—looks like the future. And so we lobby Dad, a frequent traveler to that magical land, to take us there someday.

He answers the same way he does whenever I ask him to take us bowling or to tell me what Watergate means or to explain Vietnam (or Viet Nam). "Someday," he says. "Someday."

There is a new rhyme to endure on the bus in the fall of 1972: "Nixon, Nixon, he's our man! McGovern belongs in the garbage can!" I repeat it at home. Mom is a Democrat, Dad a Republican. I've heard him say, "We cancel each other's vote." I don't know if he has come by his political affiliation after great thought or if he just wants to negate women's suffrage.

I take Mom's pained expression on hearing me trash McGovern to be disapproval, though it might just be morning sickness, for she is pregnant again, with a fifth child. Sears portrait-studio photographs of the first four of us hang in descending order—Jim, Tom, Steve, Amy—down the wall of the staircase. In a fifth frame above the bottom step, Dad—an accomplished doodler—has hand-drawn in cartoon bubble letters WATCH THIS SPACE.

Dad is in Los Angeles when Mom goes into labor. He arrives home just in time for the birth of a fourth son, who is named—with an extravagant four letters—John. To avoid confusion, Mom no longer sings to me "Diddle, diddle dumpling, my son John" but instead wakes me with just its uncoupled second line: "One shoe off and one shoe on."

She'll pass me on the couch in the middle of a Saturday morning and sing, "One shoe off, one shoe on," for that is often how she finds me: wearing one mateless sock or limping like a peg-legged pirate in a single shoe, absorbed in a waking dream about almost anything—who would win a fight between Inch High, Private Eye and the Ty-D-Bol man, for instance, and why the former wears a raincoat to receive clients while the latter wears a blazer to circumnavigate the toilet bowl. Perhaps they should swap wardrobes. And so it goes, for hours on end, until that terrible moment when *American Bandstand* begins and brings down the curtain on five and a half consecutive hours of Saturday morning TV.

For Mom, the arrival of her fifth child is fractionally eased by the arrival of disposable diapers. There is still a stack of cloth diapers and pink- and blue-capped diaper pins in a dresser drawer in Amy's room, but they are ignored in favor of Pampers, another wonder product from Procter & Gamble, the global leviathan founded and still headquartered in Mom's hometown of Cincinnati, to which she remains intensely devoted. She serves chili over spaghetti, as they do in Cincinnati, roots for the Reds with a singular passion, and believes in the sanctity of Procter & Gamble. Our dishwasher detergent is Cascade and our fabric softener is Bounce, so that

Cincinnati, like God, is always with us and all around us—on our forks and plates and underpants.

Like Ignaz Schwinn, William Procter and James Gamble were Old World men shaping my life from beyond the grave. They immigrated separately to the United States—Procter from England, Gamble from Ireland—and only stopped in Cincinnati by coincidence, both men seeking medical attention on their way west. Procter stayed and became a candle maker; Gamble stayed and was apprenticed to a soap maker. When the two happened to marry sisters—Olivia and Elizabeth Norris—their father-in-law suggested they go into business together, which they did, forming Procter & Gamble in 1837.

That they did so in Cincinnati is why my mom is now partial to Tide detergent and—just debuted in time for John's arrival—Bounce fabric softener. There is nothing P&G doesn't make, so our toothpaste is always Crest with fluoride—"clinically proven to fight cavities"—and we're occasionally allowed as a treat at Red Owl to pick out a tube of Pringles. It's also a P&G product, which is why Fredric Baur will be buried in suburban Cincinnati in the Pringles can he designed.

Mom hadn't wanted to move from Cincinnati, where Dad first took a job with 3M, to Columbus, Ohio, to which Mickey Mining dispatched him and where Jim was born. She hadn't wanted to move at 3M's behest from Ohio to greater Chicago, where Tom and I were born, and after ten years in Palatine and Lisle, she hadn't wanted to move from Chicago to Bloomington. Through all these moves, she held fast to the polestar of Cincinnati: to Graeter's ice cream and Ohio State football and the Big Red Machine of Johnny Bench and Pete Rose.

There are a few exceptions to Mom's Cincinnati loyalty—she sometimes buys Hills Bros. coffee instead of P&G's Folgers and only ever buys Dial soap, from the Dial Corporation. It is clearly the gold standard of bath soaps, literally a gold bar, wrapped in gold foil, with DIAL carved into the center. I run my hands across those letters in the bath, tracing them with my fingers, digging my nails into the soap. Tom is passing gas in the tub; I'm scrubbing my "business," which is one of Mom's many euphemisms. We're also to say "tinkle" and "BM," so that when she buys B&M brand baked beans—or, worse, B&M brown bread in a can—we make gagging sounds while carrying the groceries in from the garage.

Since there are five of us, one of those grocery sacks now always contains a receipt that is three feet long and curled up on itself like a lizard's tongue.

With the birth of John, our family is complete. We have moved again, into bigger digs, three minutes by bike on the other side of South Brook, to 2809 West 96th Street. Before Dad moved us to Bloomington in the first place, he house-hunted alone during a few idle hours away from the Mickey Mining campus and bought the house on Southbrook Drive. Mom never saw it until she moved in, but Dad knew she would love it, that it was perfect for her. She hated it instantly and immediately began looking for another in the neighborhood, part of a pattern of Dad thinking he knows what she wants, with the best intentions, while not really having a clue. When Mom begins driving across town to the Normandale Racquet Club to walk on a treadmill three mornings a week, Dad buys her a treadmill and puts it in the basement. "Now you don't have to drive all the way across town," he says. "You can walk on the treadmill *at home.*" From the day she receives it, Mom uses the treadmill only as a coatrack and continues to drive across town to walk on the racquet-club treadmill. Some days it is the only escape from her manifold domestic duties.

I am now the middle of five children, but Mom and Dad are only keeping pace with the neighbors. It's not unusual for families at Nativity to have five children, or nine. At least a dozen families at school consist of seven or more kids. Already there are more kids enrolled in school in Bloomington than there ever have been before, or ever will be again—twenty-six thousand of us. Bloomington is in peak bloom, and now so is our house. None of these entities—our town, our school, our house—will ever be fuller than they are now, never as loud or eventful or brimming with life.

This youthful vitality, this animating energy, seems to suffuse the entire country. For the first time in American history there are 25 million teenagers in the United States—kids aged twelve to seventeen—every one of them teeming with a life force in search of an outlet. Toward that end, *Playboy* will sell 8.5 million copies of its November 1972 issue, a record that will never be broken. And while I am too young to see Swedish brunette Lena Söderberg dressed for the day in nothing but a sun hat and feather boa, I am evidently old enough to see my first grown-up movie.

With five children aged three months to eleven years to look after, Mom deserves a relatively quiet evening at home, and Dad orders Jim, Tom, and me to pile into the Impala. We are going—at long last and with great ceremony, and

for the first time in my life—to "the movies." We're seeing *The Poseidon Adventure*, which sounds like a madcap
nautical escapade on the high seas. More momentously, I'll
finally set foot in Mann's Southtown Theatre, which Dad
pronounces "thee-AY-der." He has a fondness for the entire
oeuvre of Abbott and Costello and the swashbuckling adventures of Errol Flynn, but otherwise Dad is not a movie
buff. His favorite film of the last quarter century is the TV
movie *Brian's Song*, about the dying Chicago Bears running
back Brian Piccolo, which annually airs on ABC and trig-
gers Dad's annual tear, which always puts me in mind of
Iron Eyes Cody.

The Southtown Theatre is a magical non sequitur, a place
whose very existence is a mystery and a miracle, as if a Manhattan movie palace circa 1947 has fallen from the sky onto
Penn Avenue South in suburban Minneapolis, between the
Putt-Putt mini golf course and Wally McCarthy's Oldsmobile
dealership.

Southtown's klieg-lit marquee runs for miles, wrapping
around the entire pebble-dashed exterior, which glows from
its own footlights. Should Gene Hackman and Ernest Borgnine step out of a stretch limousine and onto a red carpet
at any moment, as I fully expect they will, the Southtown
Theatre is better prepared than that other great movie palace
in this same chain, Mann's Chinese Theatre in Hollywood.

The mid-century modern lobby of the Southtown is dom-
inated by a fountain filled with coins and live goldfish, and
a refreshment stand stocked with comically large boxes of
Mike and Ike and Sno-Caps. Jim and Tom and I fog the glass
cases with our breath before reluctantly moving on. Every-

thing smells headily of fresh popcorn and carpet disinfectant. Advancing past the box office and beyond the red velvet ropes of the ticket takers standing sentry above slotted gold boxes, I see the framed poster for *The Poseidon Adventure.* Bodies dressed in formalwear are raining down inside an inverted cruise ship. The tagline reads HELL, UPSIDE DOWN. I feel a dull pulsing of dread in my stomach, but it's still competing for attention with all that surrounds me.

Inside, the theater itself is vast, at least the size of the Montgomery Ward across the parking lot. The screen alone is seventy feet wide and thirty-six feet high—a foot shorter than the Boston Red Sox's famed Green Monster, the left-field wall whose height I have committed to memory and use to gauge the height of every other earthly structure. There are, for reasons I cannot possibly fathom, twelve hundred seats in the theater. With five daily screenings, it can accommodate 7 percent of the population of Bloomington every single day. Even in central Bloomington, a place of finite entertainment options—there's a hobby shop in the Southtown strip mall, and Howard Wong's restaurant is across the street—twelve hundred seats seems a tad overambitious.

Every one of those seats is a plush red-velvet rocker. I barely weigh enough to hold down its spring-loaded, flip-up mechanism and worry I'll be catapulted into the rows at the rear of the theater.

The seats at the back have ashtrays built into the armrests. When the houselights go down, ghostly blue smoke is visible, rising like a wraith through a beam of projector light. The bubble of fear in my stomach expands. I look back frequently, or a mile up at the ceiling, because it's better than looking forward, at the screen. The SS *Poseidon* looks exactly like pictures I have seen of the *Titanic,* but its fate—I learn instantly—won't be nearly as pleasant. "At midnight on New Year's Eve, the SS *Poseidon,* en route from New York to Athens, met with disaster and was lost," reads a title card in the opening credits, preempting any hope for a happy beginning, much less a happy ending. "There were only a handful of survivors. This is their story…"

On that insane Southtown screen, the captain appears at his post—white-haired Leslie Nielsen, his head seventy feet tall, looking grave and important. When a kid named Robin Shelby staggers onto the deck, rain-lashed and wind-whipped, I become that little boy for the next two hours, my only ambition to remain alive against all odds. A "seaquake" has triggered a tidal wave on the *Poseidon*'s final voyage. It is ninety feet tall, more than twice the Green Monster, and serves—when it turns the ship upside down—as yet another sign of nature's malevolence: earthquakes, tarantulas, quicksand, the Devil's Triangle, the Loch Ness Monster, killer bees, Bigfoot, Venus flytraps, and raging infernos are all much on my mind, several of them fodder for a disaster film still to come, many of them by this film's producer, Irwin Allen, creating the disaster-epic genre before my very eyes, which are already obscured behind my splayed fingers.

The forecast is dire, but Mr. Linarcos, a representative of the ship's owners, insists that our captain, Mr. Nielsen, power onward to Athens, full steam ahead. "You irresponsible bastard!" Nielsen shouts at him, and my ears burn at the language. Likewise, young Robin tells his big sister, Susan, "Why don't you shove it! Shove it, shove it, shove it!" I fear

I'll be punished just for hearing these words, but Dad is happily eating popcorn, unmoved by the profanity.

The only swear word Dad ever says is "God dammit." Mom says "Jesus, Mary, and Joseph" or "God bless it" when she's angry. These are stand-ins for profanity. She says "Jesus, Mary, and Joseph" instead of "Jesus Christ" and "God bless it" instead of "God dammit." It's a clever bit of Catholic alchemy, turning blasphemy into praise. What I've heard other grown-ups call "dog shit" is always, in Mom's phrasing, "dog doo."

Dad doesn't mind the language on the SS *Poseidon,* though to be fair he might be distracted by the spectacle of Pamela Sue Martin and Stella Stevens. They have been ordered by Gene Hackman to remove their dresses, for safety reasons, before climbing a Christmas tree to higher ground as the ship is consumed by biblical fire and flooding, necessitating many upshots of the two scrambling nearer to God in hot pants and underwear, respectively. The ship's lounge singer, Carol Lynley, spends the entire film in a soaked, skintight sweater, so whenever Ernest Borgnine screams "You son of a bitch!"—which he seems to do every five minutes—Dad doesn't quite appear to notice.

And neither, eventually, do I. Poised on the edge of my opulent seat, both from the excruciating tension of the film and to keep that seat from ejecting me into the black void—this place is practically a planetarium—I am desperate for Robin to survive. When the boy and a few near-naked ladies are finally spirited to daylight and into a rescue helicopter—Stella Stevens, for safety reasons, remains stripped of her dress but is still wearing six-inch silver heels, God bless her—my every nerve ending is alive with feeling. I smell of relief, urine, and secondhand Winstons. But the greatest of these is relief, a profound relief to be in the cool evening air in the Southtown shopping center parking lot and no longer upside down in the SS *Poseidon.*

This same sense of relief supervenes whenever the commercials air during NBC's annual Easter-season screening of *The Wizard of Oz,* a movie that instills no wonder in me, only terror. The music alone ignites the acids in my stomach, yet I sit in front of the Zenith with my terrified brothers and sister in a five-way game of chicken, each of us holding our hands to the flame, refusing to flinch, exhaling only when the commercials abruptly appear. They act like smelling salts or a bucket of cold water thrown over a drunk, snapping us out of one world and returning us to the real one. I am grateful for their temporary respite from tornadoes and witches and flying monkeys. "Plop, plop, fizz, fizz. Oh what a relief it is."

And then the movie is back on, and I am envious again of John, in his football pj's, too young to be terrified, or already too tough.

Even before he can walk, John is conscripted into our basement games, placed like a sack of laundry in front of our floor-hockey goal as we practice rifling tennis balls past him. By the time he can stand he is "roughing up the crease," raking his stocking feet over the basement concrete as if coarsening freshly Zambonied ice with the blades of his goalie skates. He seems to enjoy the hockey as much as we do. Only rarely do we have to duct-tape him to the uprights to keep him in goal.

Amy is largely protected from this violence. Dad dotes on his only daughter. He calls her Amelia Bedelia and often sings "Once in love with Amy, always in love with Amy…" Jim, Tom, John, and I are The Boys. "Where are The Boys?" Mom will ask, often with an air of suspicion. "Amy, have you seen The Boys?" *Like the singin' bird and the croakin' toad,* I want to tell them, echoing a song on the radio, *I've got a name. I've got a name.* The house has now divided, like Viet Nam, into Amy, with her beautiful strawberry-blond hair, and The Boys, with their basement boxing bouts and bathroom sword fights.

Dad will hear another parent say of his own five kids, "I have one redhead and four shitheads." This is exactly what he has, exactly what we are, though the math is complicated. Jim is also a redhead, so we are technically two redheads and four shitheads, though there are only five of us, because one of our redheads is also a shithead.

Amy has a doll named Baby Tender Love. This sounds like the title of a Barry White song, or the Captain's pet name for Tennille, but in fact Baby Tender Love is an object of such all-consuming affection that it is, for a time, Amy's *only* doll. My sister will not countenance any rivals. So it is that when Amy descends to the basement one Saturday morning to find us using the disembodied head of Baby Tender Love as a hockey puck—Tom has torn the hair from Baby's scalp, and left it at the side of the basement like roadkill—our sister is momentarily struck mute.

She stands frozen on the stairs, her open mouth a black rictus. And then suddenly her tonsils twitch to life and she screams. It is so shrill, so piercing, we fear it will shatter the glass in the little basement windows just beneath the beams, the way Ella Fitzgerald's voice—first live, and then recorded—shatters a wineglass in the Memorex commercials on TV. Dad despises these commercials, because they're memorable and Memorex is a rival brand of recording tape. "Is it live, or is it Memorex?" is the kind of catchphrase Scotch brand recording tape would kill for.

But despite this unwelcome reminder of Memorex, or the sight of his only daughter trembling with sorrow and rage, or the thought of The Boys in the basement still going top-shelf and five-hole with the now-bald head of Baby Tender Love, Dad remains calm. He might even have a grudging respect for The Boys. Not that he will say so. On the contrary, after a stern but rather wooden reading of the riot act to us—an unconvincing actor running his lines—he turns to Amy and says, "I can fix this."

After five minutes bent over his basement workbench, Dad emerges with Baby Tender Love's head. Her scalp has been restored, though a green glue is oozing from her hairline. And Baby Tender Love's expression, though unchanged—eyes wide, brows raised, mouth open in a pink pout—now appears to contain a hint of horror rather than wonder. So does Amy's, it must be said.

Mercifully, and at long last, I've discovered a world beyond The Boys, playmates independent of the three other shitheads, for love is in bloom at Nativity. At school, in our first-grade classroom, behind the little window in the door that Mrs. Streit has obscured with a HAVE A NICE DAY sticker—the smiley face brilliantly hiding her classroom from looky-loos like Sister Roseanne Roseannadanna—I have found a best friend. It is necessary to have a best friend, to have an answer to the questions "What's your favorite color?" and "When's your birthday?" and "Who's your best friend?" Mike McCollow and I share a love of the Vikings, can both imitate Rod Carew's batting stance, and quickly begin to speak to each other in a kind of twin language or Navajo code talk.

In years to come we'll stand with our palms church-steepled in prayer in our First Communion photo, drag his mother's couch cushions into the backyard to soften the landing when we shoot each other off a ladder as stuntmen (after seeing Burt Reynolds and Jan-Michael Vincent in *Hooper*), ride Sting-Ray knockoffs over homemade ramps, produce our own newspaper called the *Digital Times*—with a cranky advice columnist named Dear Crabby and hilarious marital notices that go "Ella Fitzgerald married Darth Vader and became Ella Vader"—and by eighth grade be sneaking off Nativity's grounds at recess to search for naked ladies on the Ohio Players album covers in the bins at Harpo's Records 'n Stuff on 98th Street. We'll con our parents into letting us see Gabe Kaplan—TV's Mr. Kotter!—do stand-up comedy at the University of Minnesota's Northrup Auditorium, as Mike's mom shakes her head at the profanity and the blue material, mostly about women having their periods, and I strike exactly the same posture I did when pretending not to hear the profanity in *The Poseidon Adventure*.

But for now we are content to make signs for Vikings games and hold them up in front of the TV as if the players can see them. If Miss Betty was able to see us through the TV on *Romper Room*, surely Fran Tarkenton can. Perhaps our signs will be captured by TV cameras and shown to the nation and spur the Vikes on to the Super Bowl at Tulane Stadium. WE'RE VIKES FANS AND HERE'S OUR PLANS. WE'RE GONNA PACK OUR JEANS FOR NEW ORLEANS. If Doris McCollow is unhappy that her son has Magic-Markered that phrase onto her bedsheets, she doesn't say anything, at least not to us.

I'm leading a kind of double life, for in addition to my best friend at Nativity I also have a best friend in South Brook. School and neighborhood are two distinct worlds, with almost no crossover. Neither knows about the other, and I feel no guilt when I go to Kevin Sundem's house in South Brook to play driveway baseball or backyard football, running there through a dozen backyards, a landscape I now know intimately, and "intimate" is the right word, given the off-white brassieres hanging on the backyard clotheslines. I blush as I run past them, smell the Tide blowing off them, and try not to think of the moms and big sisters to whom they belong, all these over-the-shoulder boulder holders, rippling in the wind.

Exploring South Brook by backyard or bicycle, I develop an expert knowledge of the neighborhood topography, whose yard I cannot enter to retrieve a ball (the Sea Hags, the two elderly ladies we seldom see) and in whose house I should decline the milk (the Sundems serve skim, and my body is accustomed to the higher-octane 2 percent). The Redmonds have central air—stepping across their threshold is like stepping into a refrigerated boxcar—and the Raichs have a basement beer-can collection. The McCarthy boys are allowed to collect pop cans, while the Rushin boys are allowed neither. Mom might not think it's hillbilly, stacking beer cans in the basement, but she wants the trash brought out of the house, not in.

There is one other way to glimpse domestic life in South Brook, one that feels even more intimate and intrusive than stealing a peep at my neighbors' brassieres. That way is to watch my envious siblings trudge off to school while I remain gloriously, blissfully sick in bed, suddenly part of—and privy to—the secret world Mom inhabits all day.

Young life holds few pleasures greater than the school sick day. The hourly ministrations of Vick's VapoRub, the back of Mom's hand on my hot forehead, the thermometer jutting from my mouth like a Chesterfield cigarette, Mom tucking and retucking the powder-blue acrylic blanket so that the satin trim is just under my chin—all of these little joys must be indulged with a grim face. "You poor thing," Mom says, feeding me a St. Joseph chewable children's aspirin as I knit my forehead and nod dolefully. With many a cough and sniffle, I finally work up the energy to ask if I might be allowed to convalesce on the couch, beneath the knitted afghan, in front of the TV and the comforting visage of Wink Martindale.

And so the day passes in a blur of Broyhill furniture, Amana appliances, and other game-show giveaways. The announcers' product plugs and prize descriptions are instantly committed to memory:

"Rice-A-Roni, the San Francisco treat!"

"From the Spiegel catalogue, Chicago, Illinois, 60609!"

Whatever illness I am suffering is replaced by a feverish craving not for the saltines and chicken noodle soup on a tray beside me but rather for all the wonderful objects on offer on *The Price Is Right*.

When Bob Barker says "Tell 'em about it, Johnny," I hang on Johnny's every inflection, delirious from fever and the gleaming Ford Mustang slowly rotating on an automotive lazy Susan.

"It's a new car! It's a 1974 Malibu eight-cylinder Chevelle sedan with molded full-foam seating, new grate-pattern grille treatment, and a wide-stance chassis with a look all its own from Chevrolet! It comes fully equipped with deluxe bumpers; outside remote-control mirrors; body side molding; door edge guards; rack-and-pinion steering; steel-belted, white-striped radial tires; Turbo-Hydramatic transmission; deluxe seat belts; and tinted glass!"

And what else do you have for us, Johnny?

"It's a trash compactor! From Whirlpool, the company that believes quality can be beautiful, comes this Trashmaster compactor that mashes a week's worth of trash into a tidy disposable bag a little larger than a grocery bag. No more kitchen clutter, Bob."

I want every one of these things, want to live in a modern California home with a Turbo-Hydramatic transmission and an absence of kitchen clutter and a canary-colored range that cleans itself like a cat. Tell us about *that*, Johnny.

"It's a range! Monarch's double-oven electric range features two stay-clean continuous-scrubbing ovens plus a lift-up cooktop, from the Monarch Range Company, Beaver Dam, Wisconsin, leaders in quality since 1896!"

The contestants from these shows are all from Southern California towns with names—West Covina, Thousand Oaks, Pomona, Fontana, Escondido, Encinitas—that sound like poetry. I am instantly envious of every child who lives in such a place and of the places they go on vacation, which sound nothing like Wisconsin Dells. Tell us about *those* places, Johnny.

"It's a trip to Hawaii! We'll fly two of you round-trip economy on American Airlines from Los Angeles to Honolulu, where you'll spend six days and seven nights at the Ala Moana Hotel at the entrance to Waikiki! You'll enjoy the Ala Moana's nine exotic restaurants and Polynesian-themed swimming pools! The Ala Moana, an American Hotel, part of a prize package worth $8,397!"

There are only three holiday destinations that these game-show contestants ever go to in 1974—Waikiki, Acapulco, and Puerto Vallarta—but all three sound like exceedingly pleasant places when Johnny says "We'll fly you and a companion *round-trip* to the exotic El Mirador hotel in the beautiful port city of...Acapulco!"

When *Love of Life* comes on channel 4 after lunch, ushering in a dispiriting block of soap operas on all three networks, I turn to channel 11 and the Minnesota sick-day standby *Mel's Matinee Movie,* hosted by Mel Jass, who introduces *Hook, Line, and Sinker,* a 1969 comedy starring Jerry Lewis as a dying man traveling the world and maxing out his credit cards.

Mel's Matinee Movie is hosted from a Twin Cities studio whose set is so dark—an ink-black void—it apparently wants to mimic the surroundings of its viewers. Most of them are shut-ins or nursing-home patients—or kids like me, curtains drawn against the workaday world, half asleep on the couch beneath an orange afghan, in a happy torpor, in the medicated bliss of a school sick day.

5.

Wish Book

The only thing better than a sick day is a snow day, which is a sick day without the sick. It begins like any other. Mom sings the *Boone and Erickson* theme song, pulling up the shades to flood the room with light. Startled awake, my heart hammers out the drum riff from "Wipeout" while my Vikings book bag hangs in rebuke from the headboard, filled as it is with half-done homework. A familiar dread sets in until I see, through the frost-fringed window, a world outside covered in snow, as thick and muffling as fiberglass insulation.

I bound downstairs to hear Charlie Boone, or possibly Roger Erickson, reading the alphabetical listing of school closings on WCCO. He is only just past Bloomington— "Brooklyn Center, Brooklyn Park, Burnsville"—and the tension as he runs through the whole alphabet is almost unbearable. By the time he is back to the *B*s again, I am reminded of a roller coaster, ratcheting up a hill. Then it crests—he gets to *B*—and I hear it: "Bloomington schools, public and parochial—*closed.*" Instantly it's Mardi Gras and V-E Day and the Lindbergh parade all in one, and the flakes falling outside look like ticker tape.

All twenty-six thousand of us schoolkids in Bloomington feel the same way. Each of us is a death-row inmate reprieved by the governor, and we'll relish every minute of this stolen Tuesday. I'll take my hockey skates in to be sharpened, the blades throwing off sparks like a welder's torch, and then carve up the Clearys' flooded backyard next door, my wrist shots made wicked by the boomerang curve of my Sher-Wood. We'll clear the ice every ten minutes by skating with a shovel in ever-tightening ovals—because my fondest desire is someday to drive a Zamboni at the North Stars games.

I take off my skates after an hour of impersonating Bobby Clarke of the Flyers and, as always, feel a foot shorter. Inside, Mom has made hot cocoa, warmed on the same stovetop burner on which I curved the Sher-Wood and boiled my hockey mouth guard, this ancient alchemy of fire and ice.

Kevin Sundem walks past outside, dressed in the kind of snowsuit that Minnesotans call a snowmobile suit. I pack a snowball, rear back with the same windup Juan Marichal has on his Topps baseball card, and peg him in the head from sixty feet away. Then I duck behind a tree that looks—like every other tree on the block—like it's been dipped in white chocolate.

We build a fort, an impregnable igloo stocked with snowballs, from which we conduct guerrilla raids on every other fort on the street, and by day's end we will rule our block like rajas.

After lunch, my backyard becomes Metropolitan Stadium

in a whiteout. Mark Redmond is playing quarterback, his Fran Tarkenton Vikings jersey stretched over his parka so that he looks—bulging in purple—like Violet Beauregarde from *Willy Wonka*. With his unmittened hand, he throws a bomb that I catch near the sideline, which is the property line between our yard and the Clearys', and I high-step into the end zone, which is bounded by the swing set and the arborvitae. And then I Nestea-plunge onto my back and lie there a moment to catch my breath before making a snow angel in celebration.

I am so cold that I pull my parka hood with the fake-fur fringe over my authentic replica Vikings helmet. Come Sunday, while watching from in front of the fireplace some football game in Miami or Los Angeles, I'll look at all those players and fans in their short sleeves and suntans and feel sorry for them.

In the house, while my wet socks are somersaulting in the dryer—the snow having penetrated the protective layer of Wonder Bread bags—I lob a ball at the mini hoop hanging from the back of the bedroom door, counting down the final seconds of a game before the buzzer beater goes in, and the ball rebounds off the door and rolls back to my feet like an obedient dog.

This miraculous ball—made of an orange wonder substance I can't identify—was conceived just a few miles from this bedroom, by a Saint Paul native named Reyn Guyer. In the auspicious year of 1969, when my father was summoned to Saint Paul by his benevolent masters at Mickey Mining, Reyn Guyer invented a retort to all the American mothers who said "Don't play ball in the house," as Carol Brady would famously do in an episode of *The Brady Bunch*. He gave the children of America non-expanding recreational foam, whose acronym—Nerf—was almost as fun as the ball itself.

Parker Brothers sold four million Nerf balls in 1970, its first year on sale. As with the BIC Cristal, the Nerf was easily and instantly weaponized. Tom likes to fart on the Nerf ball—something in its pockets of polyester resin retain the odor—and then clamp it over my face, as if chloroforming me.

Years earlier, Guyer invented Twister and pitched it to 3M, which had a games division. But, alas, the brain trust at Mickey Mining wasn't interested. After Johnny Carson played Twister with Eva Gabor on *The Tonight Show* in 1966, the "game"—a polka-dotted plastic sheet and spinner—became a necessity in basement rec rooms.

This Chicago–Twin Cities corridor in which I am living out my childhood has become fertile soil for American home life, incubator of Nerf, Trix, Twister, Cheerios, Wheaties, Schwinn, Hamburger Helper, Mary Tyler Moore, the Spiegel catalogue—Chicago, Illinois, 60609—and me. Among the greatest of these is a direct collaboration between Chicago and the Twin Cities, the love child of General Mills in Minneapolis and Ferrara Candy Company, maker of Brach's confections, in Chicago. It was at General Mills that a product developer named John Holahan, charged with repurposing the company's existing products, paired Cheerios with a Brach's marshmallow abomination called Circus Peanuts, a pairing that gave birth to Lucky Charms. Thus a banana-flavored "peanut" was cut into pink hearts, yellow moons, orange stars, and green clovers and marketed—like every other cereal, no matter its contents—as "part of a healthy breakfast."

And recently Vikings placekicker Fred Cox, known to all in Bloomington as "Freddy the Foot," did what Parker Brothers couldn't do: he invented the Nerf football. Parker Brothers had been trying to make a football the same way they make a basketball, by cutting the object from foam. But it didn't feel or fly right, so they bought Freddy's instead. Cox used injection molding to make a football that is heavier than the basketball, with a durable skin—the perfect size and weight and density for throwing and kicking in the backyard.

There is an irresistible impulse among the boys of suburban Minneapolis to kick a football as far as they possibly can. Even among the men. Mike McCollow's dad will come home from his dental practice, having stopped at the VFW hall for a brandy Manhattan en route, and drop-kick a half-frozen football between the uprights of two barren tree branches without even setting down his briefcase. Then Mike and I will resume our field-goal-kicking contest. Perhaps it's happening everywhere in America. In all these backyards that our backyard backs on to, the boys of South Brook want to put their gym shoes of varying stripe and quality through an oblong ball. Dad tells me the kids in Germany and Italy have the same compulsion to kick soccer balls, and I've been told—by older kids in the neighborhood whose knowledge is unimpeachable—that Adidas stands for All Day I Dream About Soccer.

Cox is not the only inventor who recognized this odd but undeniable desire in the youth of the Twin Cities. So did the W. H. Schaper Manufacturing Company, founded a few towns away in suburban Robbinsdale in 1949 by a mailman named William Herbert Schaper, who in his spare time invented a game called Cootie, which he sold to Dayton's department stores, which in turn sold them to a grateful public. Schaper went on to create Ants in the Pants, Don't Break the Ice, and other games that found novel use for plastics, but the greatest of these is Super Toe, which fills a need in the 1970s for a plastic placekicker figurine that kicks plastic footballs great distances through plastic uprights whenever I bash it over the head with my fist.

I can now kick footballs in my bedroom through my plastic proxy, Super Toe, or kick them in the backyard for real with the Nerf football. The Nerf football will become the bestselling football of all time and earn Fred Cox royalties for the rest of his natural existence. It has also earned him my undying admiration.

The Twin Cities in the 1970s is Florence in the High Renaissance, and I am lucky indeed to have begun life in the shadow of the Keebler elves' hollow tree and to be growing up among all these Edisons of American childhood. As I continue to shoot bedroom buzzer beaters with my Nerf basketball, the real buzzer on the dryer signals that my socks are ready and that there is still life to be squeezed from a precious snow day.

It's already midafternoon, and I'm desperate to make the most of what little daylight remains. So I pull the warm socks from the dryer, fire a hair dryer into the boots, and plunge my feet into first one and then the other. The warmth is an illicit pleasure, like wetting my pants without the shame. I pull my sled—a plastic tray in fire-engine red—to the crest of the tallest hill by Hillcrest Elementary. Standing atop that mountain of white, I imagine I'm looking down on the bobsled chute at the next Winter Olympics, in Innsbruck, Austria, in 1976.

Bombing downhill, my every nerve alive with feeling, I become certain of one thing: the thirty minutes spent getting dressed and ascending this hill is a pittance to pay for the breathtaking twenty seconds of descent.

When I finally heed Mom's call to come inside at six o'clock, it has long been pitch-dark. My cheeks, reflected in the kitchen window, have grown red, like the Christmas lights strung above the garage, and I remove my purple toque with its Vikings patch, pom-pom, and built-in ski mask to find that every hair on my head is standing on end. Mom says it's static electricity, but I know better.

Falling asleep on December nights is nearly impossible because Christmas is coming and every waking moment and many of the sleeping ones are spent in an agony of anticipation. Childhood hours are elastic, some passing in seconds, as this snow day has, while others stretch like Silly Putty, so that waiting in line with Mom at Community State Bank for five minutes is an entire geological epoch.

But time is never slower than in the days leading to December 25. Tonight, like every night since December 1, I stare at the construction-paper chain taped to the back of my bedroom door, the green and red loops representing the number of days until Christmas. Every night before bed, I tear off one more link in the chain and toss it into the oversized Schlitz-can wastebasket in the corner, as if that Schlitz can is a Shinto shrine and every loop a Japanese prayer slip.

Then I hit my knees and pray to God that Santa Claus

will bring me a Super Bowl Electric Football game and a children's typewriter and an ant farm and a woodburning kit and a Toss Across and a Score Four and a View-Master—preloaded with *The Brady Bunch* and Pan Am's 747 discs—and a Spirograph and an Etch-A-Sketch and a pair of white walkie-talkies that "enable minute-by-minute contact with your fellow spies the moment danger strikes."

All these objects of desire, and hundreds more, beckon from America's shop window, the Sears Christmas Wish Book, whose 601 pages I have committed to memory since Mom first set it out in mid-November, a full two months after it landed like an Acme anvil on our doorstep. Jim and Tom get first crack at it and have left its pages dog-eared, glass-ringed, and BIC-graffitied until at long last—after two full days and nights—I am allowed to hold its broken spine and gaze upon its booger-encrusted pages with a longing that leaves a physical ache.

My brothers have read the catalogue from back to front, as if it were in Hebrew, for the last third of the Wish Book is devoted exclusively to toys and games and electronics. Outside of Santa's Workshop, these two hundred pages are the greatest concentration of toys ever assembled in one place, at one time, in human history.

Many of these toys appeared in the very first Sears Christmas Wish Book in 1933, including the battery-operated cars, the Mickey Mouse watches, and the Lionel electric trains. It was just called the "Sears catalogue" then—our family still just calls it the "Sears catalogue"—but enough salivating customers called it the "Book of Wishes" or the "Christmas Wish Book" that Sears officially changed its name in 1968, by which time it had grown to more than six hundred pages, of which more than two hundred were devoted to toys of every description.

The Wish Book is yet another wondrous product of the Minnesota–Chicago axis. It is the brainchild of Richard W. Sears, who started a business selling watches and jewelry in North Redwood, Minnesota, in 1886, opened the R. W. Sears Watch Company in Minneapolis, and a year later moved his business to Chicago, where he hired a watch repairman named Alvah Roebuck, who became his partner in Sears, Roebuck and Company. Their watch catalogue expanded over time into the omnibus behemoth that I am reading now, on my stomach, head cradled in my palms, in the primary-colored glow of the Christmas tree bulbs.

Unlike Jim and Tom, I read the catalogue front to back, for the Wish Book's wonders are scarcely confined to the toys I'm saving for last. The first two-thirds of the catalogue are full of insights into the world of adulthood, the secret lives of my parents, with its fondue sets and fake-fur bed-spreads and—on a heavily thumbed page sixty-six—a variety of "nylon tricot sleepthings for sheer beauty." These are pastel nighties with plunging necklines worn by models and advertised in strange proximity to an arresting array of "Fun Bags"—which turn out, alas, to be organizers for children's bedrooms and playrooms.

But still. My gaze falls on an in-car coffeemaker that would allow Dad to brew a pot of Hills Bros. on the drive to Mickey Mining, then hold the scalding Styrofoam cup in his crotch between sips. "Just hang this in your car window," the caption reads, next to a photograph of a man giddily driving to work with a coffeepot hanging in—and blotting out—his shotgun window.

Or maybe Dad would like the cocktail ice bucket shaped like a diver's helmet. Or the "Mediterranean-Style Smoker," a solid elmwood stand twenty-five inches tall that supports a green glass ashtray, so no houseguest ever has to bend to ash his or her cigarette. On the page dedicated to the kind of colognes Dad marinates in every morning, I circle in blue BIC the three brands I recognize. They are, in reverse order of expense, English Leather, Brut, and Old Spice. Every Christmas, The Boys get Dad a bottle of Old Spice. For his birthday, we spring for a can of tennis balls. Opening either one even today releases a pleasing smell I have come to associate with my father.

If Mom and Dad give us a "family gift" this year, the "Portable Color TV with Remote Control" is an impossible dream. There is no way we are getting this fifteen-inch TV in a walnut-grain plastic cabinet with a two-button remote like the *Star Trek* phaser. "You can control on/off, volume, and channel selection from any spot in the room," the catalogue claims, offering no indication at all how this miracle was engineered, except in the two-word semi-explanation at the end: "from Japan." Dad's frequent trips to Japan, where Mickey Mining is in mortal combat with Sony and TDK, color his view of all Japanese electronics, and I silently resign myself to manually turning the channels for the rest of the decade.

I turn the page and my eyes fall on the twin polestars of Dad's professional existence: an "Automated Replica of the Pan Am 747 Giant Superjet" replete with "little stewardesses that move up and down the aisle" and a variety of "Portable Eight-Track Tape Players (Cartridges Not Included)." *Don't you worry about the cartridges,* I think. Dad will jump on that 747 and sell you all the blank eight-track cartridges you will ever need for your Portable Eight-Track Tape Player, which fits in a car's glove box, dashboard ashtray, or under the seat. "Only space-age integrated circuits make it possible to pack such quality of musical performance into such a surprisingly small unit," according to the catalogue, and all I can think in reply is *What a time we are living in, with our space-age this, our superjet that, our in-car everything.*

As much as the toys, I am falling in love with the language of the Sears catalogue, with its Perma-Prest, double-knit, flare-leg slacks; its safety-stitched, rib-knit sweaters of high-ridge twill; its shirts of Textralized Ban-Lon. These are clothes that Dad literally wouldn't be caught dead in. He would rise from his casket and speed-bag the funeral director who put him in one of the terry-cloth kimonos or U-neck belted sweater vests on offer here.

There are moms and dads and brothers and sisters all voluntarily wearing matching pajamas. Who are these people, done up like quintuplets in "Warm Nightwear for the Entire Family"? They all look giddy, Dad with a shellacked helmet of hair and a mustache like Mark Spitz's, Mom and the kids smiling into the middle distance, every one of them with one hand tucked up to the knuckles in the front pocket of a robe. (The other hand always holds a mug of steaming coffee or cocoa.) I try and fail to imagine Dad, Mom, Jim, Tom, John, Amy, and me in matching anything. Mom would never put us in "look-alike nightwear done in a crisp red, white, and blue-gray geometric print," would she? Something tells me it might be hillbilly.

It is not true that all happy families are alike. The happy families in the Sears catalogue wear matching kimonos and smile at each other while playing board games like Aggravation and Sorry! in which opponents can send each other back to Start, an act of passive-aggression that always ends, in our house, with the victim flipping the board in the air and sending the game pieces scattering through the kitchen and under the fridge. "Poor sport!" the self-righteous winner will always declare, or "Sore loser!"

But even before I make it to the board games, I pause in the middle of the Sears catalogue, where a separate toy index is printed on onionskin paper. This is an alphabetical index of my dreams, an inventory of everything in the basements of everyone I know, and an epic poem as well, which I recite in my head like an incantation:

Accordions, Activity Books, Airplanes, Airports, Animals, Appliances, Archery Sets, Art Supplies, Autographs, Automobiles, Balloons, Balls, Banks, Barbell Sets, Barbie Dolls, Baseball Equipment, Basketball Equipment, Batons, Batteries, Beanbags, Bicycles, Biology Kits, Blackboards, Blocks, Boats, Books, Bowling Equipment, Boxing Equipment, Bricks, Building Toys, Bumper Riders, Candy Novelties, Cash Registers, Chemistry Sets, Clocks, Coin Collectors' Supplies, Confectionaries, Costumes, Cranes, Crib Toys, Dishes, Dishwashers, Doctor/Nurse Kits, Doll Carriages, Doll Clothing, Doll Furniture, Dollhouses, Dolls and Accessories, Drums, Electronic Toys, Engines, Erector Sets, Farm Toys, Figure Sets, Fire Engines, Floats, Food Mixes,

Foods (Play), Football Equipment, Football Posters, Frisbees, Furniture (Children's), Games, Gardens, Geology Kits, G.I. Joe Sets, Go-Cart Racers, Grampa and Gramma Dolls, Guitars, Gum, Handicrafts, Helicopters, Helmets, Hobbyhorses, Hobby Supplies, Hockey Equipment, Hot Wheels, Housekeeping Toys, Ice Skates, Intercoms, Jack-in-the-Boxes, Jukeboxes, Jumping Equipment, Kiddie Cars, Kitchen Toys, Knitting and Weaving Sets, Lego Sets, Logs, Luggage, Magic Sets, Magnetic Boards, Marbles, Matchbox Cars, Mechanical Toys, Microscopes, Mobiles, Molding Sets, Motorcycles, Movie Films, Musical Instruments, Musical Toys, Organs, Ouija Boards, Paint Sets, Parking Garages, Peanuts Articles, Phonograph Records, Phonographs and Accessories, Pianos, Pinball Machines, Playground Equipment, Playhouses, Play Tables, Pool Tables, Posters, Pottery Workshop, Preschool Books, Preschool Toys, Projectors and Supplies, Pull Toys, Punching Bags, Puppets, Puzzles, Radios, Radio Stations, Raggedy Ann and Andy Articles, Refrigerators, Riding Toys, Road Races, Robots, Rockets, Rock Hunting Sets, Rocking Toys, Roller Skates, Romper Room Toys, Scene Sets, Science Kits, Screen Printing Sets, See 'n' Say Toys, Service Stations, Sesame Street Toys, Sewing Machines, Sewing Supplies, Shooflies, Show 'n' Tell Toys, Sinks, Sizzlers, Skis and Accessories, Sleds, Spirograph Sets, Stamp Collectors' Supplies, Stilts, Stockings (Christmas), Stoves, Stuffed Toys, Talking Toys, Tape Measures, Tape Players and Supplies, Tape Recorders, Tea Sets, Teddy Bears, Telephones, Telescopes, Tents, Theaters,

Tinkertoys, Toboggans, Tools, Tops, Toy Chests, Tractors, Tractors (Riding), Trains and Accessories, Tri-
cycles, Trucks, Trucks (Riding), Tunnels, Typewriters,
Umbrellas, Unicycles, Vanity Sets, View-Masters and
Supplies, Wagons, Watches, Weather Forecasting Toys,
Wigs, Winnie-the-Pooh Toys, Woodburning Kits, Xylo-
phones, and Zithers.

Our other sacred holiday text is The Schedule, whose official
name is "TV Week," the programming guide tucked into every Sunday's *Minneapolis Tribune*. It tells us what will be on
channels 2, 4, 5, 9, and 11 for the next seven days, and it
always should be returned to the table next to Dad's Archie
Bunker chair so that he doesn't have to ask "Has anyone seen
The Schedule?" The Schedule is the only thing that can pull
any of us away from The Catalogue. As Christmas crawls
nearer, we organize our lives around it, for The Schedule reveals the airtimes of the Christmas specials that won't be on
for another year should we somehow miss them. And the only
thing worse than missing them is actually seeing them, for every one of them, almost without exception, is terrifying.

They are part of my growing catalogue of childhood
terrors—an anti–wish book that includes *The Poseidon Adventure, The Wizard of Oz,* and half the songs on the radio,
especially if Jim is playing them in the basement when the
only light is the green glow of the graphic equalizers. Among
the scariest of these songs are the spoken-word passage in
"Nights in White Satin" by the Moody Blues ("Cold-hearted
orb that rules the night…"), the whispered interlude in 10cc's

"I'm Not in Love" ("Be quiet, big boys don't cry, big boys don't cry, big boys don't cry…"), and the chilling climax to "The Wreck of the Edmund Fitzgerald" ("Fellas, it's been good to know ya…"). Worst of all are the entire lyrics to "The Night Chicago Died" by the English group Paper Lace, about a boy waiting for his daddy to come home from work. Absent daddies may be a recurring theme on the radio, but "The Night Chicago Died" is particularly harrowing.

The boy's daddy is a cop fighting Al Capone's gang on "the East Side of Chicago," which would place him (unbeknownst to me or the Nottingham-based members of Paper Lace) in the middle of Lake Michigan. There is news of a massacre. About a hundred cops are dead. His momma cries. He hears her pray the night Chicago dies. No matter how many times I hear the song I can scarcely endure the tension of that mother's prayers and tears and that clock ticking on the wall. By the time the door bursts open wide and his daddy steps inside, I'm feeling the same sense of joy and relief as when my own daddy walks in the door after two weeks in Tokyo.

So I'm afraid of the stereo in the basement and of the basement itself, and whenever I have to go down there by myself, I frantically grope for the pull chain that will bathe it in light, fearing all over again what I might see there: a snake, maybe, or the bogeyman or the books on the basement shelf, including *The Rise and Fall of the Third Reich,* with its swastika on the spine, and *Helter Skelter,* with its photographs of Charles Manson, and *Alive,* about a Uruguayan rugby team whose members survive a plane crash in the Andes and resort to cannibalism to survive.

Still, none of these things is quite as terrifying as the TV

Christmas specials that air every other night in mid-December.

They are full of malevolent grown-ups and whatever the Grinch is. The kids too are almost unfailingly mean. Charlie Brown's so-called friends call him a blockhead and a loser. No one will play with Rudolph because he has a red nose. Frosty the Snowman is locked in a greenhouse and left to die. Burgermeister Meisterburger sends the baby Claus to the "Orphanage Asylum." These Christmas worlds are populated by Winter Warlocks and Abominable Snow Monsters and apocalyptic Heat Misers and desolate islands to which misfits are banished.

In that regard, it is not terribly different from school. To judge by the ambient temperature in our classrooms, Nativity has its own Heat Miser in the form of The Sniper. He has buffed the tiles to a high sheen. The caged lights wink overhead. On his mute rounds of these burnished brick halls, The Sniper hears Christmas carols coming from every classroom.

Our last official act at school before Christmas vacation is the annual nativity pageant in the gym. An eighth-grade boy is chosen to be Joseph; an eighth-grade girl is selected to be Mary. These are the de facto homecoming king and queen of Catholic grade school. There are other roles—the rubber-doll baby Jesus, swaddled in dish towels; the magi in their Burger King crowns, bearing gifts of Kleenex boxes covered in Reynolds Wrap; shower-sandaled shepherds in belted bathrobes; the choir of angels, beneath coat-hanger haloes, which includes me.

I look out at all the parents, in their Orlon jackets with double-knit stitching, their neckties like paisley-printed paper kites. Dad is soberly resplendent in a blue suit and white shirt and a burgundy necktie of modest girth.

Some of us are just mouthing the words. A few kids at the back are quietly singing, "We three kings of Orient are, puffing on a rubber cigar. It was loaded, we explo-oh-ded..."

We sing "Hark the Herald Angels Sing" as our showstopper. In the strobing pop of the Instamatic flashbulbs, I fear I'll have a grand mal seizure and swallow my tongue. But I finish the song, and we all float back to our seats on a sea of applause, returned to our families, to the cold metal folding chairs familiar from a hundred school assemblies.

In a minute we shall be furloughed for the holidays. But first The Sniper ascends to the stage to adjust the microphone so that Sister Roseanne Roseannadanna can dismiss us. He grips the mic stand, twists its neck like he's killing a chicken, then raises it to his great height. It is only now that I notice he is in a suit, his key ring conspicuously missing, like the leg of an amputee. The Sniper clears his throat—he is a silent assassin; none of us has ever heard him speak—and a sudden dread rises up in my chest. He has located the source of that foul odor in Nativity's halls—the green sandwiches moldering in the pencil box in my desk—and is about to announce his discovery to the assembled students, parents, and faculty. I am a misfit toy, a red-nosed reindeer, the baby Jesus turned away at the inn. I shall be exiled to a land beyond the parking lot's snow hills, driven there in the bed of an orange El Camino in a Christmas narrative that is at once ancient and brand-new.

But no. As Mrs. Malone, the music teacher, sits at the piano with her hands folded in her lap, The Sniper opens his mouth and—voice quavering with sentiment—sings, "Si-i-lent night, ho-o-ly night. Alll is calllm, all is bright..."

The audience is rapt. There is not a note of accompaniment from Mrs. Malone. The gym is silent as a tomb, save for the low thrum of the forced-air heat beneath The Sniper's angelic baritone: "Round yon virgin mother and child..."

My teachers are in tears. "Holy infant so tender and mild..." Mom digs into her purse like a contestant on *Let's Make a Deal* until she finds a Kleenex she can quietly honk into. Sister Roseanne Roseannadanna is glassy-eyed behind bottle-bottom spectacles. "Sleep in heavenly pea-eace..." Dad removes his glasses to finger a piece of dust from either eye. "Slee-eep in heaven-ly peeeace."

Maybe it's the cold metal chair or the chill from the double doors opening onto the parking lot as we all file out, winter vacation unfurled before us like a red carpet, but my skin is suddenly goose-bumped and my neck hair is standing on end. Applause is still ringing in our ears. The Sniper has brought down the house.

The afternoon of Christmas Eve is spent beneath the tree, shaking the presents from Mom and Dad like maracas. Mom is in the kitchen, baking (more cookies, powdered doughballs concealing Hershey's Kisses, pretzels covered in white chocolate like birch bark) and cooking (cocktail wieners, rye rounds, mini meatballs). The smell turns the corner like a cartoon vapor and ascends up my nostrils, the way the fumes of a cooling blueberry pie find Tom's nose on *Tom and Jerry*.

The tree doesn't smell like anything. It was assembled weeks ago, a Canadian Pine from the Sears catalogue, whose line of fake trees, of faux firs, includes Blue Spruce and Mountain Fir. Each branch is color coded. Jim, Tom, and I are assigned a color—red, yellow, or blue—and slot our branches into their corresponding holes on the green pole of the "trunk."

Bathed in the blinking bulbs of the Canadian Pine, I fly baby Jesus out of his nativity manger, soaring him like Superman over the living room. Tom picks up a shepherd with his curved staff and flies him in hot pursuit. The shepherd's crook hooks Jesus and pulls him back to earth, a few inches short of heaven.

Heaven is up there somewhere. I don't know anyone who has ever died, anyone whose parents have ever died, anyone whose dog or grandma has died. My Grandpa Boyle died, but I never knew him. That was before I was born. Sometimes I think of what it must be like to be dead, to live in the clouds in a white gown, play the harp, spy on friends and family, and wear a halo that isn't made from a coat hanger. It would be cool. It would be terrifying.

At 6:30 we put on our best clothes and drive to Christmas Eve Mass at Nativity of Mary Church, next to school. The Mass takes ages. Father Gilbert tells us to get some sleep tonight. His name is pronounced "Gill-burt," but Mike McCollow and I call him Father "Zheel-bair" after the Boston Bruins goalie Gilles Gilbert, whose name is always pronounced on hockey broadcasts as "Zheel Zheel-bair."

We love these French-Canadian hockey names. The Montreal Canadiens alone have Yvan Cournoyer ("Ee-von Cornwhy-ay"), Henri Richard ("On-ree Ree-shard"), and a roster full of guys named Jacques ("Zhock"), Serge ("Serzh"), Réjean ("Ray-zhon"), and Guy (rhymes with "flea"). Jim has gone to a North Stars game with Dad. It is a portal into adulthood, with beer drinking, smoking, swearing, and lots of fistfights. And those are just the players. The adults in the seats at Met Center, like the kids on the playground at Nativity, press their noses to the Plexiglas and chant, "Fight! Fight! Fight!" Or so Jim reported while dumping his dog-eared game program on the bed for Tom and me, who are desperate to go.

"Someday," Dad promises. "Someday."

We scissor out the faces of our favorite players from *Goal* magazine and tape them to the wall in the basement, next to the reeking bags of hockey equipment. Bobby Clarke of the Flyers has a smile that looks like a crossword puzzle. Dave "The Hammer" Schultz has a mustache like the handlebars on a Sting-Ray. Jude Drouin's sideburns are two shag-carpet samples that ripple in the breeze as he skates circles in his glorious green North Stars sweater.

Father Zheel-bair shakes me out of this reverie when he says, "Mass has ended. Let us go in peace to love and serve the Lord."

I have never felt freer or more cleansed—I have never felt happier to be alive—than leaving Christmas Eve Mass, "Joy to the World" still buzzing in my ears, the seven of us piling into the clown car of the station wagon.

"I think I see Rudolph!" Mom says, pointing to a red light flashing in the sky.

"That's just..." Jim says, but Mom talks over him.

"*That's just* wonderful," she says as Jim, a mile away in the bench seat behind her, whispers to Tom and me, "That's just the red light on the tower at WDGY, so planes don't crash into it."

As New Year's Eve is to Dick Clark, so Christmas Eve is to Mom. It is the fullest expression of her mom-ness. There are presents wrapped impeccably—paper secured with Scotch tape from the Mickey Mining company store—beneath the tree. That tree is perfection itself: man, subcontracted by Sears, Roebuck, improving on God's own creation.

The rules do not apply on Christmas Eve. We snack after dinner. We eat from TV trays in the family room. Mom drinks a cocktail Dad has mixed for her. Yes, she puts an apron over her church clothes to serve us—we are not hillbillies, after all—but otherwise she is letting her hair down, at least insofar as the hair spray will let her. Spills are left for later, glasses are wantonly set on tables bereft of coasters, Triscuit crumbs disappear into the shag carpet, to be vacuumed at a later date.

But I know a secret. At the Penn Lake Library, shelves looming over me on either side like canyon walls, I eased *The Baseball Encyclopedia* from its dusty perch with two hands. It must've weighed ten pounds, and in its thousand-plus pages is listed every man who ever played major-league baseball. Opening it, I literally blew dust from its pages. On one of them I found Mom's dad—my Grandpa Boyle—who played catcher for the New York Giants in a single game at the Polo Grounds in New York, on a Sunday afternoon in June of 1926. But I learned something else from his modest entry: James John Boyle, the book said, was born on January 14, 1904, and died on December 24, 1958.

Mom's dad died on Christmas Eve, when Mom was twenty-four years old, and now—as she sits by the tree, eating Jimmy Dean sausage on a rye cracker, the Carpenters and John Denver and Anne Murray singing all her holiday favorites—I look for some sign on her face, some poker tell betraying her sadness.

But there is nothing save her lipsticked smile and wave after wave of hors d'oeuvres washing up on my TV tray. And at least, I reason, she had a father. Dad didn't have a dad of his own. Like the baby Jesus, he was the product of an immaculate conception, not in Bethlehem but in Fort Wayne, Indiana.

In bed, stuffed to the gills with Mom's cookies and appetizers, I worry that Santa's sleigh will get snagged on the Zenith's rooftop aerial. I idly wonder if he wouldn't mind, while he's up there, retrieving the tennis balls from the gutter or the Frisbee from above the garage, on our rooftop of misfit toys.

But the only stirring I hear isn't on the roof; it comes from the next room: my brothers are up. We all pop our heads into the hallway at the same time, like a collection of cuckoo clocks all going off at once. It's dark as midnight outside, but Jim says it's already 5:27 a.m., so we all tiptoe to the top of the stairs and stand there as if poised at the top of a bobsled chute on *Wide World of Sports*. The Christ above the credenza has two fingers raised on His wounded right hand, as if to shush us on His birthday.

Noisily quiet, conspicuously inconspicuous, whispering at the top of our lungs—this is how we manage to accidentally wake our parents on purpose. Mom and Dad emerge from their bedroom, blinking against the hallway light, and stagger down the stairs ahead of us. It is only when they give us the go-ahead that we tear down the stairs, past the framed portraits of our younger selves, to see the Sears catalogue sprung to life.

There are a pair of red-white-and-blue Rossignol skis leaning against the fireplace, a 110-pound barbell-and-dumbbell set sinking into the shag, an air hockey table, a tabletop slot hockey game pitting the Bruins against the Blackhawks— Zheel Zheel-bair and Tony Esposito minding the nets—and in my corner of the room, wrapped presents whose paper I tear open to reveal Vikings pajamas and a Kenner SSP Racer with "the howl of power from sonic sound." In the stocking Mom made when I was a baby—"Stevie" spelled out in green sequins—are gift certificates for McDonald's and a Book of Life Savers.

The Book of Life Savers has ten rolls of candy inside, each one as hefty and satisfying in my fist as a roll of quarters. As I pop the first prebreakfast Life Saver into my mouth—a Pep-O-Mint or a Wint-O-Green or perhaps a Butter Rum, but definitely not a Tropical Fruit—I cannot imagine wanting or needing another thing, material or spiritual, for as long as I live.

It's not yet six o'clock in the morning. Mom, in her nightgown, keeps her right hand in a permanent salute, shielding her eyes from the klieg light of Dad's Super 8 camera. With her left hand, she pats her hair into shape before dismissing Dad, filming it all in his bathrobe of sober design, a rebuke to every catalogue model in a terry-cloth kimono.

The sun coming through the living room curtains reveals a landscape reduced to a rubble of wrapping paper and ribbon. For the next hour Dad pores over assembly instructions like Rommel over a map of North Africa. It's only when a hundred batteries have been inserted into as many toy orifices and boxes have been discarded and clothes have been tried on (and modeled, at Mom's insistence) and grandmas have been hastily thanked over costly long-distance calls—the phone and its fifty feet of coiled cord passed around the living room—and Mom and Dad have made a pot of coffee and put on WCCO radio and sat down, depleted, that the children finally present them with *their* gifts.

The look on Dad's face—of cartoon surprise and delight—confirms that he never expected to receive anything. Rubbing his palms together in anticipation, wondering out loud what this wrapped cylinder could possibly be, he says what he always does when his can of Penn tennis balls is revealed: "Pretty fancy!" He makes a big display of showing it to Mom, then protests when we try to ply him with a *second* gift: "What? But you already gave me..." And then the whole rigmarole repeats itself when he unwraps his bottle of Old Spice.

Mom is last. Tom and I pooled our allowance money and bought Mom, from the Ben Franklin five-and-dime, a ceramic gnome pushing a wheelbarrow. She unwraps it carefully, like an archaeologist excavating an Etruscan vase, and turns it around in her hands. I see we've forgotten to remove its $3.99 price tag and worry that Mom will think we've spent too much. But she is moved to near speechlessness and places the gnome among her Lladró figurines from Spain, her Waterford crystal from Ireland, the lacquered geishas from Japan, and all the other treasures in the living room curio cabinet, where it shall remain for the next two decades, spotlit behind glass.

The house is filled with the plunder of Dad's trips abroad, including an enormous oil painting of a man and his donkey, which Dad bought in the Philippines for five bucks—frame included—and immediately hung above the fireplace in the family room. If a Manila mule isn't Mom's first choice as the centerpiece of her family room, she doesn't say so, even if it dwarfs the hand-carved statue of Christ the Redeemer below it on the mantelpiece, hand-carried home from Rio.

After Mom unwraps the ceramic gnome, I give her the clay ashtray, spray-painted gold, that I made in art class. "For when company comes over," I say as she removes its wrapping of tissue paper.

Mom holds it high for all to see and says, "Just what I didn't want!"

But I can see from her smile, and her eyes, that she means the opposite. When she kisses me on the cheek, she whispers in my ear, "It's perfect." And on Christmas morning she could be talking about everything.

6

As We Fell into the Sun

Dad turns forty the first week of June in 1974 and celebrates with a backyard barbecue. He shouts for me to lug the bag of Kingsford charcoal briquettes from the garage to the patio, where I find him next to his beloved twenty-two-inch Weber One-Touch Kettle grill, as black and shiny as a Cadillac hood.

In its porcelain-enameled sheen I see the fish-eye reflection of our backyard: the clothesline that opens like an umbrella from the concrete patio, the aluminum swing set beyond the sandbox, and Dad in the foreground, looking like I've never seen him. He has his burger flipper in one hand, a lowball glass in the other, a portrait of suburban *American Gothic* that he always is on the weekends. But he also wears a pair of inverted tighty-whities on his head like a chef's hat. Emblazoned on the Y-front of those cotton underpants—a birthday gift he has evidently just opened—is the phrase HOME OF THE WHOPPER.

The lowball glass is filled with scotch. Dad drank gin in the '60s, switched to scotch for the '70s, and has vowed he will try vodka for the entirety of the 1980s. It's not the only way in which his drinking is rigidly organized. At home, Dad never drinks during the week but enjoys his "libations" on Friday and Saturday evenings, usually while he's grilling: family steak, pork chops, handcrafted hamburgers the size of his considerable fists. Standing beside his Weber, Dad is a successful Midwestern salesman enjoying the fruits of another successful Midwestern salesman.

The Weber One-Touch Kettle was invented by a salesman at the Weber Brothers Metal Works in Chicago, that cradle of 1970s civilization and incubator of immortal salespeople. The company made marine buoys, but George Stephen—a father of twelve and a man who went through family steak faster than we did—saw in those buoys a better grill. He sawed one in half, topped it with a domed lid, and added vents and legs, legs that practically galloped around the world. George Stephen had invented the Weber grill. This same object of perfection is now being poked and pronged by my father, who prides himself on lighting any grill or fireplace with a single struck match, earning the self-bestowed nickname "One-Match Rushin."

He has a similar skill with constipated bottles of Heinz ketchup, striking one violent blow with the meat of his palm to the bottom of the bottle. The ketchup flows instantly.

"Like Fonzie with the jukebox," I say, but he doesn't know Fonzie. He doesn't even watch Archie Bunker from his Archie Bunker chair. He watches four things: news, sports, Johnny Carson, and the world's most boring show, *Wall Street*

Week on PBS, hosted by a man in what looks like a George Washington wig.

I drag the bag of Kingsford to Dad. It's all deadweight. He strikes a match and the Weber goes up like the *Hindenburg.*

"I think I'll have a libation," Dad says whenever he grills, in case Mom wants to join him. She almost never does.

The liquor cabinet in the kitchen is filled with sapphire-blue and emerald-green spirits that are intoxicating even from a distance. The beefeater on the Beefeater bottle, the clipper ship on the Cutty Sark, the Dewar's bagpiper, the crown on the bottle of Crown Royal—these are adult analogs of the icons on my cereal boxes: King Vitamin, Cap'n Crunch, the Lucky Charms leprechaun, the Trix rabbit.

Unlike the cereal, the booze has a whole kitchen drawer devoted to its accessories. The corkscrews, stoppers, shakers, strainers, jiggers, muddlers, zesters, and reamers are of mysterious utility yet vital to Dad's weekend rituals. In that same way, they remind me of the censers, snuffers, cruets, chalices, and ciboriums that Father Zheel-bair avails himself of when I'm serving Mass at Nativity.

The full alcoholic arsenal is on display tonight during Dad's fortieth—the olives, the maraschino cherries, the little bottle of lime juice, the Schweppes tonic water, the bitters, the tiny plastic swords, the miniature umbrellas, the faux-leather ice bucket and stainless-steel tongs—all these trappings of religious sacrament.

We retreat to the basement during my parents' parties and can do whatever we please down there without fear—or hope—of intervention. We can pee in the drain in the floor on the unfinished side of the basement rather than go all the way upstairs to the bathroom, which has been stage-dressed with a burning candle, milled hand soaps, and towels I've never seen before. The buzz from overhead—and the hard-soled shoes clomping across the kitchen linoleum—ensure no adults will hear our screams when Jim administers a 99 Bump or a Knuckle Floater. No referee will descend the stairs to stop our boxing matches. We can whip each other with an orange length of Hot Wheels track until one of us cries "Uncle" or "Mercy" or "I give." The safe word is constantly changing and is often known only to Jim.

Long after our regular bedtimes, we're summoned upstairs as an afterthought. Before we're exiled to our bedrooms, however, we're paraded in our pajamas in front of company, like the Von Trapp kids but without the voices. The formal living room, with its curio cabinet, crushed-velvet couch, and carpeting as soft and white and muting as fresh snow, is ordinarily off-limits to us. It's reserved "for company," as Mom often reminds us whenever she catches Tom or me spinning endless circuits in the upholstered swivel chair or finds our footprints after the fact in the fresh Hoover tracks on the carpet.

Seeing the living room lit up like this, filled with men and women drinking and smoking, cocktail wieners impaled on toothpicks, ashtrays scattered everywhere, matchbooks bearing the logos of the kind of restaurants Mom and Dad don't take us to—Camelot, Lord Fletcher's, Rudolph's—is to see a stage set come to life on opening night.

In the morning, I'll rifle the cushions for the change that fell from all the Farah slacks the night before. The ashtrays will still be full of crushed-out cigarettes with lipsticked filters. On every end table, empty beer cans will hold down cork coasters. I'll pick up a can of Hamm's Preferred Stock, smell the rim, shake it. A pull tab will rattle at the bottom like a nickel in a tin cup. I'll swig the dregs. They'll taste warm and gritty, with a texture like pulped orange juice. Someone will have ashed her cigarette in my beer.

But that's in the morning. Tonight, I lie awake and listen to the chatter, the too-loud laughter coming up the stairs and under the door like a vapor. I hear it through the floor, muffled, a hum, a buzz, a rumble, frequently pierced by a howl of laughter. I walk to the top of the stairs and lie down on the carpet. Christ above the credenza looks down in rebuke. Downstairs, Dad is telling a story.

"I became an area manager in 1965," he says. "We were living in Chicago, but part of my sales territory was Detroit. I met a couple of my Mickey Mining friends there one night for dinner, after a long day of sales calls."

In the glass fronts of our framed photographs on the staircase, I can see Dad reflected back, talking to Mr. Cannady.

"At dinner, we had a few drinks," Dad says. "We had a *zillion* drinks. And a colleague who lived in Detroit suggested we go to this little ski hill that he knew. It was just like Hyland Hills." Hyland Hills is Bloomington's own little alpine resort: half a dozen slopes, a chairlift, and a warm chalet with hot cocoa and Hostess apple pies.

"We decided we would share one lift ticket to save money," Dad goes on. "We hadn't thought this through thoroughly, but we had some kind of competition in mind. There may have been a bet involved. I may have challenged the other two guys to a downhill ski race at dinner. Anyway, I decided that I would be the first to ski."

"Are you a good skier?" Mr. Cannady asks.

"I have never skied in my life," Dad replies. "In 1965, I had never even seen a ski hill in person."

"And yet you challenged these men to a race?"

"Exactly."

"Go *on*," says Mr. Cannady.

"So I went to this little shack where they sold lift tickets and rented skis," Dad says. "And the guy behind the little counter there said to me, 'Do you always dress like that to go skiing?'"

"Always dress like what?" says Mrs. Deasey. A few more grown-ups have gathered around Dad.

"This was at the end of a day of sales calls," Dad says. "I was in a blue suit, black polished wingtips, a white shirt, a tie, a wool topcoat, a snap-brim hat, and kid gloves."

The guests are laughing in anticipation. Everyone's listening to Dad's story. I imagine him on *The Tonight Show,* sitting on the couch, telling the story to Johnny.

"Anyway," he says, "the guy gave me the skis and boots, the poles, and *stapled* a lift ticket to the front of my topcoat, and I skied over to the three hills.

"The first was a bunny hill," Dad says. "The second hill was intermediate. The third hill was clearly for advanced skiers. And I decided—though I'd never worn skis or even seen a ski slope—that I had to be better than that bunny hill. I went to the intermediate one."

Downstairs, the party has gone quiet, everyone hanging on Dad's story. The raised right hand of Christ above the credenza seems to be telling me, "Keep it down. I want to hear this."

"I had no idea there would be a rope tow, or any idea how to use it," Dad says. "It never crossed my gin-soaked mind to line my skis up parallel. I just walked up and grabbed on as tightly as I could. And the rope threw me over"—he demonstrates with a violent jerk—"headfirst into a snowbank."

The other twenty people in the room are laughing, but Dad is serious as can be. He hates exaggeration and doesn't abide self-aggrandizement. This is what he prefers—objective self-ridicule. "It knocked the skis and boots off me, broke my glasses, and bent one of the rented ski poles in half."

"What did you do?" someone asks.

"I picked up all this stuff, walked back to the little rental shack, and—not five minutes after renting everything—said to the guy there, 'Hey, I just had a little accident.' The guy looked at me like 'What the *hell?*'"

My parents' friends are howling. There's no music playing, only the music of Dad's story, but it feels as if a beat and a rhythm are coming up the stairs.

"He gave me a new pole," Dad says. "Someone showed me how to grab the rope tow the right way. The palms were ripped out of my kid gloves, but I made it to the top of the bunny hill and even managed to get down. But at the bottom of the hill, there was a little warning bump. It warned you that the next bump was the parking lot. And it was then that I realized I hadn't the vaguest idea how to stop these damn things. I was later told you point 'em together like a V, but I hadn't heard that before, so I thought I'd just ski into the parking lot and run into a car. And that's exactly what I did."

I don't see Mom's face reflected in the Sears portrait-studio pictures on the stairs. Perhaps she's busy in the kitchen, rinsing glasses and crumbing trays. If she's listening to Dad, I can't pick out her laugh in the crowd. But more often on nights like these, during a party such as this, she'll leave the cleanup until the next morning and allow herself to be swept away on the tide of conversation and laughter.

Suddenly, from the kitchen, Mom says, "He brought me a present. Did he tell you? From that trip to Detroit."

Dad sighs, as if half hoping she'd forgotten. "There was a gift shop in the restaurant where we came up with the skiing idea," Dad says. "After dinner, and way too much to drink, I bought a goofy little long-stemmed thing that held water. It was like a pitcher for watering flowers that were hard to reach—or something. I really wasn't sure what it was. It looked like something I'd swiped off another table, to be honest. But when I had this sales territory in Detroit, I would drive there from Chicago and didn't have to worry about stowing things on an airplane. So I bought this useless pitcher thing that I thought she'd like, and when she saw it she said, 'How much did you have to drink before you bought this thing?' And the answer is a *lot*."

The laughter that follows sounds like applause. The way Dad tells a story, how he holds for a punch line, the details he parcels out—the kid gloves, the stapled lift ticket, the image of him spread-eagled on the hood of a Buick like a highway deer—I admire all these things from the top of the stairs.

It's another peek behind the curtain of the grown-up world. This is what happens when Dad is on a business trip. This is what a grown-up party looks like. Adulthood is what happens after bedtime.

*   *   *

Mom and Dad argue too. "They're fighting," Jim or Tom might say in a whisper. From behind the closed kitchen door, while they're reviewing the day over coffee after dinner, we might hear a hand slap on the table and the silverware jump. The argument arrives as a low, urgent murmur through the closed door. We turn the TV up louder and try not to listen.

Some nights, though I maintain eye contact with the TV, I can't un-hear what's said in the kitchen. Mickey Mining wants to transfer Dad. *Overseas.* To Belgium, which I know only from the Perkins menu as a modifier of waffles.

"It's only for five years," Dad says.

"We'll miss you," Mom says.

"It's a promotion," Dad says.

"Jim starts high school in a year," Mom says.

And that's it. Moving to Brussels is never again mentioned in our house.

At bedtime, I'll listen down the hall. Sometimes Mom goes to bed before Dad. They watch the ten o'clock news together, but Dad stays downstairs to watch Johnny Carson's monologue. This summer, it's all about Watergate: Watergate lawyers, Watergate burglars, Watergate hearings, the Watergate building. I don't know what Watergate is, but it sounds like Mickey Mining, like a brand name affixed to everything.

On nights they've argued, I'll listen down the hall to see if Mom and Dad have made up. Dad says they never go to bed mad at each other, but I'm not sure. I go to bed mad at one of my brothers almost every night. And so I cock my ear toward the hall. Standing at his dresser, divesting himself of his billfold, handkerchief, change, traveler's checks, money clip, and car-key wallet—the cargo of his workaday life—Dad will often sound a low and sonorous fart that reverberates off their closed bedroom door, with its simulated wood-grain finish and simulated copper doorknob.

On nights they've fought—and a tension suffuses the house the way Pepto-Bismol paints the stomach pink in commercials—I listen for Dad's valedictory fart, the day's closing bell. Mom's reply is always the same: "Oh, Don!"

In later years, when Steve Martin briefly penetrates his consciousness, Dad will offer a theatrical reply: "Well, *ex-cyoo-oooze meeee!*" And down the hall, secure under our blankets, Tom and I will giggle ourselves to sleep in relief.

When it's summer, we can sleep in. There's no bus to catch, no gig line to check. All I have to do today is tag along to the beach with Tom and his friend Buffy Wagner. Buffy's real name is Jeff, but he has a dog called Buffy and the name somehow transferred. It could be worse, and usually is. At school, Andy Crump is Candy Rump. His brother, Buddy Crump, is Cruddy Bump. It's a delight to discover and then deploy these spoonerisms. I have classmates who answer exclusively to Ginsu and Gizzard and Spock. When the teacher calls on them in class—"Kenny?" "Joel?" "Peter?"—there's a beat before they recognize their own given names. The girls have nicknames too, bestowed by the boys, who torture their surnames into something else: the Grunter, the Crippler, the Hustler. In these nicknames are the echoes of our Sunday-morning screenings of professional wrestling on channel 9, full of Crushers and Sodbusters and Undertakers.

My brother John is Junie, short for Junior. Amy is Mrs. Beasley, for a doll she resembles. Tom is called Waxman—

we don't know why—by Jim's friends the Pikala brothers, whose own names are Porky and Shorty. If those aren't their birth names, I haven't a clue what they are. Even Mom and Dad call them Shorty and Porky. Porky Pikala has a fake front tooth attached to a retainer. When he pops it out—as he frequently does by request—his smile resembles a two-car garage with one door up. He'd fit perfectly among the NHL stars pinned up in the basement, that gallery of crossword-puzzle smiles. Jim's other friends are called Fluff and Oz. The guy who drives the Zamboni at BIG is called Posh. Jim got a job at the Met from a guy named Smoke. One of his bosses there is called Twister.

Tom, Buffy, and I are accordioned into the backseat of Mr. Wagner's green Volkswagen Beetle. The opening chords of "Band on the Run" cry out on the radio. The freshly laundered beach towel on my lap smells pleasantly of Tide. I pop the top on our bottle of suntan lotion and take a deep snort. It is a coconut-scented nasal decongestant. The summer of '74 smells like this. It sounds like the deejay True Don Bleu on 630-KDWB spinning "We had joy, we had fun, we had seasons in the sun." Everything rhymes the summer I'm seven.

We're headed to Bush Lake in "prestigious west Bloomington," as real-estate ads on the radio are suddenly calling the new neighborhoods beyond Normandale Boulevard. "*Prestigious* west Bloomington," Dad repeats, wondering aloud what wonders life must hold for the aristocrats out there, nine minutes from our home in benighted central Bloomington. Forever after, when he hears the word "prestigious," he snorts and pronounces it with the same affected accent as the guy in the Grey Poupon commercial.

Already some of our neighbors are moving out to prestigious west Bloomington, including Mom and Dad's good friends the Cannadys and the Engelharts. Mr. Cannady has a cool job selling Cooper hockey equipment and Gladding sleds to sporting goods stores. He also sells C. Itoh bikes from Japan. My baseball glove is a Cooper model that Dad got from Mr. Cannady, who in 1973 also began to carry Nike shoes, which consisted principally of the red-swooshed Cortezes. The Cannady kids didn't want to wear them, preferring (like all the other kids in South Brook) the Adidas Roms, whose three stripes were the same green color of the sports teams at Lincoln High School. But Mr. Cannady was unmoved. He wouldn't buy his children Adidas. And so they wore the Cortezes, and within a couple of years, the rest of us did too. Most of America does. I've heard it said that Mr. Cannady gets a commission on all the Nikes sold in Minnesota, Wisconsin, Iowa, North and South Dakota, and Nebraska. And so they are moving off Xerxes Circle and on to prestigious west Bloomington.

But Mom and Dad have doubled down on South Brook, adding a screened-in porch to the back of the house and expanding the family room at the front of the house. From the outside, you can almost see the mint-green aluminum siding straining to contain us, as if the buckling metal might burst all at once like a bag of Jiffy Pop.

"Jiffy Pop is a magic treat. As fun to make as it is to eat."

And anyway, our fortunes are rising. Mickey Mining has been good to Dad. He and Mom are playing tennis at the Normandale Racquet Club, supplementing Dad's other exercise routine of buying and ignoring primitive fitness contraptions: a single wheel with two handles for rolling on the floor, a spring with two handles on it for stretching across his chest, a spring-loaded pliers for strengthening his grip and maintaining supremacy when delivering the Knuckle Floater. It is a mark of the 3M Company's largesse that the annual picnic at the company-owned Tartan Park in Saint Paul has bottomless Coleman coolers filled with cans of Brimfull pop and soft ice cream sandwiches, and the children are encouraged after the sack-racing tournament—the parents appear to bet on their children as if it were a cockfight—to gorge on orange soda and Bomb Pops.

In Bush Lake, we swim all day, breaking only to shiver over a soggy sandwich on the beach, where I lie flat in the sand to warm myself, so that I resemble a breaded veal cutlet when I return to the water.

Life is a series of blistering sunburns, the skin bubbling up like the tar bubbles in the streets of South Brook. "Sunshine on my shoulders makes me happy." At home, before dinner, at the end of a perfect day, I lie on my bedspread and peel a patch of skin from my shoulder, hold it up to the light, and admire its translucence. In school, I'll spread a thin layer of Elmer's glue on my palm and let it dry. Peel it off and the strip lighting of the classroom shines through. But tonight this is my real skin, tanned to a Reese's brown. I ball it up like a booger and throw it somewhere near the Schlitz-can wastebasket.

We have central air now, but it's only turned on when the heat becomes unbearable. It's something we have but don't use, like the furniture in the formal living room, or nuclear weapons.

Dad has something else he doesn't use. As The Boys come thundering down to breakfast one morning, Jim's portrait is knocked off the staircase wall. The glass front breaks and the photo falls out of the frame. But there's another portrait behind it, used as backing paper—a sketch of Jim as a little boy. It's unmistakably him, beautifully rendered in pencil, and when Dad sees his own artistry—he has clearly forgotten ever having drawn this—he laughs in mild embarrassment.

I ask him to draw something, but he demurs. And yet he brings home graph paper and number-two pencils from the inexhaustible supply cabinet at Mickey Mining, and encourages me to draw whatever comes to mind. What comes to mind are hockey goalies. Page after page of goalie masks, goalie sticks, and waffle boards. I render the netminders of the National Hockey League as quasi-religious figures, in the style of my *Book of Saints*. I know the goalies better than the saints: Gump Worsley, Cesare Maniago, Gilles Gilbert, Tony Esposito, Bernie Parent, Rogie Vachon—the names alone captivate. And the goalie masks mean I never have to draw a face.

The hotter it gets in the house, the more expansive my icehockey drawings become, incorporating Zambonis, fogged breath, steaming Styrofoam cups of hot chocolate, like the kind dispensed from the vending machine at BIG—where the cup falls upright, if you're lucky, followed by a fire hose of hot cocoa.

At night I bring my drawings to Dad, ensconced in his Archie Bunker chair. He pores over them with serious interest—like Mr. Brady hunched over blueprints. *"Wunder-*

bar," he says, flexing his businessman's Berlitz. *"Bellissimo."* And then, when I don't respond, "Nice job." The family-room windows are cranked open. Crickets and the whir of the neighbors' AC condenser. Moths and fireflies bumping against the screen. Mosquito buzz, dog bark, John Chancellor talking about Watergate.

Back upstairs an electric fan cools my lobsterized body. Colored pencils scratch out goalies on graph paper. Separated from me by a foot of blue-carpeted DMZ is Tom's bed, where he too lies in front of the fan, waiting for its merciful oscillation. Together we look like "we fell into the sun," to quote Paul McCartney, on the radio, in Mr. Wagner's sputtering love bug, through all these sounds of the summer of 1974.

On late summer afternoons, in the interval between cleaning and cooking dinner, Mom does the crossword in ink, bending the puzzle to her will. If the clue to nine across is "Color of the sky," and she's already inked in "bl_h," she'll go with "blah" rather than do the remedial work required to make the sky "blue." "Well, the sky *is* kind of blah today," Mom might say, not incorrectly, unconcerned that all the other answers will play off these letters. The *a* and *h* in "blah" mean "cot" is "cat" and "mate" is "math." The completed puzzle is a neat grid of non sequiturs. But it all fits, the way my favorite palindromes—"Some men interpret nine memos"—are clever and tidy without making any sense.

The orderliness is what matters to Mom. A place for everything and everything in its place. It bothers only me that an "army bed" is not a "cat," that a "London pal" is not a "math," and I set about correcting Mom's crosswords when I find them on the table next to her chair, until one day she just asks me for my help.

"What's a four-letter word meaning 'Swear or repair'?"

"A four-letter word for a four-letter word?" I say, and she laughs. It's a special thrill to make her laugh. We all try at the dinner table. It isn't hard to do, especially with impersonations of teachers or neighbors. On exceedingly rare occasions, Mom laughs so hard she has to push back from the table mid-meal and run to the bathroom to avoid tinkling in her pants. Getting Mom to race to the can is an unexpected triumph, like getting three jokers to line up on *The Joker's Wild*.

"'Darn,'" I say.

"What?" Mom says.

"'Swear or repair' is 'darn,'" I say.

"Of course," she says. "I should have known that."

Mom believes in euphemisms for swearing, and she believes in darning socks. Her three-tiered sewing kit is more impressive than any tackle box in Minnesota. Among its many implements is a lightbulb-shaped device over which she pulls socks for darning. When she does laundry, she rolls every pair of socks into a ball, which is then swallowed and held fast by the elastic cuff of one of the socks in the pair. This is the right way to pair socks because there is a right way to do everything. Mom is a devout balancer of the checkbook, a priestess of passbook savings accounts. If she were a contestant on *The Dating Game,* her turn-ons would include Heath bars, Triscuits, and ironing bedsheets.

Among her turn-offs are freeway on-ramps. Just before

merging onto I-35W, which bisects Bloomington on its way from Dallas to Minneapolis, she comes to a complete stop. Then, when there is a gap the length of a football field, she accelerates from zero to fifty-five in a hundred twenty seconds in a Chevy Impala station wagon. This often results in shouts of uneuphemized profanity from outside the car, and occasionally from within.

Nor does Mom care for getting wet. She has a miraculous way of swimming—a gentle, bobbing breaststroke—that practically leaves her bone-dry. Mom floats through a thrashing crowd of Marco Polo players in the Holidome pool of a Holiday Inn, ascends the shallow-end steps, and applies a couple of light dabs with a beach towel, and it's as if she had never swum at all.

Her twin aversions to getting soaked and speeding vehicles give her a special loathing of amusement-park rides. She will never set foot on a roller coaster, bumper car, or Ferris wheel, but her least favorite of human activities is the water flume. When Valleyfair, Minnesota's own Disneyland-by-the-Dakotas, opens just south of Bloomington in 1976, Mom will stand a safe distance away, just out of misting range, patting her hairdo into shape, while the rest of us slot into a fiberglass log and go cannonballing down a steep decline that ends in a frigid explosion of white water.

Dad's turn-ons include black coffee, televised college football, and Milk Duds. And drawing, apparently. Two Christmases from now I'll get a large hardcover book inscribed to me from Dad. It's called *Fun with a Pencil* by Andrew Loomis. "I had this when I was a kid," he'll say, and something in his expression will tell me that he had this—*and only this*—when he was a kid.

The instructional book was published in 1939 and is filled with the most amazing pencil sketches of that age—gangsters in double-breasted suits, cardsharps in green eyeshades, prize-fighting palookas, icemen, beat cops, grannies. In a section called "Let's Mix Up the Races," an African man in a loin-cloth stares at a toothbrush, a cartoon question mark floating above his head. This collection of cultural stereotypes—a Chinese coolie, an American Indian chief smoking a peace pipe, a mustachioed Italian man singing opera—was Dad's first view of the wider world beyond Fort Wayne, Indiana, before Mickey Mining and the 747 conspired to show him what it looked like firsthand.

At the back of the book, as at the back of Pik-Quik, are pictures of women in various stages of undress. Two full pages are headed "Vamps" and "More Vamps": a bare-bottomed, bare-breasted Eve batting her lashes at Adam; a topless bur-lesque dancer covering herself with a feathered fan; a Holly-wood starlet prone on a bearskin rug.

It scarcely matters that they're drawings. These are the first boobs I have ever seen, if you don't count the trick in which punching 5318008 into a calculator and turning it upside down reveals BOOBIES. 710 77345 inverted on the cal-culator becomes SHELL OIL, but that trick doesn't fascinate us in quite the same way that BOOBIES does.

My next endeavor is to see a naked woman. It is the final frontier. My friend Tom McCarthy and I have already tried smoking—rolling the dried leaves in my backyard into a sheet of Mom's typing paper, then torching one end with a book of matches procured from above the range. I let Mac go first. When it's my turn, I take one deep drag and scorch the back of my throat, then fling the burning paper to the grass before my fingers also go up in flames. Stomping out the fast-growing brush fire—of paper, grass, and dried leaves—I'm cured of ever smoking again. I'm also cured like a ham, to judge by the smell of my hands and head, which I scrub meticulously under the backyard hose.

And so I've moved on to another vice. There are three places within walking distance of my house where a boy can see a naked woman—or at least a badly degraded photograph of a woman who is also, in her own way, being badly degraded.

Snake Hill is on the path that leads from the end of our block through the woods to the Bloomington Ice Garden. Up a small rise is a sudden clearing. In it, an elm tree stands surrounded by empty beer cans and crushed cigarette packs. The hollow of that tree acts as a kind of safe-deposit box for generations of Bloomington children. Stashed inside is a perpetually five-year-old copy of an off-brand men's magazine with a name like *Gent* or *Swank* or *Oui*.

It is common knowledge that another magazine featuring women disporting in the altogether is hidden under leaves in the woods somewhere behind the Torgesons' house. But the closest of these magazine stashes is somewhere in the marsh across the street from our house, a wetland that extends for many square miles and is covered in reeds taller than I am. It would take a team of archaeologists using sonar and satellites the better part of a year to find a single nudie magazine buried in this swamp, though its precise location is known to half the boys in South Brook.

"I know where it is," says a South Brook kid named Eddie O'Phelan.

I don't ask how he knows, or where it is, or even *what* it is, exactly. I just follow him into the marsh. The wetlands squish underfoot. We have to part the reeds or push them aside like stage curtains. The ground is trying to suck the shoes from our feet. There are no signposts in here, nothing to distinguish one direction from another. It's like being lost in a cornfield, and after ten minutes I stop fearing that we won't find the magazine and instead start fearing that *we* won't be found. A helicopter will locate our bodies weeks from now, lying a few feet from a copy of *Penthouse,* like Robert Falcon Scott dying just miles shy of his Antarctica supply depot.

But Eddie plows forward, as if guided by some divine hand. After fifteen minutes he pauses, seems to sniff the air, takes three steps forward and three more to his left. Then he crouches. Clearing away a tarp of dead reeds, he reaches into a small pit from which he removes a wet magazine rolled up like a spyglass. If he had just removed a rabbit I would have been no more astonished—indeed, I would have been much less astonished, as there must be a million rabbits out here, but only one magazine.

Peeling it open reveals an enormous woman, a wall of flesh in black-and-white. She looks at us balefully, as if we're not even the first young visitors from South Brook today and she only wants to be left alone beneath the reeds. The great wedding cake of her crenellated flesh is exposed once again to the world, and we stand there, in nylon shoes soaked through to sodden socks, staring in wonder and terror at the first real naked woman either of us has ever seen.

We never turn the page, just gaze at a wet magazine that for all we know is called *Wet* magazine.

After a few minutes of quietly confused contemplation, Eddie shrieks, "My dink's growing! My dink's growing!"

As is our sacred duty, we rebury the ancient artifact for future treasure hunters and set about trying to find our way out of the wilderness, our dinks leading the way like the tails of two English pointers.

Even before we're out of the marsh, I know that I won't relay this sin to Father Zheel-bair when our class next goes to confession. If God is watching, He already knows. Plus, I only ever enter the confessional with the same three sins. Like a soldier trained to give only his name, rank, and serial number, I only ever offer "I fought with my brothers and sister," "I disobeyed my parents," and "I lied." Often, telling the priest that I lied is the only lie that I've told, but a good confession requires three sins, and I'm never going to cop to the real ones, like coveting my neighbor's goods or thinking impure thoughts. If I have just committed adultery—and I'm pretty sure I have—I know from religion class that my eternal soul will be consigned to hell, forever poked and prodded like a hamburger on the Weber grill by some pointy-tailed, cloven-hoofed, trident-wielding demon. (Satan, to my understanding, looks like the logo on packages of Underwood deviled ham.) So I consign myself to warm places in preparation.

The warming houses of Bloomington are incubators. They hatch hockey players. Those hockey players become baseball players in the spring and football players in the fall. In the summer, we buy baseball cards at Pik-Quik and play box hockey, floor hockey, and air hockey in the stifling grade school gyms of the city's Parks and Rec programs.

As a spur to do homework, Mom threatens us with summer school, the worst possible fate that can befall a child, but when we get to Parks and Rec, the Bloomington public schools are revealed to be empty in the summer, desks occupied only by the chairs inverted on top of them, the petrified boogers and Bubblicious stuck to the undersides now visible beneath the strip lighting. Our counselors are in high school and cannot contain our coursing adrenaline. It's at Parks and Rec that Tom raises Mike Knapp's Sting-Ray to the top of the Hillcrest flagpole and lets it free-fall, so that Knapper has to ride it home with a wonky wheel. It wobbles off unpredictably like a Red Owl grocery cart.

And so the counselors focus our energy on sports. We are the sun, the counselors are the magnifying glass, and sports are the ants we burn through. We play Ping-Pong and dodge-ball and foosball, kickball and baseball and four square. With the possible exception of Dodgertown, the Dodgers' spring-training redoubt in Vero Beach, Florida, no American city has ever been so singularly devoted to sports as Bloomington, Minnesota, is in the 1970s. And even then Dodgertown isn't a real municipality, and it's dedicated to only one sport and for only six weeks of the year.

The kinetic energy of Bloomington's exploding youth population is transferred from our bodies into baseballs and tennis balls and hockey pucks and anything else that can be struck furiously with a stick or racquet. As at Dodgertown, our civic self-esteem is tied entirely to athletics. We love watching the Vikings and Twins and North Stars. Seeing BLOOMINGTON in all caps in a three-day-old copy of the *Los Angeles Times* or *Dallas Morning News* that Dad brings home from his travels is still a thrill—a reminder that BLOOMINGTON has a place with LONDON and MOSCOW and SAIGON at the dinner table of international datelines.

Even in South Brook, the giants of our televised dreams walk among us. Mr. Fischer lives on West 97th Street and is the football coach at Edina High School but is much more famous in our subdivision for working on the Vikings chain gang. He appeared on the cover of *Sports Illustrated* once, framed between Vikings linebacker Wally Hilgenberg and Cowboys running back Preston Pearson. Mr. Stange, the Twins pitching coach, lives on Upton. He used to pitch for the Boston Red Sox. My Nativity classmate Andy Crump is the son of the Twins equipment manager, and Troy Chaika's dad is the innkeeper at the Airport Holiday Inn, where the Vikings stay the Saturday night before home games. No man is a hero to his valet, but these men are the valets of my heroes, and therefore heroic themselves.

By 1974, the Bloomington Athletic Association can claim to be the largest all-volunteer sports organization in the United States. It is our version of Little League, our outlet for football, hockey, basketball, and baseball, so well subscribed—we don't sign up so much as get conscripted—that the city is subdivided into five color-coded precincts: Northwest (with green uniforms), Southwest (purple), East (red), South (yellow), and North (blue). These stoke intracity rivalries where there otherwise would be none.

Every boy my age in South Brook is grateful beyond words to be in BAA North, because it means Craig Newell might be on our team instead of someone else's. Newell is eight going on thirty-five and North's wild, flame-throwing pitcher with an incipient mustache. One afternoon I watch from left field as he hits the first four batters of the game, each batter more terrified than the last. The children must be forced from the on-deck circle by their coach, then coaxed into the batter's box by the umpire. By walking in the first run, Newell secures a win for North, since the East coach—after a brief but animated argument with our coach—forfeits the game.

My baseball uniform is a pair of plaid Farah slacks and a blue BAA T-shirt. I usually forget my blue cap at home.

"You'd forget your head if it wasn't screwed on," Mom says.

That might be true. I'm riding my bike no-handed home from Kevin Sundem's one afternoon, lost in thought, my palms pressing down on my thighs to help pedal, when I crash into the back of a car parked on West 96th Street. I never see it coming, perhaps because it isn't—it never moved—but after I pick myself up and check myself for injuries, I wonder if I'm not destined to walk off a cliff absentmindedly, then fall for a full minute in the manner of Wile E. Coyote.

One evening our team is taking infield practice and I'm playing first base, daydreaming as Coach Landrus lays down a bunt. The catcher—a kid I know only as Corey—picks up the baseball and fires it to first. Corey appears to me only as a silhouette, backlit by the blazing nimbus of the setting sun. I again have forgotten my cap, and in the split-second interval between the ball leaving the catcher's hand and it smashing into my mouth, I hear Mom saying, "You'd forget your head if it wasn't screwed on."

My mouth explodes. Blood and exposed nerves. Bits of teeth on my shirt like chipped china. A crowd of teammates standing over me. It hurts to breathe in. There's a hole where I used to have my front teeth, my grown-up teeth—the first grown-up things I've ever had—already gone. We're as far from home as it is possible to be in BAA, all the way over on the east side of Bloomington at Running Park. It's surrounded by houses, and Coach Landrus bundles me into the kitchen of the nearest homeowner who answers the frantic knocks on her door only to find a child bleeding on the front stoop.

I'm in the kitchen of an old woman, older than my Grandma Boyle.

She presses a dishrag full of ice to my mouth, if only to stop me from bleeding onto her linoleum. Coach calls my mom from a phone tethered to the kitchen wall because I can't speak, except to recite my phone number. My lips are swollen to twice their size, which is saying something.

At Mom's instruction, Coach drives me straight to the dentist's office, where our South Brook neighbor Dr. Popovich opens his practice at eight o'clock on a Wednesday night to build up my front teeth with some kind of quick-hardening enamel-like substance. In doing so, he robs me of my only possible reward: playing Parks and Rec box hockey tomorrow with a Bobby Clarke smile to rival any we had scissored out of *Goal* magazine.

And though I'll never have removable front choppers like Porky Pikala's, I am grateful for my baseball coach and my neighbor-dentist and the old lady who answered her door by

Running Park and the kindness of an entire community that became a sort of dental bucket brigade the second my teeth were smashed out.

It isn't the first time I've had an emergency in a park and been rescued by a kindly stranger answering a frantic knock. Skating on the outdoor rink at Brookside Park in the winter, my bowels once began to collapse in a way that recalled very tall buildings imploding on the news. The warming house didn't have a bathroom.

So I pulled off my skates, slipped my snowmobile boots on over my bread bags, sprinted across Xerxes Avenue, and pounded on the door of the nearest house. To my profound relief, a woman answered.

"May I please use your bathroom?" I said, mentally calculating the sixteen buttons and zippers and the half dozen layers I would have to undo or remove before I could even sit down on her toilet.

"Of course," she said, eyeing my hockey stick, which was held over my shoulder like a hobo's bindlestick, the skates tied together and dangling from either side. "Just down the hall. First door on your left."

But before I could make it past her, my clenched bowels cried uncle. I froze. The woman and I never broke eye contact throughout the volcanic exertions that followed. We both knew what was happening, and we both pretended it wasn't.

Mercifully, I was wearing snow pants that cinched at the bottom. I walked like Frankenstein to the bathroom, a slow and stiff-legged gait, so that whatever was in my pants wouldn't escape into the hall. Locking the bathroom door behind me, I shook my left leg as if I were trying to dislodge a small dog that had attached itself to my ankle. But it wasn't a small dog that fell onto the bathroom floor.

After mummifying both hands with a roll of toilet paper, I cleaned the once-pristine tiles as best I could and divested myself of the mess in a series of flushes, each time giving the tank several seconds to refill. "Is everything all right in there?" the woman asked, not unreasonably, after the seventh or eighth flush.

When I finally emerged from the bathroom five minutes later, in a cloud of Glade—I'd sprayed half an aerosol can in the air and the other half down my pants—the lady looked at me and said, "Is your mother home, dear?"

"I don't think so."

"Want me to call her?"

"No, thank you."

"Perhaps I should."

"No, thank you."

"What's your number?"

I didn't want to say. But I caved beneath her skeptical gaze.

"Ay-day-date, two-weight-seven-two," I said.

"I'll be right back," she said, eyeing her upholstered chairs and sofa. "If you want, you can wait out on the front stoop."

I went outside to the stoop, sprinted across the front yard, serpentined across Xerxes Avenue, and sat in a snowbank by the Brookside Park parking lot to hide my shame and my snow pants.

The curtains parted across the street. In the window was the woman, peering out at me. Ten minutes later, Mom pulled into the parking lot, leaned across the shotgun seat, and cranked down the window. "You poor thing," she said, beckoning me to get in.

"But my pants..."

"Get in, sweetheart," she said.

I couldn't set a glass of water down without her whisking a coaster beneath it, but when I did a BM in my snow pants at Brookside Park, she rushed to my rescue without so much as a towel on the seat. "You poor thing" was all she said. "You poor thing."

That was last winter, a lifetime ago. This is summer, a vast hole to be filled, an hour at a time. Kevin Sundem has older sisters, old enough to have a record collection in which there appears, sometime in June, a double album by the Beach Boys called *Endless Summer*, which is what we have on our hands: a ninety-two-day weekend, a three-month recess, a single afternoon that lasts until all the moms of South Brook call in all South Brook's sons and daughters for supper in September.

September, like mortality, is an abstraction, too distant and theoretical to comprehend.

In the morning, with no bus to bundle us onto, and Dad in Tokyo for two weeks, Mom banishes us from the house with "Go play."

"Where?"

"Anywhere."

"But there's nothing to..."

"Find something."

A bicycle circumnavigation of South Brook turns up other kids flushed out of their houses and also circumnavigating the subdivision in search of Something to Do. We circle one another like dogs, try to sniff out a plan, ride our bikes in silence to the playground at Hillcrest Elementary.

The sun is already burning the dew off the metal slide. The few remaining drops are sizzling like batter droplets on a griddle. Climbing the ladder to the top, I imagine myself to be one of the cliff divers of Acapulco. I've seen them on *Wide World of Sports*, the men who swan-dive in electric-yellow Speedos onto the frothy shoals of the Pacific. Dad says they're *"pazzo,"* and I agree.

There's a high dive at the city pool at Valley View. Viewing it from the bottom of the ladder, I cannot fathom even climbing up, much less diving off. But now I force myself to the top of the slide at Hillcrest and look down.

Its angle of descent is roughly the same as that of the laundry chute that drops straight down from Mom and Dad's bedroom closet to the laundry room a floor below. When Mom's out of the house, Tom and I use it as an intercom system, shouting echoing messages to each other. We'd be dead meat if we were ever caught in this closet, which acts as a repository of hidden Christmas presents, unopened cans of tennis balls, walnut-handled back scratchers, long-stemmed shoehorns, dry-cleaned dresses, rolls of dimes, but not—upon thorough inspection—a single magazine featuring photographs of naked women.

At the top of the slide, I close my eyes and surrender to a scalding descent, braking halfway down with the soles of my gym shoes, though doing so risks my tumbling over the low edges and falling a dozen feet to the ground below, which is a mosaic of broken-bottle glass, cigarette butts, and used Band-Aids.

The stand-up merry-go-round next to the slide is more terrifying still. Four of us take up our positions on its perimeter while a fifth, older kid, whom I don't recognize, volunteers to spin it. He jumps on once it gets going, like a hobo onto a moving boxcar. When the merry-go-round is spinning at sixty miles an hour, I redouble my death grip on the handles and lean back to look up at the sky, which has become a whirling tie-dye of white and faded denim.

All the while, I'm aware that the playground engineers have left just enough space between the bottom of the merry-go-round and the asphalt beneath it to accommodate the skull of any eight-year-old who's been thrown free from this gyrating monstrosity.

Fresh from this experience, I lie on a patch of grass and watch the sky pinwheel. It's in this state of happy nausea—stomach churning, head spinning—that I ride my bike on a drunken slalom over the little footbridge across Nine Mile Creek.

It rained yesterday and the creek is running fast through the narrow concrete tunnel that passes under the bridge. One of the Davis brothers is standing in the raging water, holding on to a rope he's tied to the rickety fence that halfheartedly guards against children falling into the creek and being swept away like a bobbing cork.

"What are you doing?" I ask in a tone of disapproval. I'm afraid he'll die—or, worse, get in trouble. Or, worse still, die and get me in trouble for failing to tell my mom to tell his mom to tell her son to stop it.

"Water-skiing," he says, and, by God, he does appear to be water-skiing, standing still in the rapids of a swollen creek. For a moment I envy his lack of inhibition or brains.

Even when Jim and Tom aren't tucking their fists into their own armpits and flapping their elbows at me while making *bwok-bwok-bwok* sounds, I recognize myself as a chicken. Those earliest childhood fears, of swallowing my tongue, have never left me.

Whenever a wide receiver steps out-of-bounds instead of taking two extra yards and a hit, Dad winces at the TV. "Look at *this* pansy," he says. The last thing any of us wants to be is a pansy, scaredy-cat, candy-ass, or wuss—especially now, in the Summer of Evel.

The summer won't end until September 8, when Robert Craig Knievel attempts to jump the Snake River Canyon in Idaho. In the three months until then, every son of South Brook is attempting his own daredevil feats, jumping great distances on a bicycle while trying to stick the landing. This has induced in me an especially pernicious form of pansy-ism: the Rooseveltian fear of fear itself.

At Mike McCollow's, we build bike takeoff ramps of plywood propped up on logs. We jump full trash bags, a row of soup cans, and each other. One night when I'm not there and the McCollows are hosting Father Zheel-bair and the associate pastor, Father Larry, for dinner, Mike shows off by hastily assembling a ramp and trying to set a new soup-can record. But the ramp has too much pitch and he doesn't pull up hard enough on the handlebars and lands so hard on the front wheel of his grape Sting-Ray that it snaps off and his fork sticks in the wet ground like a Jart. By then, Mike has been thrown between the handlebars, as if Freddy the Foot had kicked him through the goalposts. He lands on his face.

"Father Zheel-bair gave me last rites," Mike says the next

day, his face striped like a badger's. "I'm not even exaggerating."

So I learn how to jump without really jumping anything, how to catch a pass and stay inbounds but to fall just before contact, to stray far from the boards in hockey so as never to check or be checked, and generally to give the appearance of physical bravery without ever having to be physically brave.

From the park I ride my bike to Kevin's house, where I ring the doorbell. His mom sweeps the door open, yells "Kevin!" and returns to the kitchen.

Out pops Kevin. All I say is "Garage?"

"Garage" is an abbreviation of Garage Door Baseball, in which a batter stands in front of the garage door and a pitcher fires a tennis ball at him from the foot of the driveway. The Sundems' garage door is mottled with ball marks, the graffiti of a thousand games of Garage. There are two kinds of moms: those who allow their garage door to be used as a backstop and those who do not.

We know from Twins games on TV what Harmon Killebrew's dad in Idaho told Harmon's mom when she complained about their lawn being ruined by ball games: "We can raise grass or we can raise boys." The Killebrews chose to raise boys, not grass, and the Sundems and Rushins have made the same choice.

In Kevin's driveway, I swing a bat acquired at Bat Day at the Met, where the Twins hand out wooden weapons to the first ten thousand children to pass through the turnstiles, and we children in turn wave them in unison like windblown wheat and bang them on the concrete beneath our feet to conjure thunder in the grandstand.

Every kid in Bloomington affects the batting stance of Rod Carew. He's black and left-handed with an Afro that spills out both sides of his batting helmet, but all of us—white, right-handed, un-Afroed—can lean back like Carew does and hold the bat handle in our hands as lightly as possible, as if cupping a live bird.

Other days, when I play stickball at McCollow's house with the handle of a push broom, Mike and I press Buddig brand pastrami, thin as my mother's onionskin typing paper, into our left cheeks to mirror Carew's chaw. We have read about his belief that the bulge in his right cheek pulls the skin down ever so slightly below his right eye, the one closer to the pitcher, and helps him to see the ball better. Mike and I, we don't want to be *like* Rod Carew. We want to *be* him.

There are certain improvised rules for the games we play in the streets and driveways and backyards and playgrounds that every one of my friends accepts as gospel. If we're playing a baseball game with five or fewer kids on either team, Pitcher's Hand will be in effect, and the base runner will have to stop once the ball has been returned to the pitcher. When all of a team's batters are on base, the next man up in the order will abandon his base in favor of a ghost runner. ("Ghost runner on third!" the pitcher will call before throwing his next pitch.) In football, a defensive lineman will either count to five bananas or three Mississippis before rushing the passer. That's it, bananas or Mississippis. There is no other pass-rushing currency, and the exchange rate is fixed: one Mississippi equals 1.666 bananas. The team that is scored against in backyard

My future father smokes three cigarettes and decants the last of ten beers into his ear as my future mother looks on, 1954.

Mom and Dad, aged nineteen and twenty, at Lake Wawasee, Indiana, 1954.

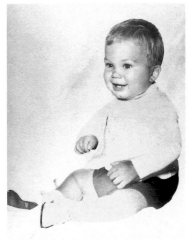

Portrait of the author as a young man, 1967.

Steve, Tom, and Jim, collectively known as "The Boys," 1967.

Jonesing for a "smoke," Tom and I clutch boxes of Pall Mall candy cigarettes, 1968.

His "nature will be an unhappy one." Crying in Lisle, 1968.

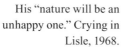

The Boys sleep Three Stooges–style beneath a Sears Orlon blanket.

The morning after the
moon landing, we stock
up on rubber tomahawks
in Wisconsin Dells,
July 21, 1969.

While Mom is locked in the
stockades at Fort Dells...

...Dad takes comfort
in the arms of a saloon
girl en route to our new
lives in Minnesota.

"You finally got one with indoor plumbing." Four months after we arrive in Bloomington, Amy is born.

Tom gleefully lands a haymaker to my left jaw as Dad captures our basement boxing bout on his Super 8.

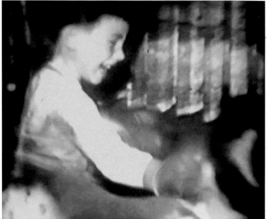

"What happened to the girl?" Mom sends me to Mass in an Easter bonnet and bob haircut, 1972.

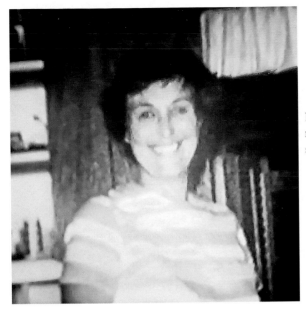

Mom arrives, radiant, in my room every morning, singing.

Dad is having a blast at Miracle Strip Amusement Park in Panama City Beach, Florida.

Unfazed by his disastrous trip to the ski slopes of Detroit, Dad takes me to Terry Peak in South Dakota in the summer of '72.

As soon as John can stand, The Boys set him up in goal and fire slap shots at him in the basement.

Mom holds Amy and Amy holds a doll in South Brook. Baby Tender Love will soon be decapitated, her head used as a hockey puck.

Los Angeles, 1972. Three Sting-Rays parked side by side turned any suburban driveway into the parking lot of a biker bar. (Getty Images)

One-Match Rushin mans his Weber One-Touch Kettle grill, filling the screened porch with smoke.

The spiral staircase of the 747 leads to a swinging cocktail party in the sky. (Boeing Images)

A book by her side,
Mom collapses on the
couch after a long day
chasing one redhead
and four shitheads.

On my seventh birthday, in a
hand-me-down Cubs jersey,
vestige of our former life in
Chicago.

Is there an ancient Chinese
secret for scrubbing the
soul? An hour before mak-
ing my First Communion.

Vikings guard Milt Sunde, pride of Bloomington, signs an autograph for me in the lobby of the Airport Holiday Inn.

Looking past Vikings cornerback Nate Wright, I hope that my hero, Alan Page, will walk through the doors of the Holiday Inn.

Tom makes a snowball assault on my fort. A snow day is Mardi Gras, V-E Day, and the Lindbergh parade all in one.

Watering John in the hope that he'll grow like his idol, the Incredible Hulk.

Family portrait, 1975. My collar threatens to flap its great pterodactyl wings and carry me away.

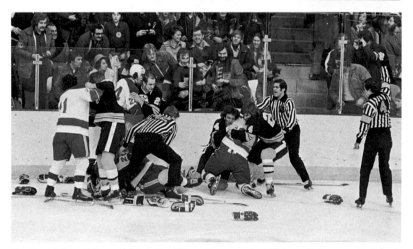

On the night of his tenth birthday, Tom witnesses horrifying violence at the North Stars–Bruins game while I stay home and watch *The Carol Burnett Show.* (AP Photo)

The 1978 Ford Country Squire, peak of the simulated-wood-grain aesthetic. Through its Magic Doorgate, I watch America recede from view on summer vacations. (Bettmann)

Disney World, 1975. Jim, the future bench-press champion of Lincoln High School, appears poised to rip my lips off.

Allowed one souvenir from the Magic Kingdom, I choose a Mickey Mouse trucker cap that brings me boundless joy, at least on the inside.

It is necessary to have a best friend: Mike McCollow and I try to look tough in front of his mom, 1976. (Dr. Terrence and Doris McCollow)

If it's the 1970s, then Dad is drinking scotch, probably in some far-flung port to which he was borne by a 747.

Tom and I are briefly BAA baseball team-mates. I kneel below him, in plaid pants.

Our BAA football team goes winless in 1976, but at least I get the number I want: O. J. Simpson's 32.

Indians, real and imaginary, are often in my thoughts. Tom (right) and Buffy Wagner pose with their baseball mascot, Chief Wahoo.

John admires Dad's new Buick Regal with the landau roof, a bridge from the station wagons of his past to the Cadillac of his dreams.

Shortly after touching down in San Francisco, Tom and I are urged by a cable car to think about smoking, 1977.

With his Super 8 camera, Dad films his seven-year-old daughter on the brink of the great precipice that is Big Sur, California, 1977.

Big Surly: Weary from the long car ride, the Rushins scowl for the camera at Big Sur, though I take comfort in my Sunkist-stained Rod Carew replica Twins jersey.

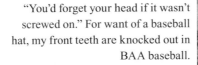

Steve Rushin makes like Steve Austin, the Six Million Dollar Man, at Universal Studios in Los Angeles.

"You'd forget your head if it wasn't screwed on." For want of a baseball hat, my front teeth are knocked out in BAA baseball.

Goodbye Yellow Brick Road: Family portrait, circa 1980, when Jim has gone off to college on a hockey scholarship—and started to wear clogs.

Fans summit the scoreboard at the Met after the final game there, a Vikings loss that leaves Bloomington bereft. (AP Photo)

Mom makes a final pilgrimage to her beloved Cincinnati, two months before her death in September 1991.

football has to walk to the other end of the field to receive the ensuing kickoff, a rule handed down through generations and known as Sucker's Walk. In some games do-overs are accepted, while others adhere to a strict code of no do-overs.

In South Brook, Kevin and I are the only ones who play Garage. The rules and customs are too complex to recite to any other kids in the neighborhood. A hit that bounces in the driveway is an out. A ball that one-hops in the street is a single. Any drive that carries the street and lands in Karl Johnson's yard is a double. We call Karl the K-Train, after the A-Train, Artis Gilmore, of the Kentucky Colonels. If a ball should carom off the Johnsons' house, it's a triple. And when one of us—usually Kevin—hits it squarely onto, or even over, the Johnsons' roof, it's a home run.

No Johnsons were consulted in these ground rules, but no Johnson has ever complained when a ball rattles their windowpanes or lands in their rain gutter and rolls into their downspout, where it stops halfway down like a marble in a windpipe.

We play for hours. The time disappears down a storm drain, along with some of our tennis balls. A right-hander pulling the ball will send it down the hill on Xerxes Circle, rolling toward the open storm drains, so we try to go opposite field. It works for Carew, who goes opposite field or up the middle—almost never pulls the ball—and he wins the batting title every year.

Occasionally we retreat to the Sundems' kitchen, where Kevin's mom serves Kool-Aid in Dixie Riddle Cups. Kevin reads his out loud to me.

"What's the best way to talk to a monster?"

"I give up."

"Long-distance."

We admire the beaded sweat on our faces reflected in the range window, then run upstairs to Kevin's room, where he withdraws a shoe box from under the bed: it's full of baseball cards, sorted by team, bound by rubber bands, each bundle smelling of gum and new shoes.

More than any book or Sports section, any liner notes or album cover, any comic strip or cereal-box side panel or Sears catalogue, these baseball cards are my literature, to be pored over, read into, gazed upon, searched for meanings hidden and overt. Toby Harrah's last name is a palindrome. Aurelio Monteagudo has all five vowels in his first name. Ed Figueroa has all five vowels in his last name. Len Randle is poised to field a ball—knees bent, head up, glove gaping—despite already holding a baseball in his meat hand. Tito Fuentes is wearing an orange terry-cloth headband around the outside crown of his Giants cap.

These men have sideburns like the snow brushes we keep in the way back of the station wagon. Their Afros make Mickey Mouse ears out the sides of their caps. Not a single player smiles as he stares into the middle distance of some sun-scorched spring-training field with a faintly menacing air of take-the-damn-picture-already impatience. And yet these men, these cardboard giants, are in almost all other ways exactly like Kevin and me.

The back of every 1974 Topps card has a short sentence about the player. And in many cases what we learn is that the player works in the real world when he isn't playing baseball. Like the records in Kevin's big sister's room—the 45s, the singles—the flip side of these cards is less prominent but often more interesting and rewarding.

Doug Griffin's fact appears beneath a line drawing of a baseball player in a carnival ticket booth, a string of tickets spilling outward like sausage links. The caption says, "Doug spends off-seasons selling tickets for the Bosox." Whatever the job, the player is always depicted in full uniform, so that pitcher Paul Splittorff is drawn making milk deliveries while dressed for a Royals game: "Paul works for a dairy during the off-season." Skip Lockwood—briefcase, baseball uniform— "works in life insurance off-season." Lee Lacy—mailbag, baseball uniform—"handles mail in off-season." Steve Busby—hard hat, baseball uniform—"is a construction foreman off-season." Chuck Goggin won a Purple Heart and Bronze Star in Vietnam and then wore them—according to the cartoon on the back of his card—pinned to his baseball uniform.

Sadly, none of the Twins has ever appeared in South Brook in full uniform to deliver the mail or fix the furnace because these gods all spend their off-seasons in sunny places with exotic names like Jupiter, Florida, and Surprise, Arizona, and Rancho Cucamonga, California.

In every other respect the men on the fronts of the cards—to judge by the backs of their cards—have interests that align exactly with ours, beginning with baseball but not ending there. Like us, Mike Cuellar "likes the comics." George Theodore "likes marshmallow milkshakes." Jim Holt of the Twins "enjoys watching television." Tom Paciorek "has a great appetite for hamburgers." Walt "No Neck" Williams's "hobby is drawing." Ernie McNally's hobby "is being out-of-doors." And the back of Hal Lanier's baseball card says, simply, "Hal collects baseball cards."

Only I don't really collect baseball cards. I have about a dozen guys no one has ever heard of standing at attention in a Velveeta box in my closet, but when I brought them to Kevin's house one day, his sister Pam's boyfriend looked at mine and casually dismissed them before gazing in exaggerated wonder and phony astonishment at Kevin's collection, in an obvious effort to ingratiate himself with Pam.

Kevin's sister is a cheerleader at Lincoln. Every kid in South Brook will go to Lincoln, which has the same green-and-gold colors as the Oakland A's. We all want to wear Adidas Roms because the three stripes are Lincoln green. It's difficult to say if it's the 48-degree chill or something else causing the goose bumps when the Lincoln cheerleaders chant at hockey games, "*Lin*-coln *Bears,* we're for *you!* I say *Ah-ah, ooh-ooh!*"

And, "*We* got the spirit. Yes, we *do! We* got the spirit. How 'bout…*you?!*"

My brother Jim will be going to Lincoln in a year. He's thirteen now, and left-handed, with a dark red Afro that makes him more like Rod Carew than the rest of us combined. He's a dominant baseball pitcher, has a terrifying slap shot, and will soon be playing varsity hockey, football, and baseball for the Bears as well as setting the school's all-time record in the bench press, a skill he has honed on the little Sears weight set in the basement. He easily pins Tom or me to the floor, kneeling on my wet-shoelace biceps while drooling onto me or administering the 99 Bump. If we give him any fight-back or lip, he says "You have made a grievous error" and redoubles his tortures.

To any question I ask, Jim usually replies "You writing a book?" Or he answers with another question of his own: "Does your face hurt? 'Cuz it's killing me." Any declarative sentence is met with "Wanna cookie?" Or "Wanna medal, or a chest to pin it on?" If I tell him I got a hit in my baseball game, he'll say "You're my hero."

Jim's "the man of the house" when Dad's away, as Dad often is. Like the monster on the Dixie Riddle Cup, the best way to talk to my father is long distance.

Dad comes home from Los Angeles one summer night in 1974 and—evidently caught short at the airport or gas station—he pulls from his briefcase a hastily purchased present. It's a three-pack of 1974 Topps cards in a cellophane wrapper, forty-two cards in all. Through the first windowpane I see the horizontal action image of Dodgers first baseman Steve Garvey. In a single act of God I have tripled my baseball card collection, and my first thought is to find Pam Sundem's boyfriend and see him try to dismiss this titanic assembly of today's superstars. Vida Blue! Joe Morgan! Rodney Cline Carew!

They all go into the Velveeta box, which I keep separate from my football cards. The football cards came with a Parker Brothers game called Pro Draft, in which players try to assemble the best starting offensive lineup from the eleven football cards they select in a "draft." There are two Vikings among the dozens of cards: Chuck Foreman and Milt Sunde. Milt Sunde is from Bloomington and went to Lincoln High when it was still called Bloomington High School. His last name is pronounced "Sunday," which is a bottomless source of fascination to me. An NFL player named Sunday is like a priest named Sunday. Better still, Milt Sunde's dad has an appliance repair shop across from Nativity. Though I never say anything to Mom, I live in silent hope that she'll one day bring our toaster in for repair and maybe the Vikings guard will be there visiting his dad, and I can meet him.

But this is an impossible dream, because the Minnesota Vikings, unlike the workaday men on the baseball cards, do not walk among us. They are colossi with steaming breath and smoldering Afros who retreat to some frozen fortress of solitude when they're not smashing one another in the mouth with what Dad always calls—with an admiration born of having played the game—a "forearm shiver." Then he slaps his right forearm into the palm of his left hand. The resulting sound—a slap that goes off like a gunshot—is terrifying and induces in me a different kind of shiver.

I wake up on a Saturday morning in August to five bracing hours of television. Starting at seven with *The Hair Bear Bunch,* I sit Indian-style five feet from the screen through *Yogi's Gang; Scooby-Doo; Inch High, Private Eye; Goober and the Ghost Chasers; Sigmund and the Sea Monsters; The Pink Panther; The Jetsons;* and *Fat Albert,* until the lunch whistle of Billy Preston singing "Nothin' from Nothin'" on *American Bandstand* reminds me that it's noon.

The *Minneapolis Tribune* Sports section sits rumpled and already read on the kitchen table. The Twins beat the Orioles last night on two doubles by Steve Brye. The Royals beat the Brewers for Steve Busby's seventeenth win. Cubs catcher Steve Swisher turned twenty-three. Steve Mizerak was attempting to win his fifth straight U.S. Open Pocket Billiards Championship in Chicago. As I read this over a bowl of Cap'n Crunch with Crunch Berries, after ten consecutive television shows, the lesson is clear: there has never been a better time in human history to be young and sports obsessed and named Steve.

The front section of the *Trib*—the wrapper that keeps the Sports section dry on our driveway—is devoted almost entirely to yesterday's resignation of President Nixon. The president was on every channel last night, smiling and waving as he boarded a helicopter. He looked happy. Whatever Watergate was—whatever this long-running series on TV and radio was all about—it's apparently over, and Nixon evidently won. He's heading to California now, to the land of *The Brady Bunch, Adam-12, Emergency!, The Carol Burnett Show, The Sonny and Cher Comedy Hour, The Streets of San Francisco, Sanford and Son,* and every game show on which every contestant is from West Covina or Oxnard or San Clemente, where Nixon's going. I envy him, going to California, to be with the Beach Boys, as my Endless Summer draws to an end.

You can't buy an 88 Vikings jersey in Minnesota in 1974. You can buy the 10 of Fran Tarkenton or the 44 of Chuck Foreman, but if you want the 88 of Alan Page, your mom has to find a blank purple football shirt and have the numbers ironed on. As far as I know, my mom is the only one who ever did. The jersey becomes my security blanket, what psychologists call a "transition object," the item that sustains a child in moments away from his mother. I have worn the shirt until it has begun to disintegrate in the wash.

I am alone among my friends in worshipping Page. I know only that he is recognizably great—the way he pulls runners down one-handed, as if pulling the cord to signal a city bus to stop. When he removes his helmet on the sidelines at the Met on a winter day, his Afro steams, as angry heads do in cartoons.

When we return to school in September, my classmate Troy Chaika invites me to a Saturday night sleepover at the Airport Holiday Inn. I can meet the Vikings when they check in and, if I ask politely and address each of them as "Mister," get their autographs, a prospect that Troy presents as no big deal but which thrills and terrifies me in equal measure.

Every night for two weeks, toothbrush in hand, I practice my pitch to the bathroom mirror: "Please, Mister Page, may I have your autograph?"

Time crawls, clocks tick backward, but after an eternity, Saturday comes. Mom—God bless her, for it must pain her beyond words—allows me to leave the house in my 88 jersey. It is literally in tatters, the kind of shirt worn by men in comic strips who have been marooned on a tiny desert island with one palm tree. Even I can see it looks hillbilly.

So I take my place in the lobby of the byzantine Holiday Inn, a low-slung maze that requires a map at check-in. BIC Cristal in one damp hand, spiral notebook in the other, I recite my mantra rapid-fire to myself, like Hail Marys on a rosary: *PleaseMisterPagemayIhaveyourautograph? PleaseMisterPagemayIhaveyourautograph? PleaseMisterPage…*

Moments before the Vikings' 8 p.m. arrival, Mr. Chaika cheerily reminds me to be polite and that the players will in turn oblige me.

"Except Page," he adds offhandedly, in the oblivious way of adults. "Don't ask him. He doesn't sign autographs."

Which is how I come to be blinking back tears when the

Vikings walk into the Holiday Inn, wearing Stetsons and suede pants and sideburns like shag-carpet samples. Their shirt collars are great wings that flap as they walk. These are truly terrifying men, none more so than Page, whose entrance—alone, an overnight bag slung over his shoulder—cleaves a group of bellhops and veteran teenage autograph hounds, who apparently know to give the man a wide berth.

The players retrieve room keys already laid on a table for them. Page picks up his and strides purposefully toward the stairwell. I choke as he breezes past, unable to speak, a small and insignificant speck whose cheeks, armpits, and tear ducts are suddenly bursting into flames.

It is to be an early lesson in life's manifold disappointments: two weeks of excruciating, Christmas-caliber anticipation dashed in as many seconds. Though I have now seen Page outside a television set for the first time in my life, I can't quite believe he's incarnate. So—my chicken chest heaving, and on the brink of hyperventilation—I continue to watch as he pauses at the stairs, turns and looks back at the lobby, evidently having forgotten something at the front desk.

But he hasn't forgotten anything. No. Alan Page walks directly toward me, takes the BIC from my trembling hand, and signs his name in one grand flourish in my Mead notebook. He smiles and puts his hand on top of my head, as if palming a grapefruit. Then he disappears into the stairwell, leaving me to stand there in the lobby, slack-jawed, forming a small puddle of admiration and flop sweat.

I am instantly aware that it will be impossible to improve upon this experience, no matter how long I live. But Troy Chaika and I try anyway: tucked away in our room at the Holiday Inn, with his father checking on us sporadically, I pass the rest of the night in a blissful blur of room-service milk-shakes and the kind of late-night television that is ordinarily off-limits to me.

Sometime in the night, I realize that the jersey Mom made me—the wash-faded, moth-eaten, hillbilly garment she let me leave the house in, against all her instincts and upbringing and better judgment—is what caught the eye of Mr. Page. Any other garment in this condition would have been thrown away—"pitched," as Mom puts it—long before it reached this state.

There is a radio between the beds and we leave it on all night, another illicit pleasure, and the songs on KDWB are incorporated into my dreams, so that in the morning I don't know if I really heard or just imagined Paul Simon singing, sometime in the middle of the night in the Airport Holiday Inn: "My momma loves me, she loves me. She gets down on her knees and hugs me..."

Summer has one last gasp. Evel Knievel tried to jump the Snake River Canyon on September 8 live on closed-circuit TV, shown to a paying audience in American movie theaters. We weren't allowed to go. A week later it is on *Wide World of Sports,* and we get to see it with our own eyes.

We already know that he didn't make it, but that hardly matters to us as Evel arrives at the launch site. It is six hundred feet above the Snake River Canyon, so he is delivered by helicopter, the way all big events in America are now going down: Watergate, Vietnam, *M*A*S*H.* They all begin or end with our hero getting out of or into a chopper.

Evel decamps to his trailer with his wife and three sons. Watching *Wide World of Sports* in a fever of anticipation, I think how terrifying and wonderful it would be to be one of Evel's sons. To have Dad on your lunch box. Just the theme music—"Spanning the globe, to bring you the constant variety of sports!"—makes my skin prickle with excitement.

Evel is carrying his customary walking stick. As every American child knows, he has broken every bone in his body. Whether this happened all at once or one by one, none of us can say. All at once, I think. Mike McCollow thinks one by one.

Even though the jump took place the Sunday after Labor Day, Evel wore white. White shoes, white helmet, white jumpsuit. Mom would not approve, though Mom isn't watching. Dad is, his eyes Kilroyed above the newspaper just enough for me to see them rolling. There's something about Knievel he isn't quite buying. Or everything—the starred-and-striped Elvis jumpsuit, the giant EK belt buckle, the Chuckles candy patch on his sleeve, the drama-queen sheriffs with their shotguns, the security in cowboy hats, the thirty thousand kids partying in the crowd, the solemnity of the announcers…Dad seems to think the whole thing is a joke. He regards the television as he did whenever Watergate news was on, with a suspicion of all things star-spangled and helicopter-borne, with a buyer-beware cocked eyebrow at anything labeled "Tricky" or "Evel."

"Here we are with the great man," says an English broadcaster, David Frost, who we'll see again in a couple of years, interviewing Nixon. "Are you afraid at this moment?"

"Yes," I say to the screen, for both of us.

"I think that a man was put on this earth to live," Evel says. "Not to exist." I nod along to this profundity.

While a crane lifts Evel into the cockpit of his steam-powered Skycycle X-2 rocket, he is left to dangle in the wind on a trapeze swing. A clock is superimposed on the screen, counting down the final minutes. *His* final minutes, perhaps. Dad snorts, but just getting into the Skycycle is a feat of derring-do. The launch angle is almost straight up. Even knowing it all happened a week ago, and that Evel is still alive, makes it no less tense.

By the time the clock is at five-four-three-two-one, I am ready to explode. Evel is shot like a bottle rocket into the sky, trailing pink smoke. Up and up he goes and then—even before he's cleared the launch pad—the whole phallic enterprise wilts with the premature release of its white parachute. "Oh, come *on!*" someone on the telecast says. The rocket begins its descent, never having reached the airspace above the river, and goes spiraling down, disappearing behind the rim of the Snake River Canyon. "Snake Oil Canyon" is all Dad says from behind his paper, whatever that's supposed to mean.

7.

Every Day's the Fourth of July

Tom turns ten on January 4, 1975, and when he opens his card at the breakfast table, two tickets fall into his lap for tonight's North Stars game against the Boston Bruins. Dad's taking him to Met Center to see Bobby Orr and Phil Esposito and the great Bs netminder Zheel Zheel-bair. All these faces Scotch-taped to our basement wall will come to life. Tom will be ushered into the foulmouthed, beer-swilling, urinal-using world of manhood. I'll stay home with Mom and watch *The Carol Burnett Show.*

For the whole of Saturday morning, I seek solace in the five-hour block of TV, but even the interstitial pleasures of *Schoolhouse Rock!* and *In the News* can't distract me from my envy, which is inflamed with every appearance of Peter Puck. The cartoon slab of eyeballed rubber promotes NBC's coverage of the NHL—and this weekend's Blues–Sabres *Game of the Week*—to North America's schoolchildren, for whom five hours of cartoon violence is a gateway drug to professional hockey.

It is otherwise the worst sports week of the year. Dad dozes all afternoon through the Hula Bowl. But this is the calm before the storm. In eight days, the Vikings will play the Steelers in Super Bowl IX. The Vikes are already the first team to lose two Super Bowls, and losing a third does not seem possible, even if the game is in New Orleans, where the Vikings hold no advantage. Last week in Bloomington, in Howard Cosell's Icebox of Met-ruh-pol-i-tan Stadium, the Vikes had beaten the Rams before the game even started. The Rams were dead meat the moment all those tanned and blond giants stepped off the plane from Los Angeles and saw their own breath escape their bodies like ghosts from a cartoon corpse.

The Vikings are proof that Minnesota is superior to Los Angeles in at least one very important way—as a football superpower—even as L.A. dominates every other aspect of American culture.

At eight o'clock tonight, after Tom and Dad have made the fifteen-minute drive across town to Met Center, the *Mary Tyler Moore* title sequence appears on CBS with Mary washing her car in her Fran Tarkenton jersey. But the show itself, I'm now old enough to realize, is really L.A. masquerading as Minneapolis. At eight thirty, *The Bob Newhart Show,* beyond the title sequence of Bob walking down Michigan Avenue, is L.A. pretending to be Chicago. Here are my two hometowns reflected back at me from soundstages in Los Angeles, their title sequences the only scenes ever shot on location. By the time Carol Burnett takes the stage at nine, however, Los Angeles has stopped pandering to me, stopped pretending to be someplace it isn't, someplace less glamorous and more Midwestern. It is now unapologetically itself. "From Television

City in Hollywood," cries an announcer, "it's *The Carol Burnett Show!*"

I imagine an actual city called Television City, where all our programming comes from. Television City is under constant siege by murderers, junkies, rapists, and madmen, which is why it is the most heavily policed municipality in the history of man, its streets kept clean by Joe Mannix and Theo Kojak; Frank Cannon and Jim Rockford; Barnaby Jones and Barney Miller and Tony Baretta; by Michael Stone and Steve Keller on *The Streets of San Francisco;* by San Diego private detective *Harry O* and LAPD partners Pete Malloy and Jim Reed of squad car *Adam-12;* by a whole *S.W.A.T.* team and *Emergency!* crew ...

With the exception of a few sitcoms and variety shows, prime-time television is devoted almost exclusively to private eyes and policemen and one policewoman—*Police Woman* Pepper Anderson—pursuing dirtbags down California freeways and South Central ghettos and through the beachfront homes of wealthy racketeers in an endlessly perilous and endlessly fascinating place called Television City.

"From Television City in Hollywood, it's *The Carol Burnett Show!*" I love the way the cartoon Carol Burnett pulls each letter of CBS like a window shade to reveal the title: C(arol) B(urnett) S(how).

Carol's "special guest" tonight is Vincent Price, star of a thousand terrifying features on *Mel's Matinee Movie,* and the old man who holds *The Brady Bunch* boys captive in a cave in Hawaii. I also know Price as a villainous voice in *Scooby-Doo,* which that *Brady Bunch* episode totally ripped off. (At the end, Price all but tells Greg and Peter and Bobby, "I'd have gotten away with it too if it weren't for you meddling kids!")

They do a sketch called "The Walnuts," a parody of *The Waltons,* the most boring show on TV, in which "John-Girl" writes in her journal about the "ecstasy of drudgery" and "memories of whittlin' and throwin' rocks" on Walnut Mound. Is that what Bloomington is, I wonder, as I trudge off to bed: a place where things—North Stars games, for instance—only happen to other people? John-Girl says, "Don't you get the idea that I'm a sissy just because I wear glasses and write."

I've begun to write—bubble captions coming out of the faces I draw, but also little stories about the games I watch on TV. I get Mom's Royal typewriter out of the hall closet, roll in a sheet of her onionskin typing paper, and tap out stories with the datelines in ALL CAPS. I have to strike hard with every keystroke, as if trying to ring the bell at the State Fair carnival midway. And indeed at the end of every line of type a bell does ring, and I throw the carriage return back with a flourish.

Is that what people think of writers? That they're sissies? No one thinks hockey players are sissies. They don't wear helmets, much less glasses. Their mustaches look like A-frame roofs over the broken-windowed houses of their hockey smiles. Their godlike qualities are enhanced by the white-columned Greek temple they play in—Met Center, whose signature seats, upholstered in alternating green, gold, and white leatherette, look beguiling on TV, which is practically the only place I see them. But tonight's game is being televised only in Boston.

The truth is, I've been inside Met Center for lesser events, like the circus, the Ice Capades, and one mind-blowing Saturday afternoon spent watching the Harlem Globetrotters perform astonishing feats. They do with a basketball what Evel Knievel does with a motorcycle—impossible things in star-spangled outfits on *Wide World of Sports*. Both have animated, action-figure, and lunch-box incarnations, not to mention names—Evel, Meadowlark—that sound almost made-up. But walking into Met Center to see the Globetrotters instead of the North Stars, and being hit in the face by the refrigerated air meant for hockey, was disorienting. It was like seeing men dressed as women on TV, Flip Wilson as Geraldine.

This is what I think about when I fall asleep next to Tom's empty bed, still made up beneath its blue bedspread. And when he enters the room very late at night, his feet falling silent on the shag carpet, I'm woken by the *smell* of him. Secondhand smoke and secondhand violence.

"You awake?" Tom says, putting on his pj's in the dark.

"Yeah, how was it?"

"Henry Boucha," Tom says, referring to the North Stars winger who is both a native Minnesotan and a real-life Ojibwa Indian, "got his *eye poked out*."

"What?"

"Henry Boucha," he repeats, "got his eye *poked out*. By Dave Forbes."

Lying there in the dark, looking at the ceiling, I see Boucha's eye falling to the ice. In my imagination, it falls like one of Dad's pimentoed olives into a glass of gin. "What are you *talking* about?" I say.

And for the next thirty minutes, like a traveler from a far-away land—like Sinbad the Sailor or Marco Polo, returning with tales of the unimaginable—Tom describes a horror unlike any conjured by Vincent Price or Television City.

What I learn from Tom, and the next day's papers, and the subscription to *Sports Illustrated* we get from Aunt Mary in Cincinnati, and the next summer's network news, and the *New York Times* that Dad will bring home from a business trip, and just about every other news organization whose dispatches reach me through the car's radio speaker or every conversation that floats up the stairs from a dinner party, is this:

Early in the first period, shortly after Tom and Dad settled into their leatherette seats of green and gold with a bucket of popcorn and two Cokes and a copy of *Goal* magazine to mark Tom's passage into manhood—his hockey bar mitzvah—Henry Boucha hit Dave Forbes with an overhand right that knocked the Bruins enforcer to his knees. Both men were given seven-minute penalties, during which time Forbes allegedly told Boucha he would "shove this hockey stick down [your] throat."

When both penalties expired, and with play stopped, Boucha skated to the North Stars bench. Forbes followed him and thrust his stick in a "bayonet or spearing type of motion" at Boucha's right eye, which began to spurt blood theatrically.

"The defendant's attack did not end at that point," in the words of Hennepin County attorney Gary Flakne, who will try Forbes on a charge of aggravated assault that summer. "Rather, as Henry Boucha clutched his eye—which he thought he had lost—and fell, stunned and bleeding to the ice, the defendant leaped on Mr. Boucha's back and began to strike Mr. Boucha's head and body with his fists. [Then] the defendant grabbed Mr. Boucha's hair and began to pound Mr. Boucha's face onto the ice as blood radiated from Mr. Boucha's head."

As every boy in South Brook knows, Boucha doesn't wear a helmet. He wears only a green terry-cloth headband to keep his onyx locks drawn back like theater drapes. He required twenty-five stitches and had a fracture of his right eye socket, but he had not—contrary to what Tom describes to me—lost his eye.

"Who won?" I ask.

"Bruins," he says. "Eight–nothing."

Eight–nothing? It's an unheard-of score in professional hockey. Tom unfurls his rolled-up copy of the game program, *Goal* magazine, revealing North Stars center Jude Drouin on the cover. His sideburns are nine inches long. His front teeth are absent as he glides, bereft of helmet, across the Met Center ice, his Christian Bros. stick poised to poke-check the puck from some unfortunate Philadelphia Flyer. Jim will wear 16 at Lincoln because Jude Drouin does. The cover will go on the basement wall to commemorate this night of nights.

Thirteen days from now a Hennepin County grand jury will indict Forbes on a charge of aggravated assault with a dangerous weapon. He'll be suspended ten games by the NHL, while Boucha will miss several weeks before returning with double vision, his promising career in serious jeopardy. Boucha will never be the same. And neither will Tom, it appears, as he lies there in the dark, past midnight, vibrating like a tuning fork.

Professional hockey is the intersection of cartoon violence and real violence. In the hours of analysis devoted nationwide to Tom's tenth birthday present, Peter Puck—the vulcanized, anthropomorphized mascot of NBC's network coverage—is seen as an accessory to aggravated assault. My Saturday morning entertainment is hitched to Tom's Saturday night entertainment.

"Peter Puck, the silly cartoon character NBC uses as a guide for new hockey fans, is an insidious commercial for the sort of hooliganism that may someday result in murder on ice," writes Gary Deeb in the *Chicago Tribune*. "Peter is the creation of Hanna-Barbera, an animation outfit with all the scruples of Attila the Hun. For years it was Hanna-Barbera that produced many of those ultraviolent cartoons that anesthetized youngsters on Saturday mornings and weekday afternoons.

"Their NHL hockey segments are in keeping with that tradition. More often than not, the between-periods cartoons feature grotesque giants belting each other over the heads with their sticks, while Peter watches and giggles in a 'boys-will-be-boys' manner.

"At no time does Peter tell viewers that clobbering somebody across the face with a stick is nearly as dangerous as whipping out a pistol and firing away from point-blank range. A youngster new to hockey can only deduce that such action is acceptable—and generally harmless.

"That a major TV network in 1975 can pump such idiocy into millions of American homes, without recognizing the subliminal danger of numbing viewers to the possible consequences, is astonishing. Deplorable too."

NBC will drop the NHL three months later. The sport won't return to network television for seventeen years. What Met Center hosted on January 4 was both a birthday and a funeral.

Met Center is Bloomington's id. South Brook may sometimes feel like Walnut Mound, where nothing ever happens, but the city has also zoned 130,000 square feet of its eastern edge as a place where everything happens. Two weeks after Tom's birthday—two Saturday nights later—Led Zeppelin opens its North American tour at Met Center in front of 18,600 pot-smoking, Schmidt-drinking, Satan-worshipping Minnesotans rocking red-tag Levi's, Nike Cortezes, untamed hair, and incipient mustaches. Jim has just turned fourteen and could be any kid on the news filing into Met Center while flashing peace signs or middle fingers at the local news crews. Except he's already bigger and looks more menacing. But he isn't there. He channels all his head-banging these days into hockey.

From a filthy paperback copy of *The Guinness Book of World Records* in the Nativity library, I know that Led Zeppelin is the world's loudest rock-and-roll band, or at least *was: The Guinness Book* at Nativity is perpetually three years out of date. But the 130 decibels the band produces, *Guinness* claims, are the equivalent of a DC-10 buzzing our house.

Led Zeppelin has chosen my hometown, in a building so close I can ride my bike to it, to play live for the first time in eighteen months. It's here that Zeppelin debuts a new song called "Kashmir," with its apocalyptic guitars leaking through arena walls and reverberating off Airport Bowl and the Ground Round and the Thunderbird Motel, still flogging its Indian theme in newspaper display ads:

BIG CHIEF THUNDERBIRD SAY SQUAW NO SQUAWK WHEN YOU TAKE HER TO THE **TOTEM POLE** FOR DINING AND DANCING. SO MAKE IT A DATE FOR BIG HEAP EVENING.

THE THUNDERBIRD MOTEL. NEXT TO MET STADIUM AND
SPORTS CENTER.

The rock critic for the *Minneapolis Tribune,* still in the
throes of tinnitus, writes that Zeppelin produced "the sound of
a dozen jackhammers digging at your cranium" at Met Center,
cementing our reputation as the foremost place in the Midwest
to induce head trauma.

It's here that the graduation ceremonies for all three
Bloomington high schools are held. We'll all be delivered
into the world from a Met Center stage, just like "Kashmir,"
though Tom has matriculated already inside this arena, aged
ten, while I sat at home with Mom, watching Carol Burnett
and wondering when life will begin.

Soon "Kashmir" is all over the radio, the school-bus driver
blasting it each morning from a single-speaker radio that
hangs from its handle on the little metal crank that opens and
closes the doors. I gaze out the frosted window as Robert
Plant wails, "They talk of days for which they sit and wait,
and all will be revealed." And so I sit and wait, wondering
very much the same.

It turns out that I sit at the center of the universe. On the
first Saturday night of 1975, Henry Boucha and Dave Forbes
necessitated a national referendum on violence here. On the
third Saturday night of 1975, Zeppelin debuted "Kashmir"
here. And on the Saturday night in between, on *The Mary
Tyler Moore Show,* the Vikings win Super Bowl IX. Lou Grant
bet two thousand dollars on the Steelers and is distraught
when they lose, but I am elated—incautiously optimistic.

"If the Pittsburgh Steelers win the actual Super Bowl to-morrow," Mary Tyler Moore says over the closing credits of the show, "we want to apologize to the Pittsburgh team and their fans for this purely fictional story. If, on the other hand, they lose, remember: you heard it here first."

Of course the Steelers will lose. In Television City, they already have. Mary knows it's the Vikings' turn, Lou knows it, Father Zheel-bair knows it but asks us to pray for the Vikings at 10:30 Mass anyway, just to be safe. Giving the world "Kashmir" *and* the Super Bowl champions on consecutive weekends will cement Bloomington's stature as the world's greatest city, I'm sure of it. Carthage, Constantinople, Babylon, Bloomington: bellwethers of a time and place.

The Rushins are seven of the fifty-six million Americans watching Super Bowl IX on NBC. I make a sign to hold in front of the Zenith. Long after I've stopped watching Miss Betty watching me on *Romper Room,* I still suspect that TV is an abyss that is also staring back into me.

I've recently discovered that "alliteration" is the word for the pleasing repetition familiar to me from a thousand broadcast phrases: "Thufferin' thuccotash" and "Peter Piper picked a peck of pickled peppers" and "Libby's, Libby's, Libby's on the label, label, label" and "Fruit Float, Fruit Float, Fruit Float."

And so I drew bubble letters last night on the graph paper that Dad rations me from his briefcase and—tongue peeking from the corner of my mouth—I colored each one purple, Magic-Markering the headline: PURPLE PEOPLE-EATERS STOMP STEELERS, VIKES VICTORIOUS!

While the final score of 16–6 is also alliterative, the Vikings aren't Victorious, Bloomington isn't Babylon, and at the end of the game—as I imagine Howard Cosell describing the action in our house—"Stevie stomps upstairs, stunned." The Vikings have now lost three Super Bowls in the 1970s, a streak that began six months after I arrived in Minnesota and unaccountably invested my hopes and dreams in these imperfect men.

Fortunately, material goods have yet to let me down the way my team has. Levi's cords are available at a store called The County Seat, whose jingle—"Just direct your feet to The County Seat"—I'm pointedly singing to Mom at the dinner table.

"No singing at the dinner table," Dad says. And so singing at the table joins running with scissors, jumping on the bed, and swimming immediately after eating on the long list of benign activities mysteriously prohibited by most parents.

Mom sighs. "Why should I buy you Levi's?"

"Because you bought them for Jim," Tom says. "And they're the best."

"Yeah," I say. "They're the best."

"How do you know they're 'the best'?" asks Dad, putting the last two words in air quotes without ever lifting his hands.

"They just *are*," Tom says.

"Yeah," I say. "They just *are*."

"You only care about the tag," Mom says. "If there wasn't a little white tag that said 'Levi's' on the back right pocket, you wouldn't know if your cords were from The County Seat or Sears."

"It's all marketing," says Dad, who has added marketing—

whatever that means—to his purview at Mickey Mining. "Ever heard of the three Ps of marketing?"

It's unlikely that any of us has, considering that we're five children ranging in age from three to fourteen, but we roll with it.

"I've heard of three peas in a pod," Tom says.

"It's two peas in a pod," I say.

"*You* pee in a pod," Tom replies before Mom snaps, "That's *enough.*"

But I know what Tom's saying. In the last six months I've taken to sleepwalking, urinating in unlikely places at three o'clock in the morning. I've whizzed in the laundry hamper in the hall closet, drawn back the shower curtain to pee in the tub, and emptied my bladder into the Schlitz-can wastebasket. Even in my sleep, it sounded like Mom filling the spaghetti pot with water from the kitchen sink.

More than once, Tom has woken to find me pausing during one of my nocturnal constitutionals, standing over him, business in hand, poised to wet *his* bed.

"Price," Jim says.

"Price," Dad repeats. "Correct. What are the other two Ps of marketing?"

Strictly for each other's ears, Tom and I whisper all the scatological P words we can think of, which is quite a lot of them.

"I'll give you the second P," Dad says. "It's product. So price, product, *and...*"

There is no sound but the hum of the fridge. Dad shakes his head in exasperation. *"Promotion!"* he says. "Price, product, and *promotion.*"

In Dad's view, his children are enamored of the third P, promotion, to the exclusion of the first two. As consumers, he says, we give no consideration to the quality of the product and certainly don't concern ourselves with the price. What is left—promotion—is The County Seat jingle and the tag that says 'Levi's' sewn into the back right pocket.

"You only care about the tag," Dad says. "Without the Levi's tag, you wouldn't wear the Levi's."

"*I* don't care about the tag," Jim says. "I couldn't care less about the tag. Levi's are the only cords that fit me."

"Me too," I say.

"You wish, squid," Jim replies.

Jim has taken to calling me and Tom "squid" as an insult. Squid is also a verb. It is not unusual to encounter Jim in the upstairs hall these days and have him ask the rhetorical question "Squid much?" We don't know what this means, but as we press our backs against the wall to let him pass we always answer "No."

After dinner, I excuse myself and retreat to Dad's workbench in the basement to shine his shoes. I pull the chain that bathes the bench in the light of a 60-watt bare bulb. Dad has shown me how he learned to shine shoes in the army. He gave me a shoeshine box with a wood-handled brush bristling with horsehair and a bottle—never used—of edge ink for the heels. There are two tins of polish: Kiwi black and Kiwi brown. There is no need for cordovan. Dad is never going to wear cordovan.

I open the tin of Kiwi black, take a deep drag of its contents, and place a chamois over the index and middle fingers of my right hand. On my left hand I wear one of Dad's wingtips like a hand puppet. I dip the chamois in the polish and cover the shoe with Kiwi black in a series of small circular motions. Then I buff it to a high shine. "I want to see my reflection in these," Dad says. When I'm finished he can shave in these shoes.

But he's upstairs for now, and I'm down here, all alone at the workbench, with all these tools for cutting and wrenching hanging on hooks embedded in pegboard. Running the length of the room is a clothesline Mom uses in the winter. Pinned to that line is a single pair of pants: Jim's navy-blue Levi's corduroys.

It is not literally a snip to remove a Levi's tag from its pocket, even using a pair of long-jawed, forged-steel cutting pliers. I have to step on the Levi's for leverage while pulling with the pliers with both hands. Even then, the white tag is a tooth that won't come out. It takes three solid minutes of yanking and twisting before the tag is pulled, trailing its roots of white thread. The Levi's are tagless, toothless as the portraits of Bobby Clarke and Jude Drouin looking down on me from the basement wall.

Dad will be proud, for I am road-testing the three Ps of marketing. If Jim really loves the product, he won't care about the promotion, the little white billboard on his butt. Emerging from the basement and into the kitchen, I place Dad's shoes on the linoleum and toss the Levi's tag on the table. Setting down her coffee, Mom regards the tag with horror. "What is *this*?" she says. It sits on the table like the severed finger of a kidnap victim.

"A Levi's tag," I say, beaming. "I ripped it out of Jim's cords. You know, to see if he'll still wear them."

"You did *what?*" Dad says.

"I ripped it out of his cords with your pliers," I say. "'Cause he said he doesn't care about the tag."

"What the hell is the matter with you?" Dad says, drawing the attention of my siblings in the next room. It occurs to me, looking at Jim fill the doorframe, that I have made a grievous error.

"I'll sew the tag back on," Mom tells Jim, but his mustache is twitching and his biceps are flexing and—to borrow a phrase I suddenly recall hearing on the radio—his hands are clenched in fists of rage.

Jim has entered a prehistoric phase of discourse, communicating in grunts and monosyllables. His caveman's club is a hockey stick. But when enraged, as he is now—contemplating life at Lincoln High School in tagless Levi's—he's given to colorful expressions of intent. He is frequently offering to "rearrange my face" or telling Tom he is "dead meat."

"I'm going to rip your lips off," he tells me, now with perfect elocution, and a facial tic I've never seen before.

I shoot up the stairs, racing him to my bedroom, where the locked door buys me ten extra seconds. While Jim finds a coat hanger to poke through the little hole in the knob, I scramble under my bed, listening for the lock to pop. And then he appears to me from carpet level as just a pair of Roms and tube socks. "Come out, squid" is all he says.

He pulls me out by my ankles. The rug burns my back. We both know the drill. He kneels on my biceps and begins to give me a 99 Bump. I'm keeping count in my head of every knuckle-blow to the sternum, but he isn't. It could end at forty-five, it could go to three hundred. A rope of drool extends from his mouth and briefly bungees above my face before breaking. I turn my head to take it on the cheek, as Jesus would.

Another summer is another funhouse, inviting me in then scaring my pants off. This is the summer of the African killer bees, making their relentless flight north, advancing at two hundred aerial miles a year from Brazil, to which a genetics professor named Warwick Kerr had imported them in 1956 before they managed to escape their confines.

This 1950s sci-fi plot—absentminded professor, cage door left ajar—is instantly recognizable from many of the titles on *Mel's Matinee Movie*. But the bees are real. And so I lie awake at night wondering if that distant buzz is the air conditioner kicking on or the ineluctable arrival of the bees, who in May were reported to have killed "dozens" and left "a trail of havoc and death" across South America. Seven U.S. senators led by Bob Dole have called for the United States to ally with Mexico, Canada, and the nations of Central America to take "joint defensive measures" against the killers. In the meantime, I run in fear from the spilled Sunkist, the dropped Popsicle, or anything else that might attract a bee bent on homicide.

Even Bush Lake beach is suddenly a place of foreboding. God knows what is hidden beneath its Coppertone-slicked surface, for this is the summer of killer sharks as well as killer bees, death from below *and* death from above, so the only safe place would seem to be my bedroom. Up here, Tom and I polish our pitch to Dad, begging him to take us to *Jaws*, despite the terrifying ads in the *Star* but also because of the terrifying ads in the *Star:* THE TERRIFYING MOTION PICTURE FROM THE TERRIFYING NO. 1 BESTSELLER.

"You'll be terrified," Dad tells us. "You'll have night-mares." But I'm having them anyway. A child does not rise in the night to tinkle in his closet because his dreams are reassuring. Mercifully, Dad will not be swayed. And so I have the best of both worlds—bravely asking to see a terrifying movie without actually having to see it.

That leaves one more menacing summer ritual to be endured and enjoyed at the same time: the Fourth of July.

The Fourth of July is frightening for all the reasons it's alluring. Staying out after dark playing with some kid's contraband arsenal of explosives—Polish cannons, cherry bombs, smoke bombs, sparklers, spinners, snappers, poppers, snakes, sky rockets, bottle rockets, firecrackers, and the A-bomb of driveway ordnance, the M-80. The M-80, according to South Brook lore, was developed for use by the U.S. Army and is equal to a quarter stick of dynamite.

To hear Mom tell it, the Fourth of July is a festival of carnage, a celebration of lost eyes, burnt eyebrows, dismembered fingers, and blown-out eardrums. She's right, of course. During the so-called fireworks season of 1975—June 23 to July 20—more than 4,500 people will be treated in America's emergency rooms for fireworks injuries. Half of all those injuries are to children under the age of fifteen. Three out of four injured are males, according to the U.S. Consumer Product Safety Commission, and the females—I am left to conclude—are little sisters who had a smoke bomb rolled under their bedroom door. According to the National Fire Protection Association, six people will be killed and eighty-five seriously injured celebrating our nation's 199th birthday, and by serious injury they mean blindness, loss of an eye, or "traumatic amputation." Isn't that the only kind?

Tom is one of the neighborhood kids who has managed to procure explosives on the Fourth. He has a long string of ladyfinger firecrackers flung over his shoulder like a bandolier. He doesn't say where he got them, and I don't ask. I'm torn between telling on him and earning his respect. But telling on him would make me a narc *and* a chicken, so I follow him out of the house with a book of matches from Mom's supply above the range.

Mom and Dad are on the screened porch with Mr. and Mrs. Leon. They live in Saint Paul. Mr. Leon looks like Walter Matthau from *Earthquake* and played minor-league baseball in the Phillies farm system. He works with Dad at Mickey Mining. Mrs. Leon went to school with Mom in Cincinnati, and they retained their love for each other in addition to all those other Cincinnati products. On the patio, smoke is issuing from the Weber—and also from Mrs. Leon, who looks elegant and sophisticated with a cigarette in her hand, like a model in a *Sports Illustrated* Virginia Slims ad.

I follow Tom to the top of the sledding hill, to the crest of the hill for which Hillcrest school is named. We are protected by woods on three sides. I give Tom the box of matches. The gold cover says CAMELOT—ADVENTURE IN DINING. Also KEEP OUT OF REACH OF CHILDREN.

Tom lights a firecracker and lets it sizzle in his hand for a second before tossing it into the woods behind him. He hands me one. I light the fuse and let it burn down in my hand for a single second before flicking it aside like a spent cigarette.

Tom throws one at my feet and I jump away. We rifle them into the air and watch them go off against the chalky clouds. We lob them down the sledding hill like grenades, just as the Creek Freak's three sons—the Dunleavy boys—ride by on their bikes. They live in the neighborhood on the other side of Hillcrest Elementary but are heading toward South Brook. They speed away from the popping dirt as if they're being shot at by snipers.

When the string of ladyfingers is spent, we go home, straight to the upstairs bathroom, to wash the sulfurous smell off our fingertips, which have somehow remained intact. They smell like the lyrics to "Killer Queen"—of gunpowder, gelatine, dynamite, and laser beams. Mom and Dad and the Leons are still on the screened porch, untroubled by the distant report of firecrackers, unaware that we ever even left. I'm on the bed still fizzing with adrenaline when Tom looks out the window and says, "Oh no."

His face has gone pale, ghostly white save for the freckles, which look like pepper on a paper plate.

"The Creek Freak," Tom says. "He's walking up the driveway." By the time I peer through a gap in the blinds, the Creek Freak's on our doorstep, his ten-speed parked in our driveway.

The doorbell rings: *bing-bong.* Tom shuts our door. It rings again, angry and impatient: *bing-bong-bing-bong-bing-bong.*

We listen through the bedroom door. We hear the slap of the screen door that leads from the porch into the house. We hear Mom's feet in the front hall, her pleasantly puzzled greeting at the door: "Hel*lo.*"

Separated from the conversation by a full floor (and an inch of bedroom door laminated in simulated wood grain), I can't make out everything being said. The Creek Freak sounds a bit like Charlie Brown's teacher. But it's clear he's accused Tom and me of throwing firecrackers at his boys and he demands to know what Mom and Dad intend to do about it.

I realize Mom doesn't want to be rude to the Creek Freak, whom she gamely addresses as Mr. Dunleavy, less out of respect, I'm certain, than an inability to recall his first name, but she is even less inclined to be rude to her dear friends, the Leons, her houseguests on the screened porch. While she's standing in the doorway, evidently wondering what to do, Dad comes into the house with some lowball glasses that need replenishing, calling after her.

Coming into the kitchen, Dad must see the Creek Freak filling our front doorframe. The Freak's a big guy, six feet five and well muscled from his morning constitutionals along Nine Mile Creek and his forays into the woods to do God knows what. "Ever eat a pine tree?" an old geezer named Euell Gibbons asks in a Grape-Nuts cereal commercial that Johnny Carson always makes fun of. "Many parts are edible." Dad has long suspected that the Creek Freak eats pine trees.

Tom and I have cracked open the bedroom door to hear what's going on. The Creek Freak's voice is loud, insistent that the Rushin boys were throwing explosives at his sons. Dad vows to get to the bottom of this and punish us accordingly, if the charges prove true, but something in his voice is skeptical. We hear the front door close. We peer through a gap in the blinds. Dad and the Creek Freak have moved into the front yard. The window is open. We can hear their voices. Dad is again reassuring the Freak that he'll make a full investigation and punish us appropriately, provided that the allegations—given a full hearing—prove true. Tom and I are both excreting house bricks, but we can't look away.

The Creek Freak wants more. Dad is explaining that he has company in the backyard—it is the Fourth of July, after all—and that he will discipline his own children on his own time.

Then it happens. The Creek Freak throws a roundhouse punch with his right fist. It catches Dad flush on the mouth.

Something—a crown, it turns out—flies out of Dad's mouth and into the newly mown grass. In our bedroom, behind the blinds, Tom and I turn to stone on the spot. In the yard, after the punch, there is the smallest pause, during which the world can be heard, on its rusty rails, slowly stopping its rotations.

Donald Edward Rushin, who was raised in Fort Wayne, Indiana, by his grandparents, by the priests and nuns of Saint Patrick's Catholic grade school, and by his single mother (if there is a Father Rushin, we have never known him); who fist-fought and joyrode and boxed his way through high school, and returned every night to the trailer he shared with his mother, employed at Walgreens; whose football coach arranged for him a summer job at a steel mill in Gary to keep him out of growing trouble with the police, telling him, "You're the first person ever sent to a steel mill to cool down"; who starred on the Fort Wayne Central Catholic High School football team, which went undefeated and were named the Indiana state champions; who left a note for his mother in his senior year at Central Catholic to say he was off to spring football practice with Purdue, where the Boilermakers had offered him a scholarship, beating Notre Dame to the punch;

who was kicked out of the Purdue residence halls and had to eat all his meals off campus after beating up a guy who threw a snowball at him from a dorm window; who once told me, "I was never a bully, but I could take care of myself with those who were bullies"; who walked out of Purdue football practice one day and never returned; whose idea of something to do on a Saturday night after transferring to Tennessee's football program was "to get in fights in bars"; who on the final play of his career incited a benches-clearing brawl in the Vols game at Vanderbilt after pile-driving a Commodore kick returner who had just signaled for a fair catch; who then hitchhiked to Cincinnati from Knoxville to be with his girlfriend, Jane Boyle, from a family so Sunday-paper perfect that they were photographed, gathered around the Thanksgiving table, for a Sunday spread in the *Cincinnati Enquirer;* who married Jane Boyle, vowed to provide for her and any future children and to drive a Cadillac one day; who *never*—to my knowledge—threw another punch again, and instead channeled his furious energies into the selling of magnetic tape for Mickey Mining and the raising of five rambunctious children, none of whom would ever have to sleep on a couch in a trailer or relieve himself in a communal outbuilding as he had done...

...this was the man who had just been sucker punched in his own front yard on the Fourth of July by a pinecone-eating pansy who had questioned his skills as a father. And it seemed to awaken in Dad a series of memories, none of them good. Some of these, it is now clear, are muscle memories.

The ensuing whirlwind reaped by the Creek Freak has the quality of an actual tornado. Dad's flying fists knock him to the ground and seem to sweep up a funnel cloud of debris and picket fences and Holstein cows. When the cloud passes, there is only silence and human wreckage. Dad walks into our house. The Creek Freak crawls toward his glasses, places them cockeyed across his nose, and endeavors to stand. When this proves impossible, he crawls to the curb and sits there. After a very long time, from somewhere across Nine Mile Creek, his wife comes looking for him. She helps him to his feet and then walks his bike out of South Brook, over the horizon, home.

Upstairs, buttocks defensively clenched against the spanking of our lives, we wait for Dad's footfalls on the stairs. There is a faint clacking sound, which I assume are from my own teeth, chattering like those novelty windup chattering teeth they sell at Spencer's Gifts at the Southdale mall. But the footfalls never come, and the clacking turns out to be a clinking of ice cubes in lowball glasses. Dad has returned to the kitchen to twist more cubes from the ice tray, to finish making libations for the Leons.

When Tom and I are summoned to eat the burgers and dogs Dad has grilled, he doesn't say anything to us. Nor does he say anything that night, after the Leons have left, and the fireworks have exploded in the distance above Southdale.

Later, lying in bed, I hear the reassuring theme to *The Tonight Show*. Ed McMahon says, "Heeeere's Johnny!" And Johnny himself opens the monologue with "Good evening. I'm gonna bring you a safe and sane Fourth tonight." There is tentative laughter from the studio audience. "Because the monologue," Johnny says, "is a dud."

Dad laughs. Carson introduces a joke about the New York

sanitation department promising to collect the garbage next year, on the bicentennial, and every two hundred years thereafter. "This is the one day out of the year," Johnny says, "that people set aside their differences and join in a calm celebration."

I fall asleep to Dad's laughter and Johnny's familiar voice making ironic references to a calm Independence Day, both men reassuring me that I'm safe beneath my Sears blanket. I sleep soundly and peacefully, even while rising in the night to tinkle, like a fountain cherub, into the laundry hamper in the hall.

Two weeks later, after two weeks of lurid testimony and a national debate about the propriety of charging athletes as criminals for violence perpetrated in the course of a professional hockey game, *The State of Minnesota v. David S. Forbes* ends with a hung jury. It will not be retried.

On an equatorial evening at the end of August, Mom is hosting her bridge club on the screened porch, which is Dad's cue to evacuate the premises. He informs Tom and me that we're going back-to-school shopping for new underwear at Korner Plaza, but just before we get there, he abruptly pulls into the parking lot of the Boulevard Theater, which has four blood-red letters on its marquee: JAWS.

It was released two months earlier, sold twenty-five million tickets in its first thirty-eight days, and has prevented me—on the basis of the poster alone—from swimming in Bush Lake.

"There are no sharks in Bush Lake, honey," Mom insisted. But I wasn't willing to take her word for it. Nor did I have any interest in seeing *Jaws,* despite my pleading to the contrary. I would *almost* rather be shopping for underwear. What is Dad thinking, acceding to our wishes—expressed on a weekly basis since the film opened on June 20—to take us to see *Jaws?* It is entirely unsuitable. In the opinion of the critic for the *Los Angeles Times,* "The PG rating is grievously wrong and misleading...*Jaws* is too gruesome for children and likely to turn the stomach of the impressionable at any age."

This becomes clear in the opening seconds—naked woman, drunken boyfriend, death by shark—but as the film's sphincter-clenching music and popcorn-spilling surprises pile up, a strange calm washes over me. I am surviving *Jaws* and even enjoying it, already composing in my head what I'll tell my friends when I return to Nativity next week.

"Did you see *Jaws?*"

"Yeah, I saw *Jaws.* It wasn't that scary."

It's the scariest thing I've ever seen, even scarier than *The Poseidon Adventure,* but seated next to Dad, sipping on a Coke, hearing him horselaugh at the scariest parts, I think of the advice I heard on TV that summer, in one of the many stories that aired about what to do in case of a real-life shark attack. "Punch it in the nose," the reporter said. And this I know Dad will do for me.

After the movie, eating ice cream at Bridgeman's when we should be in bed, I ask Dad if we're still getting underwear.

He smiles and says, "Some other time."

8.

Through the Magic Doorgate

It's nineteen feet long, weighs five thousand pounds, and gets twelve miles to the gallon, enough to get us from gas station to gas station in comfort if not style, in a giant rectangle made for squares. The Ford LTD Country Squire station wagon is to South Brook parents what the Schwinn Sting-Ray is to their children: not just a mode of conveyance but a symbol of arrival, a suburban icon of American engineering. And there is one sitting in our driveway right now, its wood-grain side panels, trimmed in true blue, blistering in the sun. The empty luggage rack is inviting us to drive to some distant vacation paradise.

The wood panels on the Country Squire are made of vinyl just as our house is covered in mint-green aluminum siding made to look like painted wood. Our basement is paneled in fiberboard printed with a wood-grain design. Every door in our house is made of a similar substrate with a wood-grain pattern of whorls and knots baked onto its surface. If my bifold closet doors weren't hollow, I'd think they were hewn from a single slab of stained oak. Our steak knives have plastic handles made to look like rutted logs, tiny versions of the flume ride's fiberglass logs at Valleyfair. We live in a place where real wood is cheap and abundant but not nearly as prized as its aluminum or vinyl analogue. And the Ford Country Squire is the high point of this simulated wood-grain aesthetic.

The car smells like its upholstery—acres of DuraWeave vinyl that radiates the intense heat of summer and the gasp-inducing cold of winter. On every August ride home from Bush Lake—the back of every thigh sizzling like the flame-broiled patty of a Whopper—I think that my thermos must be made of DuraWeave vinyl, so successful is this wonder material at retaining the ambient miseries of a Minnesota season. When I look up "Minnesota" in *The Encyclopedia Americana* at the library, I see "The winters are often severe; the summers are marked by sudden intense heat waves." It's my first inkling that the rest of the world isn't necessarily like this.

Travel confirms it. Facing backward in the way back of the wagon, I see where we've been, not where we're going. The Country Squire has dual facing rear seats, separated by a foot of carpeting, so that two or four children marooned back there on its bench seats appear to be seated at the world's smallest restaurant booth, from which the table has been removed. There is a power window in the tailgate door, which swings out instead of folding down—Ford's Magic Doorgate—offering not one but two easy ways (window, gate) to accidentally tumble onto the interstate at seventy-five miles an hour. The thought preoccupies me on long drives. Falling out the back of the Country Squire would be like falling off the lido deck of an oceangoing cruise liner, so distant is the driver and so swift is our progress. No one would hear me scream. I would simply recede from view in the asphalt wake of the LTD Country Squire.

I ask Dad what the LTD stands for.

"Limited," he says. "As in limited warranty."

"What does that mean?"

Dad sighs. He doesn't love the Country Squire as much as I do. "It just means they'll only make so many."

"How many?" I ask.

"As many as they can sell."

Into this car he will load our matching Samsonite suitcases, each one slightly larger than the next, a series of Russian nesting dolls rendered as lime-green luggage. Packing the Country Squire for vacation is a puzzle to be solved, a three-dimensional Escher drawing, and as Dad stands before the Magic Doorgate, surveying the way back of the wagon with a chin-scratching intensity, I think of the opening words of *The Twilight Zone* reruns that freak me out on weekend nights: "You unlock this door with the key of imagination. Beyond it is another dimension—a dimension of sound, a dimension of sight, a dimension of mind. You're moving into a land of both shadow and substance…"

Somehow he makes it all fit, with just enough room for me or John or Amy—sometimes all three of us—to slot into the gaps as human packing peanuts. The man is a master of packing, a ninja of folding. He can fold a dress shirt as fast and fastidiously as a Marine triangle-folding the U.S. flag. Perhaps his semiannual two-week trips to Tokyo, for which he only ever packs a small valise, have given him a taste for origami. By the time he's finished folding and packing, every trouser crease is sharp enough to shave on. With each new nose blow, he folds his handkerchief in such a way that it somehow launders itself, like Mom's self-cleaning oven.

All of which is to say that Dad can fold a shirt and pack a suitcase, and pack that suitcase into the way back of a Ford LTD Country Squire, like no man before him. Watching him prepare for a trip, I imagine this is what it must be like to see Brooks Robinson oiling his glove or Clapton tuning his guitar: the undisputed master of his craft preparing to do what he was born to do. In Dad's case, this is travel.

Through the Magic Doorgate, I have seen Houston, Texas, on a visit to Uncle Pat and Aunt Sandy's. I toured NASA and the Astrodome—"The Eighth Wonder of the World." I rode a horse, which stopped to make a prodigious BM while I sat in the saddle. (It is the last time I will ever ride a horse or watch *Mister Ed* without gagging.) I have been to Disney World in Orlando and to Tarpon Springs, Florida, where Dad held the smaller of us over an alligator pit for laughs and I cut my chin climbing into our station wagon, scarring me for life. The chin scar matches the scar I got on my forehead when I ran into a low pipe while playing tag in the Devitts' basement. Between my chin and my forehead and my fake teeth, I have had a very short time to be factory new, a scant few years with my original parts. In that way I am not unlike the Country Squire, which Dad says—when pumping its sleepy brakes or watching steam rise from its hood on the litter-strewn shoulder of some interstate—is the worst car he's ever owned. He swears he will never again buy a Ford. To pass the time on long drives, he begins composing alternative acronyms for LTD—"Less Than Dependent," for instance, or, when it's especially temperamental, "Lower Than Dogshit." These new abbreviations pair nicely with his favorite reverse-engineered acronym for Ford: "Fix Or Replace Daily."

Every other summer we drive to Chicago to visit old neighbors and then on to Cincinnati to visit our aunt and uncle and cousins and Grandma Boyle, occasionally stopping in Wisconsin Dells to top up our supply of rubber tomahawks and eat breakfast in the kind of roadside diners whose fork tines are webbed with congealed egg yolk.

And these summer vacations all start the same way. We leave home before dawn, under cover of darkness. I half expect Dad to silently push the car down the driveway in neutral, in the manner of Baron von Trapp fleeing the Nazis, so stealthy is our 4 a.m. escape and so strong his insistence on "making good time."

One way to make good time is to ignore every billboard that advertises a tantalizing attraction only thirty-seven miles off the interstate. Every wondrous cavern and canyon, every glorious glade and garden, will go forever unexplored by the Rushin family. The terrible puns I hear every day on the school bus—"Hey, Rushin, why aren't you *rushin'* somewhere?"— are answered unequivocally on our drive. We *are* rushin' somewhere, so that our only diverting roadside attractions are the billboards advertising roadside attractions, rather than the roadside attractions themselves. Their appearance every forty miles or so gives us five seconds of respite from the excruciating tedium, which is otherwise relieved by playing bruising games of Slug Bug, waiting for my bladder to pop like a water balloon, and staring glumly out the window at other children, in other cars, staring glumly out their windows at me.

The Country Squire, like the butterscotch rocket, is equipped with only an AM radio. The driver sells audiotape for a living but refuses to have a tape deck in his car, so we can't even listen to the boredom-set-to-music that is Mom's kitchen cassette collection—albums by John Denver and Anne Murray and Cat Stevens. Instead we get whichever station comes in clearest: country music, Dow Jones industrial averages, pork belly futures, and CBS News bulletins introduced by the urgent chattering of typewriter keys that turns every one of their stories—"Women admitted to Air Force Academy!" "Tension among white farmers in Rhodesia!" "Evonne Goolagong wins her Wimbledon quarterfinal!"—into a declaration of war.

We only stop for gas and at rest areas, piling out of the clown car of the Country Squire and sprinting for the picnic tables to eat the sandwiches Mom has lovingly prepared the night before departure. We are so hungry we barely bother to remove the Saran Wrap before sluicing them down with Shasta cola, which is how we know we're on vacation.

It isn't the only way we know, of course, because everything is different out the window. Illinois is exotic. We feel the gravitational pull of Chicago as we hit the rumble strips that signal a tollbooth ahead. Tossing a quarter into the collection basket is a novelty. So is the Lake Forest Oasis, where we drive *under* a Howard Johnson's restaurant and Amoco station suspended over the rushing traffic on the Northwest Toll Road. If the Astrodome is the Eighth Wonder of the World, surely this is the Ninth.

Wrigley Field is a shocking expanse of green in the city. Michigan Avenue is familiar from the opening credits of *The Bob Newhart Show*. The *Sun-Times* and *Tribune* buildings excite me and me alone. And standing beneath the three-year-old Sears Tower, staring up at its immensity while wearing vertically striped pants from Sears, I feel a sense of ownership. This is The House That Mom Built.

Simply to be in the same zip code as the Spiegel catalogue—Chicago, Illinois, 60609—is a thrill. And as we pull into The Meadows subdivision of Lisle, to spend the night in sleeping bags at our former neighbors', the Kmieciaks, and play with our former playmates, the Weber kids— there are ten of them—I envy these cosmopolitan children, growing up by the buzz and fizz of the East-West Tollway, with its rumble strips and Oases, and that great skyline rising in the distance like the Emerald City of Oz.

Cincinnati is another foreign land with its own brand of everything (Hudepohl beer, King Kwik convenience stores, Mom's beloved Graeter's ice cream) and a bewildering tapestry of indigenous customs (putting chili on spaghetti, calling ketchup "catsup," diving into third base rather than sliding feetfirst). So this is what it's like for Dad to travel overseas. Cincinnati and Chicago are my Rome and my Rio, distant lands with enviable natives whose lives crackle with an energy and glamour unimaginable in South Brook. The roller coaster at Kings Island in Cincinnati is called the Racer and it's actually *two* roller coasters on parallel tracks that race each other. The Racer cost a million dollars to build. I first saw it on *The Brady Bunch*, when Mr. Brady's boss, Mr. Phillips, invited the architect to take the whole family on a business trip to Cincinnati, where he delivered some blueprints to the Kings Island board.

Mom grew up in a trim white house on Julmar Drive with a neat lawn and a bedroom window above the garage that her brother—my uncle Pat—could sneak in and out of after hours. A few doors down is Mom's grade school and next to it the church that she and Dad were married in at age twenty-two. Both school and church are named for Saint Antoninus, who was—to judge strictly by the surroundings—the patron saint of shade trees and birdsong.

When we passed Fort Wayne on our drive from Chicago to Cincinnati we didn't stop or even slow down. There was not so much as a drive-by of Dad's old stomping grounds. But rolling down Julmar Drive in the Country Squire, it's easy to see how Dad might have promised Mom something as safe and sylvan as this, someplace called The Meadows or South Brook, a Blooming-this or Rolling-that. On this street he vowed he would—to borrow from *The Brady Bunch* theme song—somehow form a family.

While here, we stay at my aunt Ann's house, but the Bradys—in that episode called "Cincinnati Kids"—stayed at the Yogi Bear–themed Kings Island Inn, where a Ford Country Squire trimmed in blue pulled up to its motor court in the opening scene, leading me to believe that the Bradys and the Rushins travel in the same style. (This time, at least. When the Bradys went to Hawaii, they flew on a United 747.) It confers a Southern California cool on the way back of our LTD as we pull into the parking lot at Kings Island, a place curiously devoid of a possessive apostrophe but otherwise containing everything else I could want.

Our cousins can ride the Racer whenever they please and sit in the same carriage as Bobby Brady. The Cincinnati Reds are the world-renowned Big Red Machine, defending World Series champions, playing in the modern Astroturfed citadel of Riverfront Stadium. Johnny Bench is on *The Tonight Show.* Pete Rose pitches Aqua Velva. The souvenir Slushie cups at King Kwik bear the baseball-headed likeness of the team's mustachioed mascot, Mr. Redlegs. If there is a place on earth with greater cultural cachet right now than Cincinnati, Ohio, I cannot imagine it, at least not while I'm at Kings Island, spinning on a mechanical and many-tentacled octopus called the Monster.

But of course there's a place. On the eleven-hour drive home from Cincinnati to Bloomington, stopping only to tinkle and get gas and eat sandwiches at some pigeon-shat picnic table on the interstate, while squeezing the wheel to the strains of "Are we there yet?" and "Tom's on my side of the seat!" and "Can we *please* stop at McDonald's?!" after Mom announces she's fresh out of Tootsie Pops to plug into our mouths to shut us up, with the Country Squire making ominous knocking noises and steam beginning to seethe from its hood, and nothing but the bleak expanse of central Wisconsin to occupy our minds for the next several hours, Dad turns off the radio in the middle of Lou Rawls singing "You'll Never Find Another Love Like Mine" for the fourteenth time today. There is only silence and the smell of boiling DuraWeave.

"Next summer," Dad says, "we're going to California."

There's an explosion inside the car (of joy) and outside the car (of the carburetor, perhaps). When the buzz fades, he says, "And we're flying there." More cheers. I can see his eyes in the rearview mirror, gauging our reactions. He has spent part of the drive composing a new acronym for LTD: "Let's Take Delta."

In the way back of the Country Squire, I imagine the trip. Mom will buy us Adidas and Levi's. She'll not bring hillbillies to Beverly Hills. We'll walk the Boyle Heights streets of *Chico and the Man*. Sit under the zigzagging roof of the left-field pavilion at Dodger Stadium, familiar from so many Saturday afternoons watching NBC's *Game of the Week* or *This Week in Baseball*. California. The cutest girls in the world. Swimming pools and movie stars. Like Led Zeppelin, we're Going to California and we'll fly there on a 747: "Took my chances on a big jet plane. Never let 'em tell you that they're all the same."

In the yearlong buildup to the trip, Mom encourages me to read about our developing itinerary. The rest of The Boys have library cards but have allowed them to expire, like transplanted organs that failed to take. If anyone is going to bore his siblings with arcane facts as we tour San Francisco, I am the last hope. At the Penn Lake Library, bike shackled to the rack outside, I deplete the children's section of every book on the Great San Francisco Earthquake of 1906; Walt Disney and the making of Disneyland; the San Simeon castle of William Randolph Hearst (whose daughter Patty has replaced Nixon as the national story without end that grown-ups talk about at parties); the devout and miraculous cliff swallows that fly back to the mission at San Juan Capistrano every March 19 on Saint Joseph's Day from their winter home in Argentina; and the world-famous San Diego Zoo, whose Joan Embery brings animals onto *The Tonight Show* and where I might actually see—in person, through the bars of a cage—the marmoset that once urinated on Johnny Carson's head.

But really, all I can think of on my bike rides home from the library are earthquakes. The Great Quake of '06 lasted less than a minute, but the fires that followed burned for three days, killing three thousand people and reducing five hundred blocks of San Francisco to smoldering rubble, in which half the city's population roamed without shelter, foraging for food among looters and violent mobs. What if something similar happens at the Holiday Inn Fisherman's Wharf?

And Southern California will offer even less comfort. The San Andreas Fault—as the encyclopedia informs me on my next visit to the library—trumps the Bermuda Triangle and killer bees in my nightly inventory of natural terrors. California is bracing for the Big One and it may well coincide with our trip. A prominent geophysicist has predicted that another big quake will happen in the next year. Some Californians are hoarding water and contemplating the purchase of motorcycle helmets to wear at home. Dr. Steven Howard, "director of a child guidance clinic" in the San Fernando Valley, says that these imprecise predictions of a coming catastrophe are especially damaging to children, whose greater imaginations result in vivid fantasies of apocalypse. Only five years ago the Sylmar earthquake in the San Fernando Valley killed two dozen people while "shaking most of Southern California like an angry parent shakes a screaming child," as I hear one TV newsman put it, combining the two most frightening forces I can conjure: natural and parental fury.

"In pictures children drew after the '71 earthquake," Dr.

Howard says, "they had giant fists coming up from the earth and huge monsters shaking the sides of their homes."

On the Fourth of July, we park the Country Squire in the Alligator lot at Southdale and celebrate the bicentennial as fireworks explode over Dayton's department store. This was the first fully enclosed, climate-controlled shopping mall in America, built to serve our burgeoning population, and so vast is its parking lot that we can only remember where we park by identifying the animal on the sign that towers above every section: Alligator lot, Giraffe lot, Tiger lot. More than one Lincoln student has promised his prom date he would take her to Bloomington's fine-dining restaurant, Camelot, only to drive her to the Camel lot at Southdale.

The fireworks pop. Cheers and mosquitoes. Beer and the radio. "My Love Is Alive" leaking from various car windows. The fireworks remind me of the ones bursting above Cinderella's castle in the opening of *The Wonderful World of Disney*. Everything makes me think of California, and in turn, of earthquakes.

On summer days in South Brook, when the sky suddenly turns green and the tornado siren at Dwan Golf Course sounds and WCCO radio urges its listeners—all the mothers in Minnesota—to hurry to the southwest corners of their basements, I draw similar pictures in my head, terror fantasies fueled by *The Wizard of Oz*, until the tornado warning expires and Mom's head stroking, whispered small talk, and tremulous humming of lullabies is no longer necessary and we emerge from our hole in the ground like rescued miners.

But I know nature will win in the end. The best I can hope for is an occasional fluke triumph—a bloop double, a seeing-eye single. With this in mind, a bunch of fathers and sons in South Brook hack down a corner of the swamp across from our house. (It's surprising how many dads keep machetes in the garage.) Then we mow the stubble that remains until the marsh has a fan-shaped bald patch onto which we can lay a baseball diamond.

Base paths are dug up with gardening implements and overlaid with sandbox sand. A pitcher's mound is made from the sod that was dug up to make the base paths, which are covered with potting soil. Foul lines are chalked out; bases are anchored in. Mr. Raich has a sign in his garage that says MINNOWS, and he nails it to a stake that he pounds into the ground and Minnows Field is born. The sign is quickly stolen and our ballpark is renamed Bicentennial Field, but a few boys with a Toro push mower cannot compete with nature's fury, and in a matter of weeks it has reclaimed our little diamond, letting me know who's boss.

It's an unnecessary reminder. I still play BAA hockey outdoors in the winter, stuck in a snowbank between shifts, wishing I were in the warming house. My favorite part of skiing at Hyland Hills is sitting in the chalet, by the fire, eating a Hostess apple pie. I want to quit hockey this winter and try basketball but am afraid of what Dad will think. Mike McCollow plays basketball inside, in a heated gymnasium, in shorts. I've inherited my father's love of the Great Indoors but none of his toughness. His disdain for nature manifested itself in a fistfight with the Creek Freak. Mine finds an outlet in the summertime cool of the basement, away from the burrs and wasps and things that slither beneath the mower as I cut the grass.

Not that it isn't scary down there too. Jim has a new stereo in the basement—a turntable and tape deck and two tall speakers paneled in a wood laminate like the rest of our possessions. The first album he ever owns, bought at the tail end of 1976, is the Eagles' *Hotel California,* which he plays on repeat. The Hotel California itself scares the wits out of me, with its satanic guests stabbing beasts with their steely knives and its unreasonably inflexible checkout policy. This is what every hotel in California must look like, a mission-style building with a Spanish-tile roof and palm trees swaying in a permanent twilight.

That's the front of the album. On the back of the album, in the empty lobby of the Hotel California, is the hallmark of any Rushin vacation—a thrumming pop machine lit from within, its coin slot eager for my quarters. And it's this push-pull of horror and fascination, of Beelzebub and Bubble Up, of earthquake and Disneyland, that is our looming trip to California.

Listening to the Eagles at night—the lighted bars of the graphic equalizer rising and falling like an EKG, their alien green glow the only illumination in the basement—pop music becomes a game of chicken, a hand held just above the flame. "Seasons in the Sun" ("Good-bye my friend, it's hard to die..."). "Dream Weaver" ("I've just closed my eyes again..."). "Nights in White Satin" ("Cold-hearted orb that rules the night..."). "Alone Again (Naturally)" ("I remember I cried when my father died..."). "Lonely Boy" ("Well, he ran down the hall and he cried. Oh, how could his parents have lied?"). I lay awake at night, thinking of that ghostly girl in Nebraska, with the hoot owl outside her window, calling after the undead pony she called Wildfire.

Above the basement couch are two shelves mounted on brackets. They support the Rushin family home library. Most of its volumes were acquired during a brief but torrid membership in the Book of the Month Club, supplemented by fat paperbacks from the spinning racks of international airports. Mom is partial to eight-hundred-pagers with one-word titles like *Shogun* or *Burr* or *Centennial* or *Roots.* The books, like the music, are magnetizing in their horror. But I'm powerless to stop opening these doors. On page twenty-eight of *The Godfather,* Sonny Corleone and a bridesmaid named Lucy are a mystifying blur of "upper thighs" and "turgid flesh," of "savage thrusts" preceding a "shattering climax." The passage holds me rapt, which is not to suggest that I understand a word of it. For all the apparent penetration going on, the passage remains impenetrable to me.

If Mom and Dad had read any of these books they wouldn't have left them in the basement. Or maybe they left *The Godfather* here in lieu of giving me The Talk. Jim and Tom and I will never get The Talk, left instead to squint at scrambled images of sex scenes on the premium cable channels to which we don't subscribe. (Only John will be pulled into our parents' bedroom one night, fifteen years from now, to find Dad poking a finger in his chest. "Remember," Dad will say in a talk inspired by army training films and the *Scared Straight!* prison documentaries, "a hard *dick* is a head without a mind." After these ten words—the entirety of The Talk—John will be bundled back into the upstairs hallway, left to compose himself in the unwavering gaze of Christ above the credenza.)

And so most everything I know about the birds and the bees will be gleaned from books, magazines, and music, principally Rod Stewart's "Tonight's the Night" and Johnnie Taylor's "Disco Lady": "Move it in, move it out, shove it in, 'round about, disco lady."

Our home library is only forty or so books, but the terrain and hidden treasures of each become as familiar to me as the backyards of South Brook. I can skim a whole history of the United States in just a few volumes. *Miracle at Philadelphia* is about the Constitutional Convention of 1787. *The Confessions of Nat Turner* is about a bloody slave revolt in 1831. *The Death of a President* recounts every harrowing detail of the assassination of President Kennedy in 1963. The newest book on the top shelf is *All the President's Men,* about the enduring mystery that is Watergate. When I open it up, newspaper articles clipped from the *Star* rain down on me. Each has a date inked on it in Dad's handwriting. He knew I'd open this book. The clippings are his way of explaining Watergate.

Mom and Dad know that Jim and Tom aren't about to read any of these books for pleasure, and that Amy and John are too young to be interested in these grown-up hardcovers. Mom probably assumes my plate is full with the ten Children's Classics on the shelf in my bedroom. Bound in fake-leather covers, their spines beautifully imprinted in black and silver, these were a birthday present to The Reader in the Family, a role I embraced when I discovered that reading can excuse me from going out of doors. And so I work my way through them: *Twenty Thousand Leagues Under the Sea, Robinson Crusoe, The Adventures of Tom Sawyer,* but also *Little Women, The Secret Garden,* and Mom's childhood copy of her favorite book, *Jane Eyre.* There are more books about girls than there are about boys. And while I won't admit it under penalty of torture, the girls are often braver and stronger and cooler than the boys. Pippi Longstocking lives with a clothed monkey and a horse on the porch at the Villa Villekulla, where she goes to bed whenever she wants in the absence of her dead parents. Harriet the Spy lives on East 87th Street in New York City and takes the subway to a place called Far Rockaway. Jo March wants to fight in the Civil War.

The only boys I read about are Frank and Joc Hardy of crime-infested Bayport, where everyone seems to have been lobotomized. "It sure was swell of Dad to let us have them," Joe says of the motorcycles on which he and Frank chase hardened criminals. They never face danger on an empty stomach. Before Frank and Joe visit a dilapidated water tower, where they're imprisoned by a man named Hobo Johnny, Mother packs them a picnic hamper filled with roast beef sandwiches and deviled eggs. All the moms in the Hardy Boys books are greeted as "Mother," not "Mom." But it's pretty Laura Hardy who makes the best picnic baskets. "That sure would be swell," friend Chet tells her when she offers to make him one. "You make grand picnic lunches, Mrs. Hardy."

No one uses food as a weapon quite like Mrs. Hardy. Mother tells the boys to wait a minute before they go visit their friend Slim Robinson: "I'm going to bake a ham and a cake for you." In addition to Slim, the Hardy boys have friends named Chet and Biff—"the gang"—who greet each other not with Hertz Donuts or Pit Vipers, as we do in South Brook, but with ancient salutations from some distant decade that I don't recognize and that may never even have existed: "Hi, chums!" they say, or "Hi, fellows!"

There is no way for me to know that the first three Hardy

Boys mysteries—the only three on my bookshelf—were written in the 1920s not by Franklin W. Dixon, as the covers claim, but a Canadian newspaperman named Leslie McFarlane, who was paid as little as eighty-five dollars for his fevered manuscripts. Nor can I possibly know that the editions I'm reading were revised in 1959 to remove racial stereotypes. And yet, even in my revised editions, characters say things like "No workee, no eatee," while preparing dinner. An Italian immigrant named Rocco runs a fruit stand in Bayport. "You very kind boys," he tells Frank and Joe. "You better salesman than Rocco." And that's just the very first volume, *The Tower Treasure,* a book that so offends me I've read it three times.

And anyway, these characters are consonant with the other cultural stereotypes on TV. My worldview is informed by the prototypical Frenchman Pepé Le Pew, Latin archetypes Speedy Gonzales and the Frito Bandito, the Chinese characters Ah Chew on *Sanford and Son* and Hanna-Barbera's Hong Kong Phooey. Whenever Tom and I are kung fu fighting, we first bow to each other and say, "Ah-so, Fatso," before delivering every blow with a "Hi-yah!" On *The Muppet Show,* it is Miss Piggy's catchphrase.

When a British colleague from Mickey Mining visits our house for cocktails one evening, Dad instructs me to greet him with "Cheerio, ol' chap!" I'm surprised that he isn't wearing a bowler and carrying an umbrella, like Mr. Banks in *Mary Poppins* or Winston Churchill or any other Englishman I have ever seen on TV.

But what am *I?* I'm not Scandinavian like so many Minnesotans, who tell Sven and Ole jokes about dumb Swedes: "Did you hear Sven died while ice fishing? He was run over by the Zamboni."

I'm not Polish, like the "Polacks" in the "Polack" jokes that everyone else tells. "You've got to hate someone, I guess," the syndicated columnist Andrew Greeley writes in 1976. "And you can't hate the Jews or blacks or Latinos or Indians or women. Who's left? Why the Poles, of course." A study of working-class Polish Americans in Detroit this year reveals Polack jokes have left them with low self-esteem and a zeal to make their children's lives better. "Poles are far from the only ethnic group to serve as the butt of jokes," reports the *Chicago Tribune*. "They just happen to be at the top of the list right now."

The United States Supreme Court has just denied an appeal by the Polish American Congress and a Chicago man who wanted to reply—under the fairness doctrine's principle of equal time—to a TV-show skit that disparaged the Polish. In February, on *The Dean Martin Celebrity Roast,* Don Rickles tells Jimmy Stewart that the war is still on and he's needed at the front. Then the comedian looks at Nipsey Russell and says, "The black guy just went 'I didn't know the war was still on.' And the Polish kid went 'I did.'" The audience at the MGM Grand in Las Vegas roars. I'm not Polish, so I do too.

I'm not Russian either, thank God, though other kids ask me in a hostile tone: "Hey, Rushin, are you *Russian?* Are you a *Commie?*" I always assure my accuser that whatever a Commie is—and neither of us has the slightest idea—I am not one.

Johnny Carson is interviewing Frank Sinatra on *The Tonight Show* in 1976 when Don Rickles suddenly walks onto the set. "I am a Jew and you're an Italian," he tells Frank. Looking at Johnny, he says, "And you are a...What?"

Is that what I am? Am I a What? Dad didn't know his father, so he doesn't know where the name Rushin comes from. But Mom is a Boyle, her father comes from a long line of James John Boyles out of Cork, and that makes me Irish, or more Irish than anything else. Irish like my friends Mike McCollow and Danny Collins and Dan Mullen and Tim Flynn and Frankie X. Connolly and half the rest of my class at Nativity. Irish like the Lucky Charms leprechaun and the lady on the Irish Spring soap commercial, who says, "Manly, yes, but I like it too!" Irish like Patrick Pig in *Richard Scarry's Busy, Busy World,* my favorite book as a preschooler, featuring "33 Exciting Adventures" in "Many Exotic Countries," a book whose protagonists include Sven Svenson of Sweden, Hunky Dori and Suki Yahki of Tokyo, and Farmer Polka and Farmer Dotta of Poland.

Now I'm reading about the Hardy Boys and another child detective in another crime-infested hamlet, Encyclopedia Brown of Idaville. But the Hardy Boys can't do anything that Nancy Drew doesn't already do, and Encyclopedia Brown's friend Sally is the one who stands up to the bully Bugs Meany. Amy would do that—stand up to a bully. She isn't afraid of the copious bleeding in our house, doesn't blink at broken teeth and boy-on-boy violence.

"Amy's going to be our doctor," Dad says when she watches our boxing matches with forensic curiosity. She can defend herself, mix it up with us. "Manly, yes, but I like it too."

Mom watches the same thing Dad does and wonders if I might want to become a priest. Or a lawyer. "You like to read," she says. "And lawyers get to read a lot."

Mostly I read about California throughout fifth grade, through the school year of 1976–77, while staring at Sister Mariella's nut cup, at Ned Zupke's soiled rubbers, and counting the days until I can "get on board a westbound 747."

If 1977 is going to be the Year of California, I still have to get through 1976, the Year of Everything Else. It's the Bicentennial Year, an Election Year, an Olympic Year, and "The Year of the Cat," according to a song on the radio by Al Stewart, whose other hit will be called "Song on the Radio." But even in the Year of the Cat, my mind is on the Year of California.

On the Wednesday evening of September 22, 1976, ten years to the night after I entered the world to the *Star Trek* episode "Where No Man Has Gone Before," the ABC television network debuts another new show, this one called *Charlie's Angels,* about "three little girls" who graduated from the Los Angeles Police Academy but were "taken away" from their menial duties and hired, as private eyes, by an anonymous millionaire named Charles Townsend. Television has given me a tenth birthday present. Charlie first appears to America lying on his stomach, while a young woman in a bikini massages his pelvic muscles, which he has somehow overexerted. "I think it will be just a matter of some deft manipulation," he tells his Angels over a Western Electric speakerphone, "before I'm standing as erect as ever."

Charlie exists almost exclusively as a disembodied voice speaking in double entendres that I don't understand. He assigns the Angels their first case, to investigate the death of a woman driver at a dirt-track car race. Angel Jill Monroe infiltrates the infield, posing as a traveling evangelist.

"And what denomination are you, little lady?" a leering grease monkey asks her.

"Thirty-five, twenty-four, thirty-five," Jill purrs.

At school, in science class, I've seen time-lapse film of seeds growing into fully bloomed flowers, ninety days of nature compressed into thirty torrid seconds. *Charlie's Angels* acts as a similar accelerant for puberty, several years passing in the forty-four minutes of the fourth episode, called "Angels in Chains," in which the ladies go undercover in a women's prison in Louisiana. In the basement, as Mom and Dad chat obliviously upstairs, Tom and Jim and I watch in slack-jawed disbelief as a leering warden named Maxine says, "Okay, girls, strip down to your birthday suits."

Our silence is an unspoken agreement never to speak of what we are witnessing, which is Jill Monroe being strip-searched, showered, and deloused.

"Are there dressing rooms?" Jill asks.

"Whaddya think this is, Saks Fifth Avenue?" barks the warden. "Now drop the towels and get to it!"

By November, *Charlie's Angels* has forty million viewers a week. It is known to every boy in every grade at Nativity, re-hashing the previous night's plotlines during Thursday morning recess, as "Chuck's Chicks." Tom acquires a poster for our room of the actress who plays Jill Monroe, Farrah Fawcett-Majors, only the third female face to grace our walls (after the Virgin Mary and Miss Piggy, from the "Pigs in Space" poster I've taped to our door). Twelve million other kids have bought the Farrah poster for their bedrooms, nearly all of them—like Tom—spending their allowance at Spencer's Gifts, purveyors of Farrah posters, Playboy lighters, patchouli oils, pet rocks, lava lamps, black lights, greeting cards featuring morbidly obese women in bikinis, mesh-backed caps with a coil of plastic turd on the top, and—in the "Adult" section at the back of the store—personal vibrating massagers that women, to judge by the packaging, use to rub on their cheeks.

Farrah Fawcett is married to Lee Majors, the Six Million Dollar Man, and this to me is the essence of California, a place where the Bionic Man and one of Charlie's Angels are conjoined in connubial bliss. Every other husband and wife in the state seem to have their own network variety show: Sonny and Cher, Captain and Tennille, Shields and Yarnell, Marilyn McCoo and Billy Davis Jr. If Tony Orlando and Dawn aren't married, if Donny and Marie aren't husband and wife, you could have fooled me.

My California dreams are kindled by a hundred library books on the gold rush of 1849 and a prime-time lineup set almost entirely in California, an idyll of poolsides and palm trees, patrolled in the Striped Tomato by the Bay City detective duo of Starsky and Hutch, whose paid informant, Huggy Bear, is a human jukebox. Keep feeding him money and he sings. *Three's Company* debuts in the spring, set by the beach in Santa Monica. Mr. Bradford on *Eight Is Enough* is a newspaper columnist for the *Sacramento Register,* which I recognize as a fictitious paper because the real paper there is the *Bee.* I think maybe I'd like to be a newspaper columnist instead of a lawyer. I watch Twins games on the little TV in the basement, write summaries of them on Mom's typewriter, and imagine filing them to the *Minneapolis Star* or *Sports Illustrated.* I spend much of the long winter of 1976–77 in that basement, hunched over that typewriter, composing newspaper-style stories on various subjects—including vivid accounts of our epic basement matches in what I have come to call the National Indoor Ping-Pong League, or NIPPL.

In the spring of 1977, two months before our departure, Space Mountain opens at Disneyland. *Star Wars* has also come out this month, and seeing it at Southtown—knowing I'll soon be living a similar space-based adventure for the two minutes and thirty seconds' duration of Space Mountain in Tomorrowland—is almost too much to bear. I'm now allowed to ride my bike to Southtown, and that bike is a sparkling-green hand-me-down Schwinn Varsity ten-speed with ram's-horn handlebars wrapped in black grip tape. At ten years old, on a ten-speed, riding home from a PG movie, I am practically a grown-up. When I see *Rocky* at Southtown, I ride home in record time, drop my Varsity in the driveway, and begin boxing the arborvitae outside our garage, "Gonna Fly Now" playing in my head all the while.

In late June, just before we leave for California, Bloomington reasserts its position at the center of the cosmos, a status I feared had disappeared forever in January, when the Vikings (incredibly but inevitably) lost their fourth Super Bowl, this time to the Raiders. ("Look," Dad said at the start of the game, pointing out the Raiders center, who had OTTO on his back, above the number 00. "He's a palindrome." It was as good as the day would get.)

In becoming the first team to lose four Super Bowls, the Vikings don't even win a booby prize as Johnny Carson's first choice for an NFL laughingstock, an honor he has bestowed in his monologue jokes on the terrible Tampa Bay

Buccaneers. And yet here we are, less than six months later, with Bloomington preparing for its most intense and prolonged national close-up yet. On the searing Sunday afternoon of June 26, 1977, Jim drives me and Mike McCollow to the Met. Mike and I have tickets to sit in the left-field bleachers there while Jim punches in for work as the sixteen-year-old manager of the center-field commissary, where his staff of teenage flunkies prepares the food that the vendors working the bleachers will sell. When I turn thirteen, I can become one of these flunkies too.

The Met, usually three-quarters empty, is sold-out. The Twins are tied for first place with today's opponent, the White Sox, and 46,463 fans have come out to see our own Rod Carew in his summerlong attempt to hit .400, which no one has done since the immortal Ted Williams did it thirty-six years ago. Seventy games into the season, Carew is still hitting .396. The first fifteen thousand fans aged fourteen and under are handed a cotton Carew jersey on the way in. Mike and I immediately pull our new shirts over our heads and settle onto the wooden benches with an empty gallon jug. We bring it to Jim beneath the bleachers at regular intervals. He fills it, alternately, with the two pops the Met carries: Sunkist and Coke. The stadium is fizzing, and so are we.

Beneath a boiling sun, the White Sox lead 1–0 after half an inning, the Twins lead 8–1 after two innings, the White Sox draw to within 8–7 after two and a half innings, the Twins extend their lead to 12–7 after three innings, and the game goes back and forth like this, seemingly forever, until the vendors announce that the entire Met has run out of soda. Mike and I nudge our gallon jug of Sunkist under our seats, hoarding it like we're survivors of an Andes plane crash. Over the next three hours and thirteen minutes, fifteen thousand children in Rod Carew jerseys tremble with excitement and the depleted stocks of stadium soda every time our hero comes to the plate. He hits a home run that shakes the stadium. He doubles and receives another cataclysmic ovation. When the day is finally over and the shadows encroach on the grass and the hot dog wrappers blow like tumbleweeds across the warning track below us, Carew has gone four for five with six RBIs. (His teammate, right fielder Glenn Adams, has set a team record with eight RBIs.) The Twins 19–12 victory gives them sole possession of first place in the American League West, and the scoreboard flashes Carew's new batting average at day's end: .403. As the stadium trembles with the ovation, I wonder if this is what California will feel like during the Big One.

Within days, he will be on the covers of both *Time* and *Sports Illustrated,* smiling up from every waiting room, library, and end table in America: Rodney Cline Carew, named for the doctor who delivered him on a train in Panama. That is exactly the kind of storybook adventure I am waiting for in California. THIRTY-THREE EXCITING ADVENTURES! in MANY EXOTIC LOCATIONS! At long last the day has arrived.

Gonna Fly Now.

9.

Ventura Highway in the Sunshine

Two by two we board the great beast, animals onto the Ark: Amy and John in new Keds, Tom and I in Adidas Gazelles—he chose red, so I chose blue—and Mom in lockstep with Dad, who shoos us forward, his five kids' tickets fanned out in one hand like a straight flush. Jim is a brooding hulk bringing up the rear, resplendent in white Tigers. When I step from the Jetway into the jumbo—past the spiral staircase leading to the lounge, in pants Mom pressed for this occasion, on a 747 bound for San Francisco—all my worlds are coming together.

With a great scream, the leviathan is airborne. At cruising altitude, the engines and I sigh with relief. This spring, while taking off in Tenerife, a 747 crashed into another 747 parked on a runway, killing 582 people on the two planes, the deadliest accident in aviation history. It's not until we're over the Continental Divide, when we hit turbulence, that I have to say a silent "Hail Mary" and sing in my head the happy song (complete with backing vocals) that becalms me in the basement during tornado warnings.

> *C and H (C and H!)*
> *Pure cane sugar (Pure cane sugar!)*
> *From Hawaii (From Hawaii!)*
> *Growing in the sun (Growing in the sun!)*
> *When you cook, when you bake*
> *For goodness sake*
> *Use C and H (Pure cane sugar!)*
> *C and H (From Hawaii!)*
> *C and H (Pure cane sugar!)*
> *That's the one.*

San Francisco is only five months removed from its strongest earthquake in twenty-one years, but my fear of calamity recedes as the 747 sharks in over its famous bay and its minor bridges. The ground flanking the runway at SFO is dun colored. It reminds me of Luke Skywalker's Tatooine. I might as well be on a distant planet, arriving by rocket ship, touching down in California on a 747.

The animals leave the Ark. Tigers and Gazelles and Pumas, two by two, disembarking...into a Golden State. Led Zeppelin is playing in my head. The song has issued from the radio of our school-bus driver a hundred times now, the soundtrack to as many frigid mornings. "Going to California": *Took my chances on a big jet plane. Never let 'em tell you that they're all—all the same.*

Dad retrieves our rental car, a station wagon with gorgeous California plates, gold numbers and letters on a vivid blue background. The bench seat in the way back of this wagon faces backward, at the drivers behind us, making it easy to look for famous motorists on the northbound 101. Minutes after we leave the Hertz lot, Candlestick Park suddenly appears on our right, and I can scarcely believe that I am walking distance from the various Giants on my baseball cards—Bill "Mad Dog" Madlock, John "The Count" Montefusco, and relief pitcher Randy Moffitt, whose big sister (according to the back of every one of his cards) is Billie Jean King.

"That's where Willie Mays played," Dad says.

"Actually, he played at the Polo Grounds in New York for the first five years of his career," I say. "Then the Giants moved here in 1958. He played fourteen seasons in San Francisco, but his last two were back in New York, with the Mets at Shea..." Jim has opened his suitcase, pulled out a T-shirt, and is now gagging me with it.

"Shut up, squid," he says.

And so it goes all over San Francisco. I point out the famous Fisherman's Wharf sign with an orange crab on it that features in the title sequence of *The Streets of San Francisco*. Tom and Jim roll their eyes.

"That restaurant over there, Tarantino's, is also in the opening credits," I say. Tom gives me a flat tire, stepping on the heel of my new Gazelles, but my year of reading about California will not go to waste. I am powerless to stop my factual exhibitionism.

"That's Alcatraz," I say. "The Rock. They sent Al Capone there. And 'Machine Gun' Kelly. But not John Dillinger."

Tom laughs. He told me once that John Dillinger could wrap his dink around his leg two times and still have enough dink left over to tie in a bow. I said I didn't believe him, but he said it was true; he heard it from his friend Steve Raich.

"Can we walk across the Golden Gate Bridge?" Tom asks Dad.

"The Golden Gate Bridge is one point seven miles long," I say. "It's made from the same cable used in the Brooklyn Bridge, which features in the opening credits of *Welcome Back, Kotter.*"

"Make him stop," Tom says.

Dad takes over for me. "Scoma's," he says, pointing to another restaurant whose sign is in *The Streets of San Francisco* credits, "has the best abalone in the world."

"Better than Oscar Mayer?" Tom asks skeptically.

"Not baloney," Dad says. "*Abalone.* It's a mollusk."

I sing, "My abalone has a first name, it's S-C-O-M-A . . ."

"And over there," Dad says, "at the Buena Vista Café, they do the best Irish coffee in the world."

He must know that his children don't want a dinner of mollusks, washed down with coffee and Irish whiskey and heavy cream, but this too is a kind of exhibitionism, designed to remind us that he knows things, has been places, has favorite bars and restaurants in cities around the world. Oftentimes this knowledge will flatter Bloomington. "I've traveled everywhere," he likes to say, "and Bloomington has the best tap water in the world." And he's right. Bloomington's tap water—from kitchen sink, from backyard hose, from burbling hallway fountain at Nativity—is renowned.

Other times, Bloomington suffers from Dad's worldliness. In a couple of years, when Bloomington gets a Tony Roma's rib restaurant, Dad will mortify all his children by asking our waitress there, "Have you ever eaten at the Tony Roma's in Shinjuku?" In reply, she will stare blankly into the middle distance. "The Tony Roma's in Shinjuku?" Dad will say again, as if trying to jog her memory. "In central Tokyo?" Our waitress, a sophomore at Jefferson High, will confess that she has not yet been to central Tokyo or even outer Tokyo or anywhere else farther afield than Grand Forks, North Dakota.

Nor have I. Cincinnati is the eastern frontier of my world. I have never been farther north than north Minneapolis nor farther west than Rapid City, South Dakota. Until now. San Francisco is unlike anything I have ever seen—not the hills and cable cars, which books and TV had prepared me for, but the exotic objects that pass for everyday life out here. At the curb in front of our hotel, the Holiday Inn at Fisherman's Wharf, I pick up an empty sixteen-ounce Coke can. I've seen sixteen-ounce beer cans on Snake Hill—"silos" of Schlitz Malt Liquor—but never pop. I ask Mom if I can bring it home and give it to my friend Tom McCarthy for his pop can collection and she instantly assents. At home, Mom will seize and discard a not-yet-empty pop can before I can set it down, lest it leave a condensation ring on the counter. At the Holiday Inn, however, she happily stuffs a piece of San Francisco street litter into her Samsonite suitcase because she is a different person on vacation, free of care. And so am I, never once rising in the night to tinkle into the wastebasket or onto the rotary shoe buffer in our room.

The hotel is a short walk to Lombard Street, with its eight switchback turns in a single block that descends vertiginously from Hyde to Jones Street.

As we gaze down its serpentine descent, Dad says, "This is it—the crookedest street in the world." He sweeps his hands like a *Price Is Right* hostess showcasing a new car.

"Most crooked?" I say.

"That's what I just said," Dad says.

"You said crookedest," I tell him. "'Crookedest' isn't a word. It's *most crooked*."

Jim announces his intention to violate me with the crookedest stick he can find, but Dad is holding my gaze and nodding in a way that says he is impressed. At home, whenever I stumble on a word in the newspaper and ask Dad what it means, he always says "Look it up" while hooking a thumb at the red American Heritage dictionary he keeps next to his Archie Bunker chair.

"What is 'tendentious'?" I'll say.

"Tendentious," he'll repeat, nodding sagely. "Look it up. If I tell you, you won't remember. But if you look it up, it will stick in your brain. This is a good vocabulary lesson."

So I look it up and shut the dictionary with a satisfying *clap* and go back to the story in the *Star,* only to have Dad clear his throat. "Well," he says. "What did it say?"

"Oh," I say. "You know. 'Favoring a particular point of view' or 'Trying to provoke a reaction.'"

But he doesn't know. Only after I've looked up a hundred or more words at his insistence does it occur to me that *I'm* giving *him* the vocabulary lesson.

"You didn't know the definition until just now," I say. "Did you?"

He is hidden behind the business section of the *Star,* but his laughter through the paper is a kind of confession. He sticks his head out from behind the wall of newsprint and says, "*Now who's being tendentious?*"

Dad first came to San Francisco in 1939, when he was five years old, put on a train in Fort Wayne, Indiana, with his aunt Juanita to meet his biological father, with whom he would live for a month in a two-story walk-up at 532 40th Avenue, in the windswept and fog-shrouded Outer Richmond district, at the outer edge of the city, at the far reaches of the known world.

Dad's father was a carnival pitchman, liquor distributor, and nightclub fixture named Jack Rushin, who spent the summer of 1939 working the Midway at the Golden Gate International Exposition—a world's fair nicknamed "The Magic City"—on San Francisco's Treasure Island. Dad's mom, our seldom-seen Grandma Miranne, would remarry several times, including twice to a man named Ted Dixon, whom she also twice divorced.

To well-traveled adults, the Golden Gate Exposition was a wonder, a fairy-lit confection whose man-made glow was visible at night from a hundred miles away. To a five-year-old fresh off a train from Fort Wayne, Indiana, this Magic City on Treasure Island was a waking dream.

The Midway of this electrified dreamscape was called "The Gayway," and to the passing throngs in the summer of 1939, Jack Rushin hawked a jumble sale of dodgy products. In the official directory of exhibitors, he was listed as a purveyor of "lavender and rose beans, orange blossoms and lavender, plastic and wood names, Rushin linens, Rushin gadgets, Rushin leather goods, Stromberg condensers, kitchen utensils," and "cookie cutters." Dad remembers him flogging paper flowers soaked with cheap perfume, which he billed as "Perpetual Roses" guaranteed to "never lose their scent." Jack Rushin also stood by the pay phones and made not-quite change for a dollar, accommodating anyone who needed to break a bill by giving them eighty-five cents in change. A man who sells fly-by-night products is naturally used to flying by night, and so Jack Rushin had lived in Brooklyn (where he and my grandmother shared an apartment on Flatbush Avenue) and Detroit and other points unknown before alighting in San Francisco.

Jack apparently wore the most beautiful silk shirts on The Gayway, and bought his five-year-old son a cowboy suit before sending him home on a slow train to Fort Wayne.

These are almost all of Dad's firsthand memories of his father. He later learned that Jack Rushin managed a nightclub on Kearny Street called The Top Hat, married a waitress at The Sea Horse named Mildred, and in 1946 opened his own bar at 609 Market Street called Jack's. When the great neon sign he ordered came back misspelled, Jack couldn't bear the expense of changing it, so he called his new joint "Fack's."

Fack's (and its later incarnation, Fack's II) became a famous nightclub in the 1950s, showcasing everyone from Frank Sinatra to Louis Armstrong to Lenny Bruce, but by then Jack Rushin no longer owned the place. By the mid-1950s, he had vanished from San Francisco, or at least from the historical record.

None of which explains how Dad became what he is now—a husband, a Dad, a necktied, gig-lined, seven-to-six soldier in the service of Mickey Mining, diligently doing his own taxes on a card table in the basement every April 14, wanting to send every penny he owes to Uncle Sam, though not a penny more, because it's important to make *exact* change for a dollar. Maybe this is why he despises vending machines that rob a man of his hard-won nickels.

While I copy Dad—abhorring nature, mocking bozos, howling at Carnac—Dad has had no one to copy. He has played it all by ear. In a few weeks, when we've returned to Bloomington from California, Elvis Presley will die on the toilet at Graceland. Dad will express mild disbelief at the magnitude of the world's mourning. Every Elvis hit that plays over TV and radio in tribute to the King is new to him. "I completely missed Elvis and the Beatles," he'll say, as he has always said. But even *I* know Elvis and the Beatles. When I ask Dad how it was possible to grow into adulthood in the 1950s and early 1960s without hearing or even overhearing the most popular musicians of the day, he'll say, "I didn't have *time* to listen to Elvis or the Beatles." What he won't say, because it will go without saying, is "And that's why you have the time you do."

Every roadside restaurant south of San Francisco is more exotic than the last. When Amy throws up her lunch from the Happy Chef in the way back of the wood-paneled wonder wagon, on its stately progress down Highway 1, Dad forever after calls that hamburger chain the "Happy Barf." He pulls over to the shoulder and cleans up the mess with a pair of paisley boxers fished from his suitcase. Then he throws his vomit-covered underpants into the rolling blue of the ocean that gave this road its name.

But the Pacific Coast Highway, in my mind, is Ventura Highway in the sunshine, 'cause the free wind's blowing through my hair—literally, all six passenger heads are stuck out an open window like dogs to avoid the baking barf smell inside the wagon. It's in this posture that we roll up— exhausted and exhilarated—to a Best Western at Big Sur. After hours of serpentine driving in a wood-paneled sick bay, the kids fall out of the car like five marionettes, our limbs returning to life joint by joint, until suddenly we're all fully functional and sprinting to our adjoining hotel rooms, where I step through a door to see John standing in a geyser shooting from a burst pipe in the bathroom.

"Dad!" I yell. "Hurry! It's John! There's an emergency!"

The movie *Earthquake* was chockablock with bursting pipes and breached levees and busted dams, combining my fear of drowning (earned while enduring *The Poseidon Adventure*) with my fear of falling masonry (cultivated by the illustrations in a dozen library books on the Great San Francisco Earthquake of '06). Had I missed the first tremor that severed the pipe in the bathroom and sent a water cannon straight up to the ceiling, where it returned to the bathroom floor in the form of rain? I can't tell if my knees are shaking independently or in unison with the ground. If this is the Big One—"Cal-i-for-nia, tumbles into the sea," as I heard Steely Dan sing on one of Jim's albums—then why isn't Dad coming?

"Dad!"

Dad is schlepping two suitcases in from the car when he hears me, drops the bags, and comes running down the hall.

"What in the *hell?*" he shouts, steaming into the bathroom like a sea captain into a squall. "God *dammit.* We haven't been here for *one minute* and you've *destroyed* the place. What the *hell* is the matter with you...?"

"Is it an earthquake?" I ask him.

The geyser has stopped, and Dad and John stand dripping on the bathroom floor, clothes sodden.

"It's not an earthquake," Dad says. "It's a bidet."

"What's a bidet?"

But Dad is in no mood to explain. He waits two hours, until after dinner, to tell us what a bidet is, and what French people do with it, and how they're common in European hotels and homes. I sit there agog, marveling at the infinite variety of human beings and silently thanking God that Mom never let Dad move us to Belgium, where kids have to sit bare bottomed on a fire hose.

"John thought it was a drinking fountain!" Tom says.

"Shtop it, shtupid!" John cries. He slurs his *s*'s. He'll see a speech therapist for this. But until then, we call as much attention as we can to it, asking him all summer to say the name of the thoroughbred racehorse aspiring to the Triple Crown. And John will dutifully shout, "Sheattle Shlew in sheventy-sheven," showering us with spit.

Tom is telling on him now. "John was trying to drink out of the..." The new French word eludes him, and Tom finally says, "John was trying to drink out of the butt washer!"

In the morning, we visit William Randolph Hearst's castle at San Simeon. I'm wearing my giveaway Rod Carew jersey, dyed with so many orange Sunkist soda stains that even Mom's many ministrations with Clorox couldn't remove them. "Say 'Sunkist soda stains,'" I tell John. He says, "Shunkisht shoda shtains," spraying saliva.

"Say 'spraying saliva,'" I say, but he says "Shut up, Shtevie" instead.

"Say it, don't spray it," I say.

I read all about Hearst Castle at the Penn Lake Library and so I lip-synch along with the tour guide's spiel about "La Cuesta Encantada," or "The Enchanted Hill," where publishing magnate William Randolph Hearst set down 127 acres of swimming pools, guesthouses, his own twin-towered castle, and dozens of fountains, each one burbling like the bidet in our Best Western bathroom.

Standing next to the Neptune Pool, frozen in a waking dream like one of Hearst's Roman statues, I think, *This is the reward for a life in the newspaper business.* Everything I know or will know about print journalism issued from California. In the fall, I'll watch *Lou Grant,* about a gruff television editor from Minneapolis station WJM who moves to Los Angeles to run the *L.A. Tribune.* Tom Bradford on *Eight Is Enough* lives in a big white house bought with the salary earned from his *Sacramento Register* column. I know from careful viewing of *The Odd Couple* that while Oscar Madison is a sportswriter for the *New York Herald* and has a gigantic apartment at 1049 Park Avenue, the show is filmed on the Paramount lot in Los Angeles.

And William Randolph Hearst built this joint on the proceeds of his newspaper empire. I want my second home to be a 165-room estate overlooking the Pacific. So I tell Mom and Dad I want to be a writer.

I carry a notebook like Harriet the Spy, a sheaf of stationery from the Holiday Inn and the Best Western, and keep my eyes peeled for celebrities. We missed Michael Douglas and Karl Malden on the streets of San Francisco, but somewhere on the California coast is Bay City, home of Starsky and Hutch and the Bay City Rollers. I have no idea that the Bay City Rollers are Scottish and randomly named their band for Bay City, Michigan, but that hardly matters. When Dad unfolds his ten-square-foot map of California on the Best Western bedspread, plotting tomorrow's movements like General Patton, he informs me that there is no Bay City. "It's all fake," he says, presumably so we don't have to stop there. But what does *he* know? He says the same thing about pro wrestling.

"It's all fake," Dad says again, by way of reassurance, on the tram at Universal Studios, when the mechanical shark jumps out of the water and scares the bejabbers out of me. We pass the *Psycho* mansion, narrowly escape a mechanical rockslide, and gape at the facade of the Munsters' house on 1313 Mockingbird Lane. Oddly, it's on the same street as Beaver Cleaver's house, and he lived at 211 Pine Street. "The magic of Hollywood," Dad says, pointing out the beams and braces and brackets behind all the various false fronts, the bogus backdrops.

Many years ago, when Dad required U.S. government security clearance for a Mickey Mining project, the forms asked for his father's legal name and date of birth. A marriage certificate coughed up the details. It identified my grandfather as Nathan "Jack" Rushin. His place of birth was listed as Kingston, Jamaica. His religion was listed as Jewish. But here, at Universal Studios, I don't know any of this yet. I haven't a clue what's behind the facade—the Irish-Catholic kid I think I am—or if it matters that I'm really an Irish-Catholic Jamaican Jew. The truth is I feel like a Rushin, a Nativity-ite, a South Brooker, a Bloomingtonian, a Minnesotan, and an exiled Chicagoan, in that order.

It is here, in the Universal Studios live animal show, that we spot our first California celebrity. Fred the Cockatoo, Robert Blake's wisecracking parrot sidekick on *Baretta*, is riding a tiny bicycle for our amusement. "The magic of Hollywood," I say to Dad.

"No, that's real," he replies. But how can I know it's the same bird from the show? They all look the same.

I've come to California, braved the San Andreas Fault, and the only thing that's shaken so far is my faith in what's real.

At the end of the tour we're offered the chance to sit in "the live studio audience" for a new show. As I beg Dad to please let us watch it, he blithely declines the tickets to *Carter Country*, saying we don't have time, though I fear he has spurned the show on political grounds, since he voted for Ronald Reagan, and doesn't want to sit through a three-hour taping with a bunch of hillbilly characters from Plains, Georgia.

And yet a few hours later I *feel* like a hillbilly, a Midwestern rube, as we visit one of Dad's Mickey Mining colleagues at his house in Anaheim Hills, near Disneyland. It's a contemporary that looks like Mike Brady designed it and smells of something we don't have in Minnesota: frangipani or eucalyptus. Perhaps this is "the warm smell of *colitas* rising up through the air" the Eagles are always going on about in "Hotel California."

Dad's friend has a fourteen-year-old son with long wavy hair and a surfboard in the garage. And though the boy never says anything to make us feel less than right at home, everything about him suggests that his Hollywood nights are better than our Sting-Ray afternoons. Tom and I vow, that very night, to pool our allowance when we get home and buy a skateboard like this kid's, with polyurethane wheels, that we can use in drained swimming pools, should South Brook ever get any swimming pools, and those pools ever get drained.

And yet the solicitous manner of our host family's father, and some offhand reference to his sales territory, gradually reveals that this guy works for Dad and not the other way around, as any ten-year-old would conclude from our respective homes in Southern California and South Brook.

For the rest of the trip, I persuade myself that California is and always has been my home. At the Big A, I cheer for the California Angels, whose roster (Bobby Bonds, Bruce Bochte, Dick Drago) appeals to my love of alliteration. At Disneyland, Mom and Dad let me get a Space Mountain T-shirt and a mesh-backed hat with Mickey Mouse on the front. I assume this is Orange County camouflage, and I want to pass for a local. A two-hour wait in line at Space Mountain yields two and a half minutes of space-age carsickness, a short, strange ride through an alternate reality that evidently leaves Dad wanting more vehicular madness and alien culture, given his impulsive decision to alter our itinerary.

And so, after a brief stop in San Diego to visit their world-famous zoo—Joan Embery is not in, dashing our last chance to see a celebrity—Dad announces that we're all going to Mexico. As with Space Mountain, there is another epic wait in an endless line. We present our documents (an E ticket at Disneyland, a driver's license at border control), and for the first time in my life I am on what TV newscasters always call "foreign soil." Mom is not pleased to be in Tijuana, but then she has never liked crowds or chaos, both of which are abundant here. When she joined Dad on a Mickey Mining trip to Rome, her fierce devotion to Catholicism was defeated by her aversion to mobs at Vatican City. She loathes Las Vegas and will never join Dad on his annual January pilgrimage to the Consumer Electronics Show there. A decade from now, Mom will attend the Summer Olympics in Seoul on a Mickey Mining boondoggle and tell Dad, "If the Olympics are held in Bloomington, I won't attend them again."

So Tijuana is a tough sell, made all the more difficult by our mode of transport there—"a Tijuana taxi," Dad says with delight as the seven of us pile in, Dad riding shotgun, a rosary swinging from the rearview mirror as we rocket through the streets, Mexican pop blaring on the radio and white-knuckled Mom frantically searching her purse for her own rosary beads to clutch.

Careening through North America's largest red-light district, Mom and Dad have an urgent conversation, and Dad—suddenly chastened—asks the driver to return us to our rental car, ringing the curtain down on my forty-five minutes abroad.

The next day, at LAX, the fever dream of this vacation about to break, I spot in our terminal a group of men with identical haircuts and identical facial hair, wearing identical satin tour jackets that identify them as members of Al Stewart's band. And at the center of this entourage is Al Stewart himself, giving us a certifiable celebrity sighting in the final seconds of our vacation, in the tail end of summer, in the Year of the Cat, though to me it will forever be the Year of California.

Back in Bloomington, Mom gets the vacation photos developed. Dad travels with a Kodak Instamatic, just as he travels the world with his Super 8 movie camera. If he had a baseball card, the back of it would read "Don enjoys photography." It will be years before I discover how long he has nurtured this compulsion.

After his trip to San Francisco as a five-year-old, Dad saw his father a second time, in Chicago, where Jack Rushin was again hawking his old wares at the Chicago Railroad Fair of 1948. Jack asked his son what he wanted to be when he grew up. Dad, now a seventh-grade boy—only a year older then than I am right now—thought for a moment and said, "A promoter."

So powerful is a boy's urge to be like his father that it doesn't even require the presence of the father.

The camera is Dad's Rosebud, though he'll never say so explicitly. All he says is this: "In seventh grade, when I was living in a trailer in Fort Wayne, after my mother's second marriage to Ted Dixon, she said to me, 'Your father is in town. Do you want to go with him to Chicago?' Well, hell, I'd never been anywhere, so I said, 'Sure.' We stayed downtown at the Maxwell House, I think. In those days they had these big boxy cameras, and I saw a used camera in a secondhand store window and my father saw that I was admiring it. And he bought me that camera. I don't know if I ever took a single picture with it. We spent a couple days in Chicago, he drove me back to Fort Wayne, and that's the last I ever saw of him."

Dad is in hardly any of our California pictures or any of our other family photos, because he's always the one taking them. It's his effort to preserve in amber these moments with his children, as if he's pinning a butterfly to a page.

10

Play That Funky Music, White Boy

As California expatriates now living in Bloomington, Tom and I split the twenty-seven-dollar cost of a lime-green skateboard with space-age polyurethane wheels that can roll over any sidewalk debris like a panzer tank. Thirty minutes after we walk out of Westwood Skate and Bike, I'm standing at the top of the tallest hill in Bloomington, watching Tom go bombing down the sidewalk, a vertical descent of concrete, high above the parking lot of Normandale Community College, whose various disparaging nicknames include Harvard on the Hill, Cornell by the Creek, and Thirteenth Grade.

"I'm going to UCLA," seniors at Lincoln High School like to say. "University Closest to Lincoln Area."

Tom is halfway down the hill, leaning into the breeze at a ski jumper's angle, when a polyurethane wheel meets a moderate-sized pebble and the wheel stops instantly. The skateboard skids but Tom continues headlong down the hill at forty-five miles an hour, now without a skateboard beneath him. He breaks his fall with his right forearm, which snaps in half like a piece of chalk. Tom lies in the grassy median between the sidewalk of West 98th Street and the campus of Normandale Community College, a.k.a. Princeton on the Prairie, attempting (with the fingers at the end of his unbroken arm) to gingerly probe his brand-new wounds. And those wounds are manifold. Angry and red. He looks like one of the lepers that Saint Damien of Molokai tended to in my *Book of Saints,* except that Tom is floridly issuing all the swear words I have ever heard and many that I have not.

All my fears are absent in Tom. He's not afraid to break bones, talk to girls, or swear. He's thirteen now, and I can feel him riding away from me, disappearing down the road, the reflector on the back of his ten-speed glinting in the sun. Very soon—at least two years before he's licensed to drive—he'll take Dad's car for an occasional, illicit spin around South Brook. It's the only four-wheeled conveyance available to him, because Mom—after driving Tom to the hospital, where his arm is put in a cast—makes the skateboard disappear. It simply vanishes, like Jimmy Hoffa or Patty Hearst or the kidnapped Italian prime minister Aldo Moro.

Speaking of whom, I bring a note home from my seventh-grade teacher, Mr. Berglund, that Mom shows to Dad, who reads it first in disbelief, then in apoplexy. Mr. Berglund, Dad informs me, says I'm struggling in our weekly class discussions of current events. The next day, for the first time in his life, Dad pays a visit to one of my teachers, driving to Nativity instead of 3M to ask Mr. Berglund how this can possibly be. "Steve reads the newspaper every day, cover to cover," he says, in a conversation he'll recount to me years later. "He wants to be a newspaper writer."

Mr. Berglund says I don't appear engaged at all in the weekly oral quizzes about the news and that furthermore...

"What are these quizzes about?" Dad says.

Mr. Berglund cites the new Susan B. Anthony coin, the death of Pope Paul VI...

"He's bored," Dad says. "This stuff is too easy. Ask him about Rhodesia. Or the Camp David Accords."

"*Those* are not boring?" Mr. Berglund says, not without justification. "Most of our seventh-graders..."

"Ask him about Jonestown," Dad says. "Ask him..."

"I hardly think the Jonestown Massacre is appropriate..."

"Try it," Dad says. "Please."

For the rest of the year I will get a separate quiz on current events, except on those days when we have a substitute teacher, when instead we will take the day off to watch filmstrips and devise diabolical new ways to torment the sub. A few of the girls in the front of the class quietly seethe as the boys in the back plot their schemes against the new teacher, but those girls also inadvertently act as a human screen. So when Ricky Furness asks a question and the teacher turns to the board to write the answer, Ricky climbs out the classroom window, walks back into the school through the front door, and then—in full view of the sub now—walks into our classroom, which he never walked out of, as the bewildered teacher wonders how this Houdini of classroom cutups managed to do what he just did.

One morning, to stifled applause, Sister Roseanne informs our class that we've required, at the last minute, a substitute teacher who shall arrive here shortly. As she steps out of the classroom, we sit at our desks, trembling with anticipation, plotting ever-crueler practical jokes, which I secretly want no part of even though I usually play along with them. These pranks invariably involve thumbtacks and spitballs and wholesale seat swaps every time the teacher's back is to the class, a plot the boys are hatching in the cloakroom when Sister Roseanne returns from the hallway and we all jump back into our desk chairs.

"Your teacher is here," the principal informs us, sweeping open the door to the hallway. "Class, say hello to Mrs. Rushin."

The world goes silent around me. I have the sensation of being underwater, of drowning, of seeing everyone around me without being able to speak or hear or breathe. Every classmate has swiveled his or her head toward mine. A few of them are pointing at me, and when I finally gasp for breath and can hear again—it's as if I've resurfaced after sixty seconds—the first sound is Kurt Mason saying "Our sub is your *mommy!*"

"Mister..." Mom scans the seating chart on Mr. Berglund's desk. "Mister Mason. I'm sure if *your* mommy were teaching today, you would show her the proper respect and see to it that your friends did the very same. Isn't that right?"

"Yes, Mrs. Rushin."

"You will raise your hand if you have anything else to say, is that understood?"

"Yes, Mrs. Rushin."

"That goes for all of you," she says. "Very well, then. Let's get started. Open your math textbooks to page forty-seven..."

Every textbook, wrapped in brown grocery-sack paper

from Red Owl or Penny's Supermarket, is dutifully opened. As the morning wears on, Mom demonstrates a mastery of mathematics and American history and literature that I'd only ever seen her exhibit in the form of balancing a checkbook or reading another John F. Kennedy biography or foisting her threadbare childhood copy of *Jane Eyre* on me. She also demonstrates a firm grasp of classroom discipline. I don't relax, exactly, and I certainly don't raise my hand once, not least because I don't want to reveal the growing sweat stains beneath my flagrant armpits.

But I do glimpse her previous life, and her alternate life, the one she might have had teaching instead of raising five children, fighting the daily tsunami of laundry. (Is this why they call it Tide?) Mrs. Rushin, I realize, has kept one redhead and four shitheads in line while Mr. Rushin is in Tokyo for two weeks at a time eating spareribs at the Tony Roma's in Shinjuku. When she has to, she rules our house with an iron fist, gloved in yellow latex, clutching a wooden yardstick from Lattof Chevrolet. From the opening seconds of class, as she chalks her name onto the board in that impeccable Palmer hand, it is clear to my classmates that nobody at Nativity of the Blessed Virgin Mary—twenty years after Mrs. Rushin last taught full-time in Cincinnati—will be writing "Pussy" on *her* blackboard.

"That wasn't so bad, was it?" she asks me back home when I've gotten off the school bus, unable to bring myself to ride home with the teacher.

"Don't ever do it again," I say.

"Why, were you embarrassed?"

"Obviously," I said.

"Of your own mother?"

Sigh.

"I'm just teasing," she says. "Of course you were embarrassed. Come here." She removes a Kleenex from her purse and wipes an Oreo crumb from the corner of my mouth. And instead of resisting, as I usually do these days, I let her do it.

It's suddenly rare that I'm home after school instead of at basketball practice. When I worked up the nerve to tell Dad that I wanted to quit hockey for basketball, he said, "Great." He didn't enjoy standing in a snowbank any more than I did. And what a relief it is to be indoors, in shorts, in a heated gym, playing against opponents who aren't brandishing sticks or wearing sharpened blades. The new seventh-grade coach at Nativity is a second-year student at Harvard on the Hill. He's a short, white, nineteen-year-old man from Michigan who blasts Earth, Wind, and Fire on a portable cassette player the size of a suitcase, its eight D batteries turning the sprocketed wheels of a cassette tape. The audiocassette tape is the new paddle wheel of the Rushin family economy, displacing the eight-track tape, its success allowing us to make upgrades small (from Hydrox to Oreo) and large (from Ford Country Squire to Buick Regal). The maroon Regal, with its white landau roof, is the evolutionary missing link between the station wagons Dad has always driven and the Cadillac he long ago promised his mother-in-law he would one day drive.

One snowy morning Dad is driving his boss to Holman Field in Saint Paul, where the two of them will get on the Mickey Mining corporate jet to some far-flung locale bereft of magnetic tape. Dad is snaking his way down Shepard Road, high above the Minnesota River, when the car slides off the pavement, through the guardrail, and down the embankment leading to the icy river below.

This is the Valleyfair water flume ride in real life, the fiberglass log replaced by a burgundy Buick Regal with a landau roof. But instead of ending in a cascade of white water and Mom standing at a safe remove, patting her hair, the car is stopped, as in a Warner Brothers cartoon, by a lone tree on the river bluff.

Scrambling out of the car, up the hill, and back to the roadway, gig lines intact, Dad and his boss walk to the nearest pay phone and arrange to have the car towed to a body shop in Saint Paul and themselves delivered by taxi to Holman Field. They'd have done the same had the car gone into the river. If one of them had perished in the accident, the survivor would have made the flight. Such is the one-track mind of the eight-track salesman.

From the pay phone, Dad makes a second call, asking Mom to drive to the body shop and sort out the details of repair and payment, which she dutifully does, despite an hour round-trip in the snow to the kind of place she dreads and where she feels preyed upon—an auto-body shop.

Relieved but also exasperated, Mom expresses to Dad her mixed feelings about the presence of that tree. For now, Dad is the hero of the story, and Mom is the comic bit player. It will be years before I see that the opposite is true.

The restored Regal reminds my brothers and me of the cars driven by detective-show pimps and other police informants. Mike McCollow's dad, a dentist, likewise now drives a baby-

blue Bonneville Brougham with simulated crushed-velvet upholstery. Huggy Bear would look at home behind its burled-
walnut steering wheel. Mike and I read the cues from our male
authority figures and begin to believe—despite all evidence
to the contrary—that we are black.

Mike checks a nonfiction book out of the Penn Lake Library called *Heaven Is a Playground,* about a group of black
teenagers playing pickup basketball at Foster Park in the
Bedford-Stuyvesant neighborhood of Brooklyn. I read it five
times. The kids in *Heaven* have names like Fly and Pontiac
and call the basketball a "rock." We begin to lard our conversation with their slang and to take fashion cues from another
library book: *Rockin' Steady: A Guide to Basketball and Cool,*
by the splendiferous New York Knicks guard Walt "Clyde"
Frazier. He drives a Rolls-Royce with New York license
plates WCF. I'd drive to school in a wide-brimmed fedora and
a double-breasted suit with fur lapels set off by an ornate
walking stick, if only Sister Roseanne Roseannadanna would
relax the uniform code.

Our basketball coach is named Jim Thomas, but Mike and
I privately call him "Jamaal Tahoma." In addition to his studies, and coaching us, he works the graveyard shift at The
Embers. He can hit shots from the corner of the court, where
the sideline meets the baseline. On his boom box, we listen to
Earth, Wind, and Fire and the Commodores and long for our
own R&B delivery system—what Jamaal Tahoma calls his
"box." Our fantasies are fueled by a new television show that
debuts when our basketball season does. *The White Shadow* on
CBS is set at an urban school in Los Angeles called Carver
High Scho_l. (The second *o* is missing from the sign on

their crumbling building.) The basketball team there is mostly black, the coach is white but streetwise, and their opponents have a respectful fear of Carver. And so Mike and I come to believe that our opponents in the CYO league have a similar fear of Nativity's seventh-grade team, coached by its own White Shadow. We wear BVM across our chests, and while it stands for Blessed Virgin Mary, we've decided that Bloomington is Bed-Stuy, and that BVM is a basketball power known far and wide as the "Buh-vum." We imagine other seventh-graders in and around Minneapolis see the BVM on our chicken chests and say in a reverential whisper, "They got some bad fly muthas at the Buh-vum."

Ever since my preschool screenings of *Sesame Street* I have wanted to live in a city and play a radio on the stoop and wave to the merchants and Muppets walking by on the sidewalk. When I mention this dream to my parents, they surprise me on my birthday with a radio. Not a boom box I can carry on my shoulder like a pirate's parrot, not a Samsonite-sized South Brook blaster with speakers the size of dinner plates kicking out the bass line to "Brickhouse" and vibrating molars throughout the subdivision. Rather, they surprise me with an AM/FM clock radio I can put on the shelf next to my bed, its lighted digital numbers casting a green glow in the room at night, like the green light I've seen emanating from the underside of the escalators at Dayton's. And to my own surprise, I love it, and spend an hour running my fingers over its many buttons, switches, dials, and speaker holes, until Mom has to drive me to football practice.

In my absence, Tom studies it with envy. He takes the gooseneck reading lamp off my desk and shines it on the radio, illuminating its snooze bar and dimmer switch. Beneath the 100-watt bulb of my reading lamp, he memorizes its functions in the instruction booklet, which remains next to the lamp that still burns with a white-hot intensity when I get home from football and run upstairs to my room.

Tom is long gone. As I approach the birthday present I unwrapped only three hours ago, my mouth is a rictus of disbelief. The lamp has melted the white plastic casing that houses the radio. It's literally melting, like one of Salvador Dalí's clocks.

And yet I still love it, *truly* love it, not for the way it looks on the outside—like an electronic stroke victim, its left half now cooled into a permanent sag—but for what it has on the inside. Music. Twins games from the West Coast that play until midnight, Herb Carneal on WCCO radio singing me to sleep with an anti-music of Twins names: Dave Goltz, Paul Thormodsgard, Craig "Mongo" Kusick.

The Dalí clock radio isn't a boom box. On the contrary. It never strays from the shelf next to my bed. It's tethered to the wall socket by six feet of electrical cord but also tethered to the broadcast towers of WLOL and KDWB, playing "Baby Come Back" or "Kiss You All Over" in such heavy rotation (and even while I sleep) that it's impossible to imagine a day when their lyrics can't be summoned in my head at a second's notice. I will never grow so old as to forget a single word to "Whenever I Call You Friend."

But I also discover at night, after dark, if I position the Dalí clock radio just right and spin the dial to the far left, I can conjure the low-watt signal of 88.5 KBEM or 89.9 KMOJ out of north Minneapolis and hear through the crackling static R&B

artists that I'd never heard *of* much less heard on record. The names alone are musical: Con Funk Shun, Bootsy's Rubber Band, L.T.D., Funkadelic, Fatback Band. Their music reaches the southern suburbs like the smoke from a distant fire, to use a phrase in frequent rotation on the pop stations that come in loud and clear.

It's the R&B that's suddenly captivating, and certain phrases and words and inflections find their way into my vocabulary, and Mike McCollow's. We say "thang" instead of "thing." I'm still afraid to say "shit" but have no qualms saying "shee-yit." I persuade myself, with a linguistic sleight of hand, that South Brook is the South Bronx, two gritty urban streetscapes I come to think of collectively as SoBro.

Before or after basketball practice, Mike and I start running a couple of blocks from Nativity to Harpo's Records 'n Stuff, where we head straight for the "Records," uninterested in all the "Stuff"—incense, roach clips, rolling papers—kept in a glass display case at the counter. It reminds me of the candy case at the Southtown Theatre, if Zig-Zag Super Quality Slow-Burning Gummed Cigarette Papers had replaced the Mike and Ike Tender, Chewy Assorted Fruit Flavored Candies.

Alone, watched only by the Styx and Foreigner posters, we nonchalantly race-walk to the *O* bin, where the Ohio Players album covers reliably feature a naked or near-naked woman brandishing a honey pot or a fire hose, objects that somehow remain single entendres to us.

Cassettes are what we really want—tapes to feed the boom boxes we don't yet have. Dad could supply me with all the blank tape in the world, miles of it, courtesy of the Mickey

Mining company store, and I could tape albums or songs off the radio and use paper-route money to buy my own D batteries, which the "boxes" eat like Pop Rocks. I see myself dangling a pulsating boom box from the ram's-horn handlebars of my Schwinn Varsity. It's a grown man's bike, emblematic of my incipient maturity and an acknowledgment that Sting-Rays are over, already displaced by dirt bikes among the little kids of South Brook, a designation that no longer applies to me.

These transitions—from young to less young, from innocence to experience, from pop to funk, from white to black—are evident in our last two summer vacations of the 1970s, our post-California road trips. In the summer of '78, we made our every-other-summer road trip to Chicago and Cincinnati, where my older cousin Johnny Burns held us all rapt in his basement bedroom playing "Life's Been Good" and "Smoke on the Water" on his electric guitar. We walked to King Kwik for Slushies in a commemorative Reds cup that Mom let me take home in my suitcase, and Johnny produced a telescopic golf-ball retriever to scoop cigarette butts out of Winton Woods Harbor. Johnny called the device a "wub fisherman," "wub" being Cincinnati high school slang for what we in Bloomington call freaks, burnouts, dirtballs, or gumbies—Dad still calls them "hippies." They're a subset of youth that my friends and I ridicule, following the lead of our older brothers. Secretly, though, I also fear the freaks, with their cigarettes and Kawasakis and boots called shitkickers.

The photographic negative of freaks are jocks. As Lincoln's standout jock, Jim is the anti-freak, a football linebacker, baseball pitcher, and the dominant hockey center in a hockey town in the state of hockey. He wears number 16 in homage to center Jude Drouin of the North Stars, whose colors—green, gold, and white—Lincoln shares. Except that Jim is bigger and more fearsome than Drouin. He is not afraid, in his description, to "speed-bag" any opponent. "Speed-bag" is a verb. It means to punch a person in the head repeatedly in the rhythmic manner of a boxer working a speed bag.

He is a talented, hardworking team player of growing renown. The *Minneapolis Tribune,* which I now deliver throughout South Brook on Sunday mornings, has the same postage-stamp-sized photograph on page one of each section every day. It's a familiar icon that helps the reader find the way to his or her favorite subject. And so the IDS skyscraper is the logo for the Metro section, a dollar bill anchors the Business section, an open book orients to the Arts section. And even an illiterate buyer of the *Minneapolis Tribune* will know he or she has stumbled on the Sports section by seeing, at the top of the front page—every day of the week for a couple of years—an action photo of my big brother. In it, Jim Rushin of the Bloomington Lincoln High School Bears is shoveling another shot past some helpless sieve of a goalie who made a grievous error by skating out to cut off the angle on my big brother. Clancy the Great. Look at him skate.

In the summer and fall Jim still works at Met Stadium, managing a commissary and watching all the Twins and Vikings and Kicks soccer games he wants, not to mention concerts, so that he finds himself on the evening of August 1, 1978, standing beneath the second-deck overhang in a driving rainstorm as the Eagles, the Steve Miller Band, and Pablo

Cruise perform on the Hotel California tour before sixty-five thousand Minnesota kids high on pot and Grain Belt Premium. Jim alone is dry, sober, and high on life. Jim alone is there to hear Pablo Cruise.

Like other Minnesota-made mascots—the Pillsbury Dough-boy, the Jolly Green Giant, the Lucky Charms leprechaun—Jim is an icon, fielding scholarship offers in every sport and dating a cheerleader whose name is Peggy Golden. (Could it possibly be otherwise?) Girls want to be with him, and twelve-year-old boys want to *be* him. Strangely, I am no exception.

Except that now I'm basketball obsessed, thanks in part to another Jim—Jamaal Tahoma, our pasty, freckled, floppy-haired emissary from Harvard on the Hill who wears three pairs of socks like Pistol Pete Maravich, prompting McCollow and me to do the same. Jamaal Tahoma plays "The Groove Line" by Heatwave or "September" by Earth, Wind, and Fire before practice and I've never been happier, shooting jumpers—"Js" in our new vernacular—while singing "Never was a cloudy day, yow."

In class, Mike sketches basketball warm-up suits bedazzled with stars and stripes and zigzagged bell-bottoms and tries to choreograph a pregame routine for the Buh-vum that involves rhythmic handclaps and complicated handshakes and a mix-tape for the layup line worthy of Foster Park in Bed-Stuy, Brooklyn. The fact that we're Buh-vum and not Bed-Stuy doesn't register.

And so I have separation anxiety from my rubber Spalding basketball when we fly to Washington, DC, on our last family vacation in the summer of '79, passing a happy interval at Virginia Beach and an unhappy one at Colonial Williamsburg, where the butter-churning tedium in the dog's-breath heat of a mid-Atlantic August makes all of us pine loudly for the Holidome pool at the Holiday Inn. We race from our rental car to our rooms and from our rooms to the pool, shouting an ancient childhood mantra: "Last one in is a rotten egg."

But it's the three days in DC that enchant, and not just because I see a newly acquired object at the Smithsonian, the real Archie Bunker chair, after all these years of getting evicted from Dad's various Archie Bunker chairs. What's fascinating to me a month before I turn thirteen aren't the museums and monuments but all the black teenagers wearing PRO-Keds and shell-toed Adidas Superstars with colored laces and intricate lacing patterns and white tube socks pulled to their kneecaps, all of which I'll endeavor to replicate with my own shoes and socks when I get back to the Holiday Inn in Arlington, Virginia, for our end-of-day swim and Dad's evening libations.

We've strayed far from the National Mall when Dad leads all seven of us into a tiny liquor store late on a Thursday afternoon to buy enough booze to drown a horse. "If I don't see you before then," the guy behind the counter says, "have a nice weekend." Dad finds this hilarious, and as he leads us out of the store with a heavy paper sack under one arm, I ask him to explain.

Dad says, "For a lot of his customers, a bottle of scotch and a twelve-pack of beer is apparently a one-night supply."

I don't answer, but having begun to imagine myself as a poor city kid, I feel protective of this threadbare neighborhood and its liquor-store clientele, even if I'm protecting it from an actual poor city kid who has spent his life putting distance between himself and poverty.

At the Holiday Inn in Arlington, Dad puts the beer on ice in the bathroom sink. In the adjoining room, I reflexively turn on the TV and crank up the volume, to hear it above the hum of the overworked air conditioner.

The voice is David Brinkley's, on NBC, familiar from a thousand similar evenings at home. What he says as I lie on the bed makes me jackknife forward to attention.

"New York Yankees catcher Thurman Munson was killed today in a crash of a small airplane at the Akron–Canton Airport in Ohio."

I shudder. The sudden chill has nothing to do with the arctic AC blowing on my sweat-soaked T-shirt.

The news is unbelievable. I literally can't believe it. Major League Baseball players are invincible, and New York Yankees are immortal, the principal players in America's favorite soap opera. This summer's biggest book is *The Bronx Zoo*, by the former Yankees relief pitcher Sparky Lyle, and while I cannot spend $8.95 for a hardcover in B. Dalton Bookseller at Southdale, I check it out of the grown-up section at Penn Lake Library and read about Lyle's clubhouse affinity for sitting naked on birthday cakes.

Munson was the captain of these Yankees, the first person I know, or feel I know, who has died. I've committed to memory his baseball cards and their B sides. Bats: Right. Throws: Right. Born: Akron. Lives: Canton. And this unforgettable fun fact: "Thurman's nickname is Squatty."

That Munson died in a plane crash, three days before we

have to fly home, adds another fear to all the usual ones (death, vampire bats, Ouija boards) while joining a burgeoning category of new ones (girls, mockery, loneliness).

Munson was thirty-two, thirteen years younger than Mom and Dad, fourteen years older than Jim, in that generational gap occupied by professional athletes and rock stars and most of the people on TV. Any of them could vanish like that, *will* vanish like that. Just days after we get home, Jim himself is leaving for college, having finally accepted a hockey scholarship—"a full ride" is the congratulatory phrase he hears often these days—to a hockey power on the East Coast, which might as well be Narnia.

Five minutes before Jim leaves for the airport, bound for Providence College, he comes up to my bedroom to give me a valedictory 99 Bump, a few sternum welts to remember him by. Supine on the floor next to my bed, biceps pinned to the carpet, I scream and spit and tell Jim I hate him, that I'm happy he's going, that I hope I never see him again. He tells me I've made one last grievous error and loses count on his way to ninety-nine, forcing him to start over, hammering my chest with a single knuckle as if he's drilling for oil.

Mom and Dad wait downstairs, station wagon idling in the driveway, listening to the fight as if it's a favorite song on the radio they might never hear again.

And I kind of understand. They want to preserve this time in a locket, freeze us as we are now and will never be again.

John is about to turn seven, slurring his way through his killer Steve Martin impression at dinner parties ("Gotta condo made-uh shtone-uh, King Tut").

Amy is nine, with a Shaun Cassidy poster taped to the door

that keeps The Boys out of her bedroom. ("Do you love him more than you love me?" Dad asks Amy, standing before the poster, the teen idol's satin baseball jacket unbuttoned to his navel. Amy thinks for a minute and says, "The same.")

Tom is fourteen, a freshman at Lincoln, strong enough now to punch a hole in the wall of our bedroom when I score on him in our handheld game of Mattel football. (He steals a piece of drywall from a construction project outside the Bloomington Ice Garden, patches the hole, and puts one of Jim's football recruiting posters over the white spot on the blue wall, where MONTANA STATE WELCOMES JIM RUSHIN will stay until Mom decides—as she does every five years or so—to paint the room another color.

Jim, of course, is eighteen. "Flying the coop," as Dad says, off to college this very minute while I stay upstairs, snuffling back snot and tears on the bedroom carpet.

Tom is out. He has more friends than I have acquaintances. Amy and John have gone with Mom and Dad to see Jim off at the airport. So I'm alone with Christ above the credenza, the house silent save for clock ticks and bird chirps and the distant buzz of a push mower. It's an hour that seems like forever.

Dad tells a story when they get back. Just before he boarded the plane for Providence, Jim shook hands with John. "Well," John said, chin quivering. "You've been a great brother."

Mom was in tears but Dad howled. "He's still your brother," he said. "He'll always be your brother. He'll come home again."

But the six-year-old is the first to figure out what the rest of us can't yet face. Summers aside, Jim won't come home again. He'll not leave every morning and return every night, season after season, year after year, as reliable as the rising and the setting of the sun. Our family of seven, our aluminum-sided house "bursting at the seams" (in Mom's words), will never again be as loud, the kids' bathroom will never again be as crowded, dinners will never be so chaotic. Grievous errors will go unpunished.

Bloomington seems smaller without him. It literally is, of course, but Jim's not the only one leaving. The population is in an inevitable decline. No city, not even one called Bloomington, can remain in perpetual bloom. In February, Rod Carew was traded to the California Angels. Last year, the Vikings released Alan Page, who now wears 82 and plays for the Bears. My Vikings jersey with his number on it is now a dust rag, one more implement in Mom's Endust arsenal. The Purple People Eaters are a memory. Their Super Bowl run is over.

Mary Tyler Moore went off the air two years ago, continuing the Twin Cities diaspora: Rhoda Morgenstern left Minneapolis for New York, Lou Grant took a job in L.A., and Murray Slaughter, in an improbable career move, is now captain of the *Love Boat.*

But Bloomington remains front-page, bold type, at least for another week. Outside my bedroom window, across the marsh where Eddie O'Phelan and I first spied a naked woman, I can see a twenty-one-story hotel. At the top of it, eight lighted letters spell RADISSON, a sign that glows red at night, fueling my fantasy that I live in a city like J. J. Evans on *Good Times.*

Next door to the Radisson, invisible behind the marsh, is the low-slung L'Hotel de France, which everyone calls the Hotel Duhfrantz. It is there, in the bar of the Hotel Duhfrantz, on the evening of October 23, 1979, that New York Yankees manager Billy Martin sucker punches a traveling marshmallow salesman from suburban Chicago named Joe Cooper. Bloomington, once again, is a dateline in papers worldwide. The view from my bedroom window is national news. Many of the news bulletins mention Martin's drinking buddy that night, a "local businessman" named Howard Wong, impresario of Wong's Chinese restaurant, which is not to be confused with Fong's Chinese restaurant across town.

Martin is fired by the Yankees' volatile owner, George Steinbrenner, and to see it all turned into a running gag on *The Tonight Show* remains a thrill, even if David Letterman and Bill Cosby are guest-hosting for the week.

Johnny's hardly ever on his own show anymore. Overnight, it seems, Johnny Carson and Jim Rushin have vanished. It isn't just the decade that's drawing to a close. Bloomington's golden age is coming to an end, and childhood is receding. A month before Billy punched the marshmallow salesman, I turned thirteen and received in the mail an envelope from the Hotel, Motel, Restaurant, Bar, and Club Employees Union Local No. 17 of the AFL-CIO. Enclosed was an embossed plastic card identifying me as the newest employee of the Minnesota Twins, employee 1311, eligible to work in the Metropolitan Stadium commissary for the final home stand of the Twins season and all eight Vikings games this fall. It is nepotism, Jim's gift to me, my first job, in the beating heart of Bloomington, now a decrepit ballpark that has only two years left to live.

No longer a kid, not quite in high school, and newly possessed of a haircut that is no longer modeled on Mr. Spock's, I stay home on New Year's Eve to babysit Amy and John while Mom and Dad attend a party. Tom's at a sleepover. Alone in front of the TV as Dick Clark counts down the final seconds of 1979, I'm seized with a sudden urge to say something out loud to mark the end of the 1970s. And so five seconds before the decade expires, inspired by his enormous Afro and prodigious leaping ability, Dr. J's name comes out of my mouth. Dr. J is who I now want to be, a man who wears the stars and stripes of Evel Knievel but flies on his own power.

As the ball drops in Times Square, I whisper "Julius" in an empty room.

Then it's quiet again, save for the celebrations on TV, and Dick Clark's face reassures me that certain verities shall persist. Some things will never change. And so I fall asleep in the Archie Bunker chair secure in the knowledge that Chic, Blondie, Barry Manilow, the Village People, Bo Duke, the Oak Ridge Boys, and Shortcake from *Happy Days* will always ring in the next year, and the next decade, as they are doing tonight.

At 1 a.m., the headlamp beams of the Buick Regal light up the family room, the motor drive of the automatic garage door coughs to life, and Mom and Dad walk in, smelling of secondhand smoke. I want to keep my eyes closed, pretend to be asleep, and have Dad carry me to my room, as he did ten years ago, across the threshold of that motel in Wisconsin Dells, when man walked on the moon, life was about to begin in Minnesota, and everything was possible.

But Dad is forty-five and can't carry his six-foot son upstairs to bed anymore. Nineteen eighty is just an hour old, but childhood is already drawing down.

11.

Goodbye Yellow Brick Road

Two weeks after I graduate from the Buh-vum in June of 1980, out of the clear blue sky, Tom McCarthy's dad dies of a heart attack. Arriving straight from practice, I attend the wake in my BAA baseball uniform. Mom decides at the door of the funeral home that I should take my cleats off. It's marginally less hillbilly that way. Mac is sobbing. I'm heartbroken for him but also fearful for myself. Dad is roughly the same age as Mr. McCarthy. I don't know what to say, but when Mac sees me, stocking-footed, in my clown-colored BAA double knits, he laughs. The laughter doesn't diminish in any way the sobbing, however. He's laughing and crying at the same time, and with equal intensity. It took thirteen years, but I now know someone well who has died in real life, and from this point forward death will be as contagious as a yawn.

A year earlier, another South Brook dad was killed in a transformer explosion while working for Northern States Power, an accident so improbable that I persuaded myself that nothing comparable could happen to Dad. But now Mr. McCarthy has died, and Mike McCollow's dad will soon survive a massive heart attack of his own on the golf course. And so I intensify my unconscious explorations of the house after midnight, peeing in hampers and wastebaskets. But now I am also racing up and down the hallway in a panic, my nocturnal journeys fueled by night terrors. This makes sleepovers almost unbearably stressful. At the house of a boy named Sean Burke, it's a relief to stay up all night in his basement, playing Monopoly. Sleeping over at the McCarthys', on the other hand, I wet their new fabric sofa in a kind of waking dream.

It isn't just this sudden revelation of mortality that powers my dreams. When I run from room to room, looking in on my snoring siblings, I am sleepwalking in a kind of hypnotized state, but I'm also actively engaged in a vivid plotline. Often, a storm of mathematical equations has been whipped up around me — a whirlwind of 7s and x's and greater-than signs — and I am attempting to outrun it. Sometimes it's a hailstorm of letters, an alphabet cannonade. One vivid nightmare is a cold-war fantasy of nuclear near-annihilation. That night, I run into Mom and Dad's room, throw on the light switch at 3 a.m., and shout, "They're gonna blow up the world!"

Another night I sleepwalk downstairs in my summer pajamas, sit down on the love seat, and watch *Saturday Night Live* with the lights on. I am vaguely aware that Jim is home for the summer and sitting in Mom's chair, and that his high school friends are also in the room, drinking beer. It's nearly midnight. Jim's buddies are laughing at me. But Jim just says, "You're sleepwalking. Go to bed." I do what I've always done when I'm told it's bedtime: I stand, walk over to

Mom's chair, and give its occupant a good-night kiss. Except it's Jim's cheek that I kiss, to howls of laughter from his friends. Even in my half sleep, I brace to get speed-bagged. But Jim doesn't hit me or even mock me. He just helps his little brother, on the brink of attending high school, back up the stairs and into bed.

An introverted child who spent much of the 1970s reading his parents' newspaper would have expected 1980 to be the dawn of a wondrous age. President Nixon had expected all of America's energy needs to be met by America come 1980. Dr. James T. Grace Jr., the eminent cancer researcher, predicted cancer would be cured by this year. Bell plans to put a picture phone in every home in the new decade, and that isn't even the most exciting technological promise. Once South Brook gets cable television, we'll have fifty channels instead of five. And we won't have to stay home to watch *The Dukes of Hazzard* because every house will have a videocassette recorder, releasing us from the shackles of time, so I can record *That's Incredible!* and play it back at my leisure.

Those VCRs will require Scotch brand videocassettes, ensuring the prosperity of our household for another ten years. Dad is a hermit crab, at regular intervals outgrowing one magnetic-tape format for a bigger and better one. He abandoned eight-tracks for audiocassettes and audiocassettes for VHS tapes. Except that he's still selling audiotapes too, and so he doesn't immediately dismiss my claims when I ask for a Panasonic RX-5085 boom box that weighs thirteen pounds.

This is the one thing—more than a Sting-Ray, more than Adidas, more than flying a 747 to Television City—that will make me happy for the rest of my life. I would never want anything again if I only had a Platinum Power boom box with six-and-a-half-inch woofers and one-and-a-quarter-inch tweeters and "the miracle of Ambience Sound," as Earth, Wind, and Fire sings in the TV commercials. "Stereo, AM/FM, cassette! Platinum is the power to get!"

"Two hundred and forty-nine dollars and ninety-five cents!" Mom says. "You don't have that kind of money."

I promise I'll buy the RX-5085 with the proceeds from my first job, the $3.35 hourly wage earned in the commissary at Met Stadium. "You have to save for college," Mom says. "You don't want to work at the Met for the rest of your life."

But that's exactly what I want to do! And I think Mom knows it, which is why she said it. The trouble is, I can't work at the Met forever because the ballpark has been condemned, "slated to close"—as the newspapers put it—after the 1981 season. Likewise, Lincoln High School is "slated to close" after the 1981–82 school year, when I'm a sophomore, at which time everyone at Lincoln will be forced to attend one of our two archrivals: Jefferson or Kennedy. Bloomington's youth population is shrinking. Not every family, it turns out, has five or six or seven kids. Only the families I know.

The Twins and Vikings are moving into a new domed stadium in downtown Minneapolis, which will rob Bloomington of its dateline status. We'll no longer appear in papers around the world or issue from the mouth of Johnny Carson or Howard Cosell. We're getting demoted from an all-caps dateline—BLOOMINGTON—to a lowercase burg that people soon enough will confuse with the Bloomingtons in Illinois and Indiana.

Pity, because it's a dream working at the Met, preparing the food that the vendors hawk in the stands. This is the fantasy I'd choose on *Fantasy Island,* without the bit where everything goes wrong in the end. Breezing past the employee entrance while I flash my Minnesota Twins pass, Jim (back from college, working his old job again), Tom, and I punch in at the Main Commissary, a windowless expanse in the bowels of the Met. It's hotter than the engine room of a burning tugboat down here. The metal doors to Main are graced with permanent graffiti: MAIN IS HELL. Hung above the entrance to the center-field commissary is an ancient hot dog, shriveled and black with age, and frequently likened to the unfortunate appendage of a frostbite victim on Everest. Attached to it is a sign: GOOD LUCK FROM EDDIE AND THE BOYS.

Why Twins "executives" never ordered the petrified hot dog taken down and the signs scrubbed away—and, on the contrary, seem to enjoy the message as a welcome-to-the-big-leagues kind of hazing—says from the moment of arrival everything I needed to know about this place.

Drinking as much soda as possible from the company's endless stores of CO_2 canisters is encouraged, as long as you bring your own cup. (The wax cups emblazoned with the Coca-Cola logo are meticulously inventoried.) For the same reason, infinite hot dogs may be eaten so long as I never consume a single bun. My coworkers often smuggle in a twelve-pack of buns from Red Owl because the buns are inventoried but the dogs are not. "You do the math," my coworker and South Brook colleague Jim Clancy says. "Seventy-five cents times twelve hot dogs equals nine bucks. The pack of buns cost eighty-nine cents." Clancy clears $8.11 on the black market in a single day but feels so guilty afterward that he puts his entire profits into the collection basket during Mass at Nativity the following Sunday.

Free to eat all the bunless hot dogs we want, commissary workers appear to be chomping on cigars as we go about our business, but the smoldering Cohibas plugged into various mouths are in fact steaming Schweigert hot dogs. A vast walk-in meat freezer holds endless reserves of those wieners and boxes of Northland Dairy Frosty Malts, but this same freezer—a ballpark food Fort Knox—is also used to lock away any commissary workers who "fuck up." (The Met's introduction of daily profanity into my life is another Rubicon crossed, an irreversible passage.) Anyone caught warming their hands on the bare bulb suspended from the freezer's ceiling has their sentence extended.

Commissary crimes might consist of anything: singing the wrong lyrics to whatever song is on the radio that plays pop music throughout the Twins games. (The radio never, ever plays the Twins games themselves.) It might mean failing to boil the hot dogs long enough, so that an irate fan gets a frozen franksicle from a vendor. Or it might mean boiling the hot dogs too long, so that they all split down the center to form a little flotilla of meat canoes. These dogs are bunned split side down, so that the vendors (and the spectators they sell to) are none the wiser.

The Met introduces me to a whole new lexicon, not all of which is profane. "Dogs" are "stabbed"—forked out of the boiling water—then "bunned." (We're taught to break a dog open and lick the inside to see if it is hot enough for serving to Twins fans. The licked dogs are thrown away or, more often, eaten on the spot.) We "cup corn"—scooping cups of yellow popcorn from enormous clear bags whose corners get nibbled by mice whenever the Twins are out of town. (Veteran corn cuppers vigilantly screen out any mouse turds.) "Sodas" are "pulled": a tray of two dozen wax cups filled with ice is slid onto a stainless-steel rack; each cup is machine-filled and topped off by hand with a soda squirt gun—eighteen Cokes, six Sunkists; a sheet of cling film is stretched over the tray; and an ancient device is pulled down over the rack, sealing the cups and trimming off any excess cling film. At least one time a superfluous bolt falls off the sealing contraption and is entombed inside a cup of Coke. "Missing something?" says the unlucky buyer of that soda, presenting the bolt at the commissary door, to which he was directed by the vendor who sold it to him.

The vendors are arbitrarily our enemies. A sign in the commissary reminds us that we're not allowed to give them food. DO NOT FEED THE ANIMALS, it says. Some of these animals are our high school classmates; others are thirty years our senior. None of them complains directly to us because Jim is our manager and he frightens everyone, including—especially—Tom and me.

One night in the seventh inning of a Twins game, after the commissary shuts down and a fellow fourteen-year-old is mopping the floor, an irate drunk walks in, demanding to speak to the manager. "I'm the manager," Jim says, "and we just mopped that floor so please don't..."

But the drunk keeps walking, stepping up to Jim aggressively. The man is brandishing a hot dog. It's squeezed in his fist like a bouquet of flowers. Every commissary worker turns to watch, curious which one of us fucked up and how. There is silence save for the radio—Eddie Rabbitt singing about windshield wipers slappin' out a tempo.

"Notice anything?" the drunk says, thrusting the fisted bun in my brother's face. Jim leans back and slips on the freshly mopped and highly polished concrete floor.

We all know that any number of things could be wrong with the man's dog. Perhaps there *was* no dog in the bun when he bought it, or the dog had a bite taken out of it in advance by a hungry commissary worker. All I know is that Jim is fueled by testosterone and two gallons of Coca-Cola. He picks himself up off the floor, his T-shirt wet and soapy, and drops the complaining customer with a left cross. When the guy doesn't get up fast enough, Jim grabs him by the belt and collar and slides him across the soap-slick floor and through the commissary door like a curling stone.

I know exactly what will happen next: nothing. The drunk doesn't return with a cop. He doesn't return with a friend. He doesn't return with a broken beer bottle or any other weapon, because he has learned what I knew all along, without Jim ever having had to say so: that he has made a grievous error. The drunk just melts into the crowd.

Except that there's never a crowd at Twins games. In 1981, their final season at the Met, the Twins average 8,529 fans in a 45,919-seat stadium. Just before one sparsely attended game, a commissary colleague whom everyone calls Ziggy retreats to a men's room stall, shits in a paper cup, and beckons several of us to the empty second deck of the stadium to see what happens next. Holding the cup over the railing, he decants its contents onto the first deck below, safe in the knowledge that these sections down the right-field line are yawningly empty.

After seven innings, we can punch out, unless we're sent to Trays. Trays is another windowless room, down the tunnel from Main, where the vendors' empty hot dog coolers—reeking of boiled sausage and stained with ketchup and mustard—are stored after every game. The unlucky commissary worker sent to Trays has to wash all of these coolers out with a single filthy rag, watched by an overlord named Twister.

Commissary workers are sentenced to Trays for errors of omission (giving a vendor thirty-five hot dogs instead of thirty-six) and errors of commission (Ziggy, on a dare, also took a dump in a hot dog vendor's empty cooler). If there is no obvious candidate, the commissary manager—often Jim, or his friend Dobesh—holds a contest. All the workers line up against the wall as if to face a firing squad. Instead, they face a guy called Gumper, who—at the count of three—rolls up his T-shirt, exposing his vast, fish-white belly. The first one to laugh goes to Trays and spends an unhappy hour with Twister. If no one laughs immediately, Gumper is asked to jump up and down. It never takes more than fifteen seconds before someone breaks. Gumper is happy to participate because it gets him out of Trays.

I almost never go to Trays because Jim is my ride home and he doesn't want to wait around. Come fall, when he's back at Providence and the Twins are playing out the string and the Vikings are starting their season, Tom drives or we get a ride with a coworker. One day Ziggy gives us a ride and—on a dare from Tom—takes a shortcut. A middle-aged man is sitting in an aluminum-framed lawn chair on the concrete front stoop of his corner-lot house when Ziggy, driving his father's Oldsmobile Cutlass, abruptly turns off East 86th Street and cuts across the guy's front lawn. As we pass, not ten feet away, the man throws down his newspaper and actually shakes his fist at us in anger. I've ducked below the window line, fearful that any transgression I'm a party to will go down—in Mom's words—on my "permanent record."

We have a growing appetite for these pranks. Anything we find funny is "good yuks." Tom and his friend Rye enjoy crank-calling phone-in radio shows and insulting the hosts. I record the exchanges on a handheld cassette recorder and we play them back for good yuks. Tom and his buddies attend pro-wrestling matches at the Saint Paul Civic Center. When the house lights go down, they throw Mom's potatoes into the ring. The taped matches air on *All-Star Wrestling* every Sunday morning before Mass on channel 9. Tom tunes in to see one of his own potatoes suddenly materialize from the dark and strike a klieg-lit Iron Shiek on the shoulder.

When Dad reads about other teens doing idiotic things, he'll sometimes say, "If I *ever* hear you've pulled a stunt like that..." "Stunt" is a word he uses when he's mad. Dad has other angry poker tells, like addressing one of us as "buster" or using the phrase "God dammit" or reflexively raising a backhand. "Only two things work," I've heard him say, of trying to persuade The Boys to do anything. "Bribery and intimidation."

Whenever I protest that I didn't *try* to break Mom's vase or leave the fridge open all afternoon, he plays the rhetorical trump card: "You didn't try *not* to."

After *All-Star Wrestling* and Mass one Sunday morning,

Dad threatens us all with what-for if we don't stop fighting on the drive home. But we don't stop fighting. Which is how it happens that ten minutes after leaving Nativity, Dad parks the car in the garage and sprints around the back to catch up with Tom, who picks up a hockey stick to block the backhand he knows is coming. Dad's hand hits the Sher-Wood and instantly swells up like a foam fan hand at the Met. Without breaking stride, Dad gets back into the car—shotgun seat this time—and Mom drives him to the hospital. When he comes home with his hand bandaged, again in the shotgun seat, Dad doesn't say a word. It's the only time I have seen Mom drive when Dad is in the car. It's the absence of the steering wheel, not the presence of the bandages, that makes him look injured.

(Dad will be Mom's passenger one more time, in my senior year of high school. On the morning after his fiftieth birthday party, aggressively celebrated on our screened porch, Dad has to catch a flight to Tokyo. Mom drives. When she pulls up to the departures terminal at MSP, Dad opens the shotgun door and stands there for a moment, hands pressed to his temples, nursing his crippling hangover. Tires squealing on her new car—she has given Jim her station wagon and downsized to a Honda Accord—Mom leaves Dad there to contemplate the error of his ways and the two lonely weeks ahead, eating ribs as a party of one at the Tony Roma's in Shinjuku.)

But if seeing Dad reduced to riding shotgun is a first, the summer of '81 is mostly filled with lasts. Things are all coming to an end. The last year of Lincoln High School looms, and the Met is already reduced to a handful of Twins and Vikings games when yet another ending comes. On May 29, the Twins join their colleagues in the rest of Major League Baseball in voting to go on strike. They won't return until August 10. On reflection, theirs is the greatest job in the world, not mine. I am utterly at a loss to understand how Butch Wynegar can be paid $460,000 to play catcher for the Minnesota Twins in front of nearly eight thousand people and be anything less than deliriously happy. And because he evidently isn't, I will be deprived of my $3.35 an hour for most of the summer. I'll be denied the fruits of my labor, that Panasonic boom box with the miracle of Ambience Sound.

Thanks to annual increases in the federal minimum wage, my hourly pay has risen, like an aging pitcher's earned run average, from $2.90 in 1979 to $3.10 in 1980 to $3.35 this year. And still it's taking me forever to save $249.95. I make a modest side income delivering the *PennySaver* circular throughout South Brook every Wednesday. The job becomes less onerous when a former delivery boy tells me that he—and all my predecessors on the *PennySaver* route—just ditched the bundles in the Dumpster at Hillcrest Elementary School. No homeowners are expecting them or will ever know they're missing. By delivering the *PennySaver*s I'm doing a disservice to Dumpster-using delivery boys in adjacent neighborhoods. So I stop.

Dad knows that even if the striking Twins return to the Met and give me a dozen or so five-hour work dates at minimum wage minus FICA, tax, and union dues; and even if I continue to deliver (as far as he knows) the *PennySaver* in perpetuity; and even accounting for the shoeshine money he gives me once a week, I can never save enough in a single summer to buy what even he has come to call "this boom box." And so he tells me that he'll pay for half of it as an early birthday present.

Beyond that box camera he saw in a shop window in Chicago in seventh grade, Dad has never wanted anything, as far as I know. He still coos over the tennis balls and Old Spice we give him every birthday, Father's Day, and Christmas. And yet he understands the symbolic power that an earned object holds. It helps that for once my interest—requiring, as it does, regular feedings of Scotch brand magnetic tape—align with his. But mostly, I think, he recognizes that a shiny metallic object adorned with countless knobs and buttons can spur a man to work. The longer it remains out of reach, the better.

For me, it's the boom box. For Dad, it's the Cadillac he promised his skeptical mother-in-law when he married Mom, now twenty-five years ago.

As a surprise gift for Mom and Dad's twenty-fifth anniversary, Jim arranges for Mr. Cole, our next-door neighbor—a photographer known to us as Old King Cole—to take a portrait of the five Rushin children. The day before our sitting, in Mr. Cole's basement, Tom and I have a fistfight. With one punch, Tom tears a strip of skin off my right cheek. Jim is furious and threatens to give Tom one for symmetry. When Mom and Dad return from their anniversary trip to San Francisco, Jim presents them with a sepia-toned portrait of their five children, ranging in age from twenty to nine. The middle child's prominent scab from a bare-knuckle fight the night before is preserved for posterity inside a golden frame. Captured in amber, as it were.

Mom sighs. She could have said "Just what I didn't want." Instead, she says, "Perfect."

*   *   *

On a Saturday morning in the summer of 1981, after the Twins and I have returned to our respective jobs, which we both continue to perform poorly, and before my sophomore year begins, Dad tells me, "Get in the car." We drive a few miles to a row of corrugated metal warehouses in an industrial park. He won't say why. A steel garage door is rolled up on one warehouse that we pass. "That's Mr. Costa's," Dad says. Mr. Costa is better known in South Brook as Champagne Tony. He has a son, Nicky, who is my age. Champagne Tony is in the amusements trade. His warehouse is filled with pinball machines and arcade games. The pinball machines are festooned with familiar faces and logos: Charlie's Angels, Evel Knievel, Playboy, Kiss, and the pinball wizard himself, Elton John, who wears suspendered white bell-bottoms and blue platform boots on the Captain Fantastic machine by Bally. Even I am vaguely aware that the men on these machines and the machines themselves are icons of a vanishing age. Goodbye Yellow Brick Road.

At the front of the warehouse are their boxy replacements, the games that have taken over the lobbies at the Southtown Theatre and Lyn-Del Lanes and Airport Bowl, and necessitated an entire stand-alone arcade called Beanie's, next to the White Castle on Lyndale Avenue. These games—Space Invaders, Asteroids, Galaga, Centipede, Frogger, Donkey Kong—are the next big thing, but I'm still unaccountably attached to the pinball machines. I'm oblivious to the notion that all these endings (Lincoln, the Met, childhood, pinball, freedom from work or care or responsibility) also mean something else is beginning (a new high school, a new ballpark, Pac-Man, adulthood, a driver's license, pocket money).

Even Champagne Tony's van, parked outside the warehouse, is beginning to age. It has a metallic burgundy paint scheme, a tinted bubble window on one side, and a scene of the desert at night with a billion stars all around, so that I can never watch it go past our house without hearing the Eagles sing "Peaceful Easy Feeling."

There's a little ladder to the roof of the van—its purpose, I've concluded on my own, is for rooftop sunbathing—and its interior walls are covered in a plush carpet. The overall effect of the van—the carpet, the sunroof, the desert vignette—is of a water bed on wheels. It embodies everything that was cool about the 1970s, especially when parked outside a warehouse filled with coin-operated wonderments, machines devoted to the Harlem Globetrotters and Led Zeppelin.

"This door here," Dad says.

We step into a carpeted showroom filled with brand-new electronics and cases of Scotch brand recording tape. Like the pinball machines next door, the boom boxes on display are all lights and knobs and shiny surfaces. The room pulsates with sound. The man working here recognizes Dad, seems to be expecting him, has the air of someone who owes him a favor. "This it?" Dad says, hefting the RX-5085 by the handle, doing a thirteen-pound wrist curl, a weight that will seem to double with the insertion of eight Rayovac D batteries. There is a muttered exchange between Dad and the sales guy, a brief exchange of paperwork, and then we're suddenly outside, in the parking lot, and I'm walking past Champagne Tony Costa's Peaceful Easy Feeling van with a Panasonic boom box on my right shoulder the way Dad might carry a case of beer.

The R&B stations out of north Minneapolis don't reach South Brook in the daylight hours, so I'm left to listen at night, with a blank Scotch cassette, and press PLAY and RECORD at the same time when I hear something I like— "Burn Rubber on Me" by the Gap Band, "Fantastic Voyage" by Lakeside, "Double Dutch Bus" by Frankie Smith. Only when I've built up a solid forty-five-minute side of tape do I ride around on my burgundy Schwinn World Sport ten-speed playing "Let's Groove" by Earth, Wind, and Fire on my brand-new South Brook blaster.

Quite what the neighbors think as the Sugarhill Gang's "8th Wonder" rings out on Xerxes Circle, I can't say. All I know is I'm steering the ram's-horn handlebars of my Schwinn with my knees, a rubber Spalding basketball ("my rock") under one arm and the RX-5085 ("my box") in the other, and all the while I'm singing along to the cassette: "Go dang-diddy-dang-dee-dang-dee-dang, diddy-diddy-dang-diddy-dang-dee-dang-dee-dang…"

The World Sport is my first brand-new Schwinn. My Sting-Ray dreams have gone wherever they go when a fifteen-year-old has followed the biblical prescription to put away childish things. Those dirt bikes that the little kids in the neighborhood are riding now are all knobby tires and padded handlebars. These kids today. Sometimes I ride the World Sport with a canvas sack of *PennySavers* slung over my shoulder. The custodian at Hillcrest Elementary complained to the distributor that his papers were being disposed of in the school Dumpster. Dad said, "Never pull that stunt again, buster," and I never will.

But there are other stunts. When Lincoln High School closes forever after my sophomore year, it's as if a government has fallen. Lincoln's vast storehouses of treasure are looted. Sweatshirts and basketball uniforms and baseball Windbreakers are liberated from The Cage, where the sports equipment is stored. A classmate we call Rodney, after a streetwise character in *Heaven Is a Playground,* acquires a two-and-a-half-gallon stainless-steel fire extinguisher with LHS Magic-Markered down the side. One summer night I join Rodney and four other kids in joyriding around Bloomington with the fire extinguisher at our feet. "Excuse me," a kid named Gary Dombrowski says, rolling up on a middle-aged man walking his dog. "Would you happen to have the time?"

"Why, yes," the man says, rolling up his sleeve and checking his watch while walking over to the curb. "It's..."

But before the man can tell us, Dumbo is strafing him with a high-pressure rope of Bloomington's award-winning tap water, the fire-extinguisher foam having long since been depleted. Dumbo soaks the shirt of the Good Samaritan, who can only return a stream of profanity as we squeal away from the curb.

Another night, in the drive-through at the Valley West McDonald's, we fire-hose the seventeen-year-old who passes the sack of Quarter Pounders through the window.

Ten minutes later, we ask a man for directions and strafe him. We roll up on a car at an intersection and shoot its passengers through the shotgun window.

And though I never pull the trigger—never even touch the canister for fear of leaving fingerprints on its silver surface—

I've seen enough TV shows to know I'm an accessory, an aider and abettor, a possessor of stolen goods, a party to vehicular something or other, a so-and-so after the fact.

Even my new friends in high school have discovered my timidity. One night, at the McDonald's on Nicollet Avenue, everyone gets their order but me. Instead of returning to the counter and demanding the Quarter Pounder with cheese I paid for, I simply sit at the table, watching the others eat and repeatedly asking in a small voice, "Where's my burger?" Since then, in moments requiring bravery or recklessness, my friends have provoked me with that catchphrase: "Where's my burger?"

But it's not a fear of staining my permanent record that keeps my hands off the fire extinguisher. It's the unmistakable knowledge, slouched down in the back of a Plymouth Duster, that our targets are the kind citizens of Bloomington, every one of them ostensibly offering us assistance. These are the people who took me in when my front teeth were knocked out, who offered their phone as I bled on their linoleum, who called my mother as I stood in their foyer after shitting my snow pants. They repaid cruel nicknames by buffing the gym floor to a Comet-commercial gleam and then sang "Silent Night" to our moms and dads. They coached me, cleaned my teeth, overpaid me to shovel their driveways, bought all the fund-raiser candy bars I could flog, applauded my every groundout, insisted I take that second sucker from the little basket on the liquor-store counter. They could have been the Nativity teachers and priests who were unfailingly decent and generous people.

Given Mom's separate fears of freeway merging and

splashing water, this drive-by dousing would be the worst thing I could do to her. There is a terrible irony at play. I spent nine years at Nativity worried about getting into heaven, and now a fire extinguisher, of all things, has consigned me to an eternity of flames.

Of the five kids in this car, I'm the only one going to Kennedy High School next year. Many of my friends will be "redistricted" to Jefferson, including the best friend I've made at Lincoln, another basketball-obsessed white boy named Keith Opatz. When *The Empire Strikes Back* comes out, Ope and I pretend to play Frogger in the lobby of the Southtown Theatre for ten minutes, then ask a ticket taker if we can use the men's room beyond the velvet ropes. When he obliges, we hide in adjacent stalls for half an hour until the movie starts, then casually walk into the auditorium. And thus begins a fruitful collaboration sneaking into movies and the YMCA.

Separately, McCollow, Opatz, and I tell the front-desk attendant at the Y that we've lost our membership cards. From beneath the desk she pulls a basket that is full of lost cards and invites us to have a rummage. We each choose one with a distant expiration date and insinuate ourselves into the regular noontime "runs" at the Y—the pickup basketball games contested by middle-aged men on their lunch breaks and now us: three strutting teenagers wearing "Curtis Js." These are sweatpants jaggedly cut off at the knees, as worn by Curtis Jackson on *The White Shadow*. Ope wears as many as five pairs of socks at any given time, so he can't even lace his shell-toed Adidas. Mike takes pull-up jumpers from forty feet and shouts—in the face of his forty-five-year-old defender, as the ball rips through the net—"Three!" It's all the more infuriating to the lunchtime lawyers and accountants that Mike is playing in a knit watch cap. As fugitives on fake IDs, the three of us are careful to call each other by the names on our membership cards—Milt, Chaz, Farouk. For all this, in our pickup games against responsible adults at the Southdale branch of the YMCA, it is *we* who find *them* ridiculous, with their beer guts and bald spots and black-framed Rec Specs (as well as their paychecks and wives and new cars).

The imminent closing of Lincoln High School will rearrange the three-way friendship among Mike and Ope and me. Ope will go from Lincoln to Jefferson. Mike will go from Jefferson to Kennedy. And while I will also go to Kennedy, my own brother will go to Jefferson, joining the citizens of prestigious west Bloomington without moving out of our house. As a senior-to-be, Tom is allowed to choose which school he attends. As a junior-to-be, I'll go where I'm told, and South Brook, in the center of Bloomington, will be placed in the Kennedy catch basin. Indeed, some kids at Jefferson will be forced to attend Kennedy. Mike McCollow, from whom I was separated after graduation from the Buh-vum, is one of them. It is difficult to fathom Tom or me attending Lincoln's archrivals, forsaking the Bears to become Jaguars and Eagles, respectively. Dropping the green-and-gold color scheme of the Swingin' Oakland A's for the powder-blue of Jefferson or the navy of Kennedy. As the fire extinguisher proves, fifteen is an age before empathy.

But our bus of Lincoln refugees will discover that other students—kids who grew up in the Jefferson and Kennedy districts, and get to remain in them—are no more excited to see us than we are to see them. A large dead fish will be rotting on the front walk into JFK when we disembark the school bus for our very first day there. Written in fish blood on the concrete: NEWCOMERS DIE.

As with the greetings in the Met Stadium commissaries—MAIN IS HELL, and that shriveled hot dog wishing us GOOD LUCK—we're left to wonder how this bloody message has remained, how no grown-up has ordered it cleaned up.

But of course no teacher has seen it yet, and when the first one does—within the hour—the message in fish blood is hosed away, and I'm left to wonder if it was ever there in the first place. Nothing remains but the faint smell of fish.

Childhood disappears down a storm drain. It flows, then trickles, then vanishes, leaving some olfactory memory—of new tennis balls, Sunday-morning bacon, a chemical cloud of Glade—to prove it ever existed. It seldom ends on a sixteenth birthday or an eighteenth birthday or some other calendar date, and rarer still is it stamped with a time of death.

But sometimes it is.

The snow-covered parking lot at the Met is the usual tailgating tableau on Sunday, December 20, 1981. Weber grills and Winnebagos. Snowmobile suits and horned Hägar the Horrible helmets. It's ten degrees. A man has set up his living room in the lot: a sofa, easy chair, and coffee table anchored by an orange rug. His TV is hooked to a generator to watch the Vikings final home game of the season, against the Kansas City Chiefs, on the NBC television network.

But this isn't an ordinary Sunday. It's the last game ever at the Met, and Bloomington's final day in the sun for some time, at least until the nation's largest shopping mall—

planned for this frozen plot of land—opens in another eleven years. Fans file in with signs—BLOW UP THE DOME, THE MET'S OUR HOME, U BET WE WON'T 4-GET THE MET, and this one, spray-painted on a bedsheet, a Krylon-on-Orlon epitaph: DEATH OF A TAILGATER, 12-20-81.

As the one o'clock kickoff approaches, men file into the stadium concealing hacksaws and pocketknives, wrenches and wire cutters. The local news has reported that any fans attempting to leave the Met with stolen property will be arrested and charged with a crime, but it's a hollow threat against 41,110 potential suspects. Larceny is in the air as the game gets under way. FOR YOUR PROTECTION, the scoreboard pleads, PLEASE HAVE MERCY ON THE MET.

For the last time, I stride past the fans and through the employees' entrance with the hauteur of a professional athlete. Whatever impulse toward kleptomania those fans may be feeling, the commissary workers are reminded of our sacred duty to inventory every hot dog bun and wax cup. But by the start of the second half, some fans have already set about loosening the bolts that anchor their own seats to the stadium floor. Northwestern Bell, anticipating today, has already denuded the Met of its pay phones. In the fourth quarter, fans in the bleachers pull down the U.S. flag, which has flown over center field forever. I can't help but think of them as stagehands striking a set. Those of us who grew up here will all go on to other roles. But the curtain is ringing down on a long-running production that will never be revived.

With five minutes left in the game, a man in a gorilla suit breaches security and appears on the field. With fifteen seconds left in the fourth quarter, the Vikings have fourth and goal at the Chiefs three-yard line, trailing 10–6. Quarterback Tommy Kramer throws in the flat to tight end Joe Senser, but the pass is batted away by Chiefs safety Gary Barbaro. The Chiefs take a knee on the next play and fans begin to pour over the walls around the field—a drunken, adrenalized waterfall of humanity. Instantly, one goalpost is scaled and felled, then the other. Both are covered in fans, like ants on a Popsicle stick. They're marching an upright into the stands and down a tunnel and out into the parking lot while a lone spectator with a hacksaw works at removing the remaining yellow stump of one felled goalpost.

Many of the fans who remain in their seats are trying to uproot them. There is, in the words of *Tribune* columnist Joe Soucheray, "a terrible rending... the stomping of thousands of boot heels on chairs, the cracking of wood, pounding and tearing and pulling."

Men with knives are sawing up segments of the frozen turf. Two men punch each other in the face, fighting over a stadium loudspeaker that one of them has torn from its moorings. Did the Beatles play "Ticket to Ride" through that speaker here in 1965? Had that speaker throbbed with "Hotel California" in 1978? There is no question that many of the souvenirs being spirited out of the Met with impunity lack any sentimental value whatsoever—metal folding chairs, ancient handrails, trash cans, toilet seats. It's as if the people who have stormed the field—almost all of them men in their late teens and twenties—require some token of a dying age, something to remember their childhood by. I stash a swatch of field-goal netting in my coat pocket simply because it's there, where I'm standing in silence on the frozen fringe of the field. The lighted message on the scoreboard reads FAREWELL TO THE MET—THANKS FOR THE MEMORIES.

The news will say there are only nine arrests. The prevailing attitude of police seems to be "We get it."

A handful of bozos have scaled the scoreboard, an Everest of lights, letters, and numbers, with billboards near the top for Marlboro, Union 76, and Dial Sports, whose phone number—1-976-1313—is the portal to a modern miracle: instant scores of games in progress, accessible from your wall-mounted telephone. At the summit of the scoreboard is an analog Longines clock. As these drunken mountaineers continue their ascent of the scoreboard, they begin popping bulbs and pulling wires. The clock stops with the big hand on the three and the little hand on the two. "It was frozen at 3:10," the front page of the *Trib* notes the next day, "and will be forever."

I am too, in a way. As the mischief turns to mayhem, police loose a few bursts of tear gas or Mace or some other chemical disincentive to vandalism. Then my math-anxiety dreams come to life. A fan is picking apart the out-of-town scoreboard and tossing its contents to the wind. Letters and numbers are raining down from above exactly as they do in my night terrors. I can't know it yet, but from this day forward, I will never again have those algebraic nightmares. Seeing them made real in the dying light of a December day somehow extinguishes those dreams. In their place will come the waking nightmare of migraine headaches, so that I'll be metaphorically chased to the nurse's office from Algebra I, with its malign letters and numbers and not-equal-to signs rendered in chalk. The migraines will also excuse me from football practice, until I tell Dad—a year from now—that I no longer want to play the sport. He won't call me a pansy or ask me to reconsider. My fear of telling him—as with so many of my fears—are unfounded. But I am powerless to alter the worry gene passed down from Mom. I watch the mayhem at the Met now with a growing desire to get the hell out of here before it gets any worse.

The apocalyptic images playing out at the ballpark, Bloomington's curtain call on the national stage, are being broadcast over the NBC television network. The announcers are silent. Over scenes of destruction, NBC is playing its planned tribute, a maudlin soundtrack backed by strings: Frank Sinatra singing "There used to be a ballpark right here…"

Tom drives me home from the Met one last time. I ride shotgun in the powder-blue Honda Accord that Mom has downsized into, now that she no longer has reason to drive five children at the same time. We pull into the South Brook driveway that I've shoveled countless times, in which I've shot innumerable hoops, from which I've thrown an infinite number of tennis balls against the garage door. At the top of the driveway is the single arborvitae around which Dad still strings a single strand of Christmas lights. Midway down its gentle slope is the backboard and hoop mounted on the pole that we used as home base—known in Bloomington as "gool"—in games of tag and Starlight Moonlight. It was on this driveway that we waited, one fateful Thanksgiving, for the high school fool that TP'd our house to make one more admiring pass, at which time Jim, Tom, John, and I caught up with his car on foot and ripped off his antenna as he sped away.

On this driveway, I waited in vain for hours on summer days for something to happen. Here, Jim and Tom posed in their prom tuxedoes and Mom chatted with passing neighbors after retrieving the mail. At the sound of Dad's tires traversing this curb in the evening, she applied lipstick prior to kissing her husband in the hallway. I know every dimple and divot of this driveway. The kickstands that melted into its blacktop surface have left a topographical map of childhood.

And it is in this driveway, in the not-too-distant future, that a thing of beauty will appear, shining in the summer sun. Not a Schwinn Sting-Ray but its motorized equivalent, the color of champagne, and with the same intoxicating properties.

Dad doesn't leave his new car in the driveway for the neighbors to see. If they're so inclined, they can see it soon enough, sharking through South Brook in the predawn or early evening on his travels to and from 3M. And he certainly doesn't wash it in the driveway on weekends. Senior executives of the Mickey Mouse Mining Company with a quarter of a century of tenure get their cars washed and gassed up at the corporate headquarters garage.

And yet there is an undeniable pride of ownership when Dad calls Mom's mom from the kitchen. "I told you thirty years ago that one day I'd be driving a Cadillac," he says, as Grandma pretends to remember.

"Well, I'm driving a Cadillac," Dad says.

Comfort has never been a concern of his. Dad has never owned a pair of jeans—he calls them "overalls"—and sleeps by choice beneath a single thin sheet. This car is his sole indulgence, the only material good he has quietly coveted in his life as a father.

He would have preferred to drive his champagne Seville to Cincinnati to show it to his mother-in-law in person, but those trips are in the past—all of them made in the butterscotch Impala or the blue Country Squire, or the baby-blue Impala that Jim now drives to college—trips made when five children were fighting in the back for elbow room, attention, and a sliver of air rushing in through the window vent.

In those days, tired of buying him tennis balls and socks and Old Spice for his birthday, we annually asked Dad if there wasn't anything else he would like. And he always said the same thing. He gathered us to his side—Amy and The Boys; one redhead and four shitheads—and told us that he already had everything he ever wanted. The car is just a box to keep it in.

Oh, Oh, Telephone Line

The five Rushin siblings gathered in that driveway two more times. The first was on September 5, 1991. Mom had been sick for the previous nine months with a rare disease that was eventually diagnosed at the Mayo Clinic as amyloidosis. Abnormal proteins were building up in her organs, including her heart. Her physical decline was swift, but she always put on lipstick before receiving visitors in the hospital, as she had every night when waiting for Dad to come home from Mickey Mining.

That summer, when she called me from the banana-yellow phone in the kitchen to deliver the news of her prognosis— that she might live another three to five years—I cried for the first time as an adult, alone in the squalid New York apartment I shared with three roommates. Before she hung up, she said, "I love you." It didn't occur to me until that very instant I'd never heard her say it before. To me, the declaration wasn't remotely necessary. I think she just wanted it entered into the record.

"I know," I said. And then, after a too-long pause: "I love you too." But I think by then she'd hung up. I didn't call back to say it again, even though the number still was—and will always remain—at the forefront of my brain, thanks to her: 888-2872.

Jim and Tom were living and working in Chicago at the time. Amy and John were both attending college in South Bend, Indiana—Amy as a premed junior at Saint Mary's College, John as a freshman on a hockey scholarship at Notre Dame. The little brother we assaulted with slap shots in the basement was now six feet six. He had declined football and baseball scholarship offers to Division I universities. He was drafted out of Kennedy High School by the New York Rangers. The notion that his not-yet-toothless smile might one day appear in *Goal* magazine, to be scissored out and taped to a basement wall somewhere in North America—as we had done with head shots of Jude Drouin and Yvan Cournoyer and Bobby Clarke—was yet another illustration that dreams routinely came true to the blessed citizens of Bloomington.

Mine certainly had. In 1991, I was the baseball writer for *Sports Illustrated,* whose editors had dispatched me to Chicago on the night of September 4 to write about White Sox slugger Bo Jackson. Somehow the baseball cards I'd kept in Velveeta boxes in the bedroom closet had sprung to life all around me.

After returning to my hotel late that Wednesday night from the game at Comiskey Park (the White Sox beat the Royals 4–1), I was wakened in my room by a predawn phone call. In the blackout-curtained darkness of the Marriott on Michigan Avenue, I didn't know where I was or even who I was.

But I recognized Jim's voice.

"Mom died," he said.

He had already made flight arrangements. Jim, Tom, Amy, John, and I were all meeting at O'Hare at midmorning and flying to Minneapolis. It would be an aerial version of the same trip we made twenty-two years earlier in the butterscotch Impala, but without the stopover in Wisconsin Dells.

Mom had died in bed in the middle of the night, hours after Dad had returned home from his own mother's funeral in New Orleans. Having buried his mother and lost his wife in a span of hours, Dad now awaited the arrival of all his children, our safety at the mercy of Northwest Airlines.

"If this plane goes down," I said to Tom, somewhere over Wisconsin, "Dad replaces Job as the standard for biblical suffering."

We laughed nervously and squeezed the armrests at the slightest turbulence.

The plane landed safely, and we all piled out of a taxicab like clowns from a clown car at 2809 West 96th Street. *Home again, home again, jiggety-jog.* For Dad, a firm handshake—a modified Knuckle Floater—was always the proper greeting after many months apart. But in his grief, he gave each of us a bear hug in the driveway.

In the house, through the window, we could see neighbors bearing submarine sandwiches, tuna hot dish, and other good intentions disguised as pies and casseroles. Having packed in New York for three baseball games in Chicago, I attended Mom's funeral in a borrowed suit and borrowed shoes.

A visiting priest none of us knew was assigned to say the funeral Mass at Nativity. He sat in our family room and asked each of us to describe Jane Rushin for use in his eulogy. I said she liked to do crossword puzzles and darn socks. It dawned on me as I was saying it that these were maternal acts of completion, of repairing or filling in holes. How many times had she done this for us—replenished our bellies, closed our wounds, had me rushed to Dr. Popovich to fill the space in my smile where my front teeth used to be? The priest didn't use any of this.

The funeral procession from Nativity to the cemetery was endless, a snaking automotive conga line of grief and respect: friends, relatives, neighbors, bridge clubbers, tennis partners, teachers, school parents, hockey parents, Cincinnatians, Chicagoans, and 3Mers. The motorcade was a mile-long measure of Mom's influence.

In dying, she allayed my greatest fear—of death. Dying joined shoe tying and coat zipping and bed making on the long list of acts Mom demonstrated for her children, so that we could someday do it for ourselves. Among the so-called personal effects she left behind were the collected works of Erma Bombeck, whose essays on housework, child-rearing, and other domestic mayhem reflected Mom's own experience. Opening one of those books at random—*Aunt Erma's Cope Book: How to Get from Monday to Friday in 12 Days*—I saw the author had dedicated it to her children: "If I blow it raising them, nothing I do will matter very much."

Mom was buried beneath a plaque engraved with her name and the dates 1934–1991. Dad had his name engraved next to hers, with the right side of the dash left blank. It didn't escape my attention that he'd chosen a cemetery plot in "prestigious west Bloomington," so that Dad's moment of departure will also be a sign of his arrival.

* * *

Six weeks after Mom died, I was back in Minnesota, covering the Twins in the 1991 World Series. While there, I declined to stay in a downtown Minneapolis hotel and instead slept in my old bedroom in South Brook, where the mastheads of various newspapers that Dad brought me from the road—the *New York Times,* the *Los Angeles Times,* the *Chicago Tribune*—were still Scotch-taped to my old homework desk.

When the Twins won game seven on a Sunday night in Minneapolis, I drove my rental car home from the Metrodome and wrote all night in the basement, in front of the same TV where I watched and wrote about Twins games on Mom's Royal typewriter.

In the morning, I filed the story to *Sports Illustrated,* as I'd dreamt of doing as a child.

The next time my siblings and I met in the driveway—November 11, 1995—was the last time. Dad was moving out of our house, out of South Brook, out of Bloomington, and into a condo one suburb (and a whole universe) away. "You can't defect to Edina," I told him, but Dad was adamant. In a few months, he'd be retiring from Mickey Mining after thirty-eight years. Audiocassettes had already been replaced by compact discs. Videocassettes would soon get deep-sixed by the DVD. Dad's career in magnetic tape was winding down like one of the cassettes he long championed, all the tape having transferred to the right-hand spool—what pros like him call the take-up reel.

And so my brothers and I decided that since we'd all be visiting Bloomington on the same weekend in November, we could repay Dad by removing and dispensing with a quarter century of stuff at 2809 West 96th Street. That we chose to denude our childhood home of all its objects and their corresponding memories on November 11, 1995, did not sit well with Amy. It was, after all, her wedding day.

As she has reminded her brothers on a regular basis in the intervening two decades, Amy didn't require her alarm clock that morning. "All my brothers greeted me with a wake-up call: *Get up! It's moving time!*" she wrote to me in an e-mail in 2016. "I watched as my childhood furniture of twenty-six years was moved downstairs and into the garage. The mirror that hung on my wall was carried away. Julie, my maid of honor, gasped. I just shrugged. I kept a sense of humor and was not going to let my brothers taint my special day. So we just watched as the house was slowly emptied. Furniture. Wall hangings. Kitchen items. Holiday décor. Books. My Raggedy Ann doll. My whole doll collection. My favorite stuffed Santa. I complained that there was no place to sit down—the kitchen had been cleaned out—so John brought a lawn chair in from the garage. Jim retrieved the toaster from its box. My wedding-day breakfast was toast on an aluminum-framed lawn chair in an otherwise empty kitchen. I was stuffing away an explosion of emotions as every worldly possession I had ever known and every childhood memory I ever had was swept into the garage."

In fairness, we'd been instructed by Dad to take whatever objects we wanted and to "pitch" or donate the rest. Dad called dibs on his and Mom's bedroom set, the donkey painting that he bought in the Philippines, a carved statuette of Christ the Redeemer picked up in Rio. In honor of Mom, I grabbed a Lladró figurine of a schoolteacher pointing at a globe. I did not take, to my everlasting regret, her Royal typewriter. It and nearly everything else was driven to Goodwill.

We cleaned so diligently and for so long that Saturday that Tom and John showed up late to church and missed the wedding pictures. John didn't notice that he had the rented tuxedo shirt meant for Mike, the groom, who was eight inches shorter. And Mike didn't notice that he had John's shirt. So Mike rolled up his sleeves during Mass and never removed his tuxedo jacket. At the reception, several of Mom's friends said to Amy, "Your mother is turning over in her grave right now, the way your brothers treated you on your wedding day." But the redhead knows the ways of the shitheads. Amy forgave us.

She was enrolled in medical school at the time, on her way to becoming an emergency-room doctor. None of us was surprised. Growing up with four brothers, Amy was adrenalized by chaos, unfazed by blood, inured to violence. She's raising four kids in suburban Minneapolis now. Working the night shift at the ER, saving gunshot and car-crash victims, is her way of unwinding. The Boys still take credit for her success. When we decapitated her Baby Tender Love doll for use as a hockey puck, and she saw it miraculously (if somewhat gruesomely) restored to life, a doctor was born.

Dad now has fifteen grandkids. He lives a block from Amy. Jim, Tom, and John are all successful businesspeople with families—Tom in Minneapolis, the other two in Chicago. I have a large and noisy family of my own in Connecticut. But I still feel the gravitational pull of the two cities where the rest of my family has remained. Where life began and gathered its propulsive force. Where life was never more lively.

On my desk I keep a working, banana-yellow, rotary-dial phone with forty feet of coiled cord. Every so often I pick up the receiver just to feel its heft in my hand. Then I press it to my ear and listen for some distant echo of its origin, the way you hear the ocean in a seashell. All I ever hear is the dial tone. But what I'm really hoping for, one of these days, is my sister's voice, so I can tell her to get off, that it's my turn to use the phone.

Acknowledgments

Every generation has its own Sting-Ray, or so John Parsley reassured me in the early stages of this book, which he edited with his customary grace and wisdom. John recognized that a story about growing up in the 1970s in Minnesota could also be a story about growing up at any time, in any place, and for that and many other insights I'm forever grateful.

At Little, Brown, I also owe thanks to Michael Pietsch, Karen Landry, Gabriella Mongelli, Malin von Euler-Hogan, and Elisa Rivlin, an extraordinary group of professionals who showed nothing but kindness and patience. Dianna Stirpe is a copyeditor of the first stripe, an anagram she'd recognize and gently suggest deleting. I am also indebted, as ever, to Bill Thomas at Doubleday.

Given her devotion to the Boston Red Sox, Esther Newberg shouldn't have the energy to pull for me, too, but she does, unfailingly. I am lucky to have her as my agent.

Steve Cannella and Chris Stone, my editors at *Sports Illus-*

trated, have indulged and encouraged my various whims over the years. Karen Carpenter at *SI* was also helpful, and her name belongs in a book about the '70s.

Craig Finn has made art out of the Minneapolis suburbs— and the Southtown shopping center in particular—with his band the Hold Steady. He was also kind enough to read the manuscript and point out that Eddie Rabbitt, not Eddie Money, sang "Drivin' My Life Away." As a fact-checker, he is a rock star.

Mike McCollow is my oldest friend and remembers in vivid detail every moment of our singular childhood, which we spent more or less conjoined. This story is as much his as mine. I was helped, too, by the recollections of other Bloomington friends, neighbors, and parents, among them Tom McCarthy, Jim Clancy, and Doug Cannady, all of whom once lived in South Brook, whose residents made it an exceedingly lively place to be a kid. It still is.

I cannot adequately express my gratitude to the teachers I had at Nativity of Mary. They put big ideas in my head like helium into a balloon, and with the same levitating effect. Nativity is still there for the present generation of Bloomington kids. Likewise, the Penn Lake Library remains a place to get happily lost in books. The teachers and coaches at Lincoln and Kennedy made my high school years as seamless and fruitful as possible. I am grateful, too, for the continuing friendship of Keith Opatz and Kevin Sundem.

My wife, Rebecca, grew up in Massachusetts in a family similar to mine: she was forced by her big brother, Jason, to fight her sister, Rachel, in boxing gloves in a pink bedroom out of earshot of their parents. The start and end of each round was signaled by an owl-themed wind chime. Growing up in a large, noisy, chaotic family—and then raising one of your own—is not for everyone. But noisy families have been the great blessing of my life. If writing is a solitary pursuit, my children—Siobhan, Maeve, Thomas, and Rose—ensure that it's never a lonely one. Tara Collins and Jessie are family, too.

The heroes of this story are my parents, Don and Jane Rushin. They passed along to all their children the richest possible inheritance: a sense of humor. Dad is the most modest man I've ever known. He's allowed me to write about him for my sake, not his. It's one more of the countless gifts he has given me.

Despite her well-deserved reputation for throwing away almost everything, Mom always saved what mattered most to me: baseball cards, books, and every photograph from childhood, with names, dates, and circumstances written on the backs in her impeccable penmanship. These photos and the memory book she kept for me were invaluable in writing this memoir. Mom, more than anyone, made me a writer. I miss her every day.

My siblings—Jim, Tom, and John Rushin, and Amy Kolar, MD—remain close, though we would never say so out loud. Despite distance and the passage of time, we'll always share a bathroom at 2809 West 96th Street in South Brook. In many ways, we never left.

When we were kids, Jim used to answer most of my questions with a hostile question of his own: "You writin' a book?"

Turns out I was.

Notes

INTRODUCTION

9 "Boys play aggressively in large groups": "Suspicion Confirmed," *Chicago Tribune*, March 1, 1973.

CHAPTER 1

25 "So I walked over to the desk drawer, got out my .22 revolver": United Press International, "Lawyers Rush to Aid Pop Machine 'Killer,'" *Chicago Tribune*, January 30, 1970.

30 "Mass travel by air": *National Defense Transportation Journal*, vol. 22–23, National Defense Transportation Association, 1966.

32 "He frequently flies to Paris": Walter S. Ross, *The Last Hero: Charles A. Lindbergh*, Harper and Row, 1968.

33 "If anyone ever flies to the moon": "Juan Trippe, 81, Dies; U.S. Aviation Pioneer," *New York Times*, April 4, 1981.

33 "I predict that we can enter the decade of the '80s without the specter of cancer": Dr. James T. Grace, *Journal of Medicine*, vol. 1, S. Karger, 1970.

34 "beer and soft drink containers, old hubcaps, iron bars": "Family Helps Clean Face of America," *Chicago Tribune*, April 2, 1970.

36 "We are a nation of pigs": "Litter of Pigs," *Roanoke Times*, reprinted in *Chicago Tribune*, July 22, 1969.

36 "will cost Illinois taxpayers 63 cents": "Highway Litter Costs Reported," *Chicago Tribune*, July 25, 1970.

41 Dr. Auerbach taught eighty-six beagles to smoke: "12 Dogs Develop Lung Cancer in Group of 86 Taught to Smoke," *New York Times*, February 6, 1970.

44 the display ad in the *Tribune*: *Chicago Tribune*, September 22, 1966.

49 "Tape playback in automobiles…boat full of life jackets": C. P.

Gilmore, "Hard-Nosed Gambler in the Plane Game," *True,* Fawcett Publications, 1966.
49 "tinkle" as he talked: Richard Rashke, *Stormy Genius: The Life of Aviation's Maverick Bill Lear,* Houghton Mifflin, 1985, p. 258.

CHAPTER 2

55 "The Zeppelin, a British four-man group": Peter Vaughan, "Led Zeppelin Was Good and Loud," *Minneapolis Star,* April 13, 1970.
62 "She saw other children using the Romper Stompers": *"Romper Room*—a Growing Family Affair," *Chicago Tribune,* April 21, 1970.
68 Preschoolers in 1971 spend 64 percent of their waking hours watching TV: "Kids' TV Addiction Told," *Chicago Tribune,* October 18, 1971.
70 23 percent of all airtime is devoted to commercials: "Assail TV Commercials, Violence," *Chicago Tribune,* September 8, 1971.
71 "relax minor tensions with a pill": "TV Helps Turn Children to Drugs: Lindsay," *Chicago Tribune,* February 8, 1970.
71 "Schools...are becoming the training ground for the next generation of addicts": Ibid.

CHAPTER 3

82 "This airplane is the finest piece of aeronautical engineering": Associated Press, "Jumbo Jet Returning," *Daytona Beach Morning Journal,* January 23, 1970.
82 "Once you have flown on this plane": Ibid.

CHAPTER 7

200 "The defendant's attack did not end at that point": Ray Kennedy, "A Non-Decision Begs the Question," *Sports Illustrated,* July 28, 1975.
202 "Peter Puck, the silly cartoon character NBC uses as a guide for new hockey fans": "Peter Puck Belongs in Sin Bin," *Chicago Tribune,* February 25, 1975.

204 "a dozen jackhammers digging at your cranium": Michael Anthony, "Music: Led Zeppelin," *Minneapolis Tribune,* January 19, 1975.
212 six people will be killed and eighty-five seriously injured: "Warning Given on Fireworks," *Toledo Blade,* June 29, 1976.
220 *Jaws* is too gruesome for children": Charles Champlin, "Don't Go Near the Water," *Los Angeles Times,* June 20, 1975.

CHAPTER 8

231 "In pictures children drew after the '71 earthquake": "Few Californians Shaking Over Quake Talk," *Chicago Tribune,* October 19, 1976.
239 "You've got to hate someone, I guess": Universal Press Syndicate, "In Defense of Polish Pride," *Chicago Tribune,* March 9, 1976.
239 "Poles are far from the only ethnic group to serve as the butt of jokes": "The Polish Joke Carries a Punchline of Sorrow," *Chicago Tribune,* March 8, 1976.

CHAPTER 11

307 "a terrible rending…the stomping of thousands of boot heels on chairs": Joe Soucheray, "Destructive Fans Bid Violent Adieu to Metropolitan Stadium," *Minneapolis Tribune,* December 21, 1981.
308 "It was frozen at 3:10": Ibid.

About the Author

Steve Rushin is a writer for *Sports Illustrated* and the 2006 National Sportswriter of the Year. He is the author of four nonfiction books and a novel. His work has been collected in *The Best American Sports Writing, The Best American Travel Writing,* and *The Best American Magazine Writing* anthologies. He lives in Connecticut.